Law in Practice
The RIBA Legal Handbook

John Wevill

RIBA Publishing

© John Wevill, 2013, reprinted 2015 and 2017

First published by RIBA Publishing, The Old Post Office, St Nicholas Street, Newcastle upon Tyne, NE1 1RH

ISBN 978 1 85946 500 4

Stock code 80466

British Library Cataloguing-in-Publication Data

A catalogue record for this book is available from the British Library.

Commissioning Editor: Fay Gibbons

Project Editor: Neil O'Regan

Typeset by: Academic + Technical, Bristol

Printed and bound by Park Communications Ltd, London, UK

While every effort has been made to check the accuracy of the information given in this book, readers should always make their own checks. Neither the Author nor the Publisher accepts any responsibility for misstatements made in it or misunderstandings arising from it.

RIBA Publishing is part of RIBA Enterprises Ltd.

www.ribaenterprises.com

For

Ben and Dora

Lyver berr yw lyver da

(old proverb)

Foreword

At every stage of a project, from the negotiation of the appointment through to the management of liability years after practical completion, the architect works within a framework established by the law.

An understanding of this legal framework, and how it applies *in practice*, is vital to the architect's skills. It is an integral part of the architect's professional duty of care to the client and it underlies the architect's approach to staying safe and running a more risk-free business, with better collaboration and interaction between parties.

Clear, lucid guidance is often hard to find. This is the particular strength of *Law in Practice: the RIBA Legal Handbook* which provides an admirably down-to-earth account of the practicalities of the law as it applies to a construction project. Beginning with the fundamentals, it moves deftly through to answer many of the legal questions that arise during the course of a project. Of particular value are the explanations of the implications of a range of bespoke contract clauses that the client may wish to assert – providing clear arguments for architects which can put them on a much stronger footing during contract negotiations.

This book will give architects the confidence that, if a legal issue arises, it will provide guidance on the matter and assist with finding the best answer. Alongside the *RIBA Job Book* and the *Architect's Handbook of Practice Management*, I hope that *Law in Practice* will become an invaluable comfort and trusted authority for the architectural profession.

Angela Brady

President, RIBA

Preface

One question was at the forefront of my mind when I was first presented with the opportunity to write this book: does the world really need another law textbook?

I have a particular interest in providing construction law advice to architects; it is the core of my professional practice. In late 2009 I had begun drafting a series of articles covering the basic principles of English construction law. I hoped to explain the fundamental issues as simply as possible, and then go into more detail and expand the articles to cover interesting current developments flowing from the basics. In this way, I wanted to make the articles useful for students of architecture and those just starting off in practice, but also to make the pieces relevant and interesting to more experienced practitioners. The articles were going to deal with the various topics from a practical perspective. I wanted to give architects practical arguments they could use in contract negotiations, and a way to find answers to the legal questions an architect is likely to encounter during the course of a project. To make sure my work was along the right lines, but not directly covered by material already published, I checked the available texts – what were other people talking about?

There were many interesting one-off articles; but there did not seem to be available to architects an up-to-date, comprehensive guide that sought to provide practical advice. There were perhaps two or three good textbooks providing a comprehensive technical summary of the relevant law. But nothing like the work I wanted to produce. The only sensible way to cover the range of topics I wanted to address seemed to be with a new textbook, so I started writing.

My focus is on the law of England and Wales and this book deals with construction law. There are many excellent RIBA books covering related areas – planning law, for example, and practice management – in much greater detail than I could in these pages. I have listed a number of very useful RIBA titles in the further reading section at the end of this book.

The aim of this book is to describe, as simply as possible, the law an architect needs to know to get through a project successfully; but then to go one step further and discuss the practical effects of the relevant law. In short, to give architects the tools that will enable them to work through for themselves queries related to construction law. As a by-product, I hope I can pass on in some way my enthusiasm for an extremely important, engaging and dynamic area of law. The law is as stated at 1 March 2013.

There are a number of people I must thank for their encouragement, practical assistance and inspiration, and without whom the completion of this book would not have been possible: my parents, Beryl and Ken Wevill; Rachel Wevill; Cameron Hammond; Philippa Varcoe, Sally Chorley, Mark Klimt, Jonathan Brown and Michelle Dowdall; Adrian Dobson, Dale Sinclair, Peter Walker, James Thompson, Alasdair Deas, Fay Gibbons and Neil O'Regan.

John Wevill
March 2013

About the author

John Wevill is one of the leading construction lawyers in the country. He has over 15 years' experience advising consultants, developers, funders, insurers, contractors and sub-contractors in relation to all major standard form appointments, contracts and sub-contracts, and a vast array of bespoke forms, development and framework agreements, collateral warranties, schedules of third party rights and other security documents. John also has extensive experience of construction dispute resolution, including litigation, mediation, arbitration and adjudication, as well as ARB and RIBA disciplinary proceedings.

Contents

Chapter 1

General principles of English construction law

This chapter

- examines what law is and where it is found;
- considers why it is important for an architect to know the law;
- describes how law develops and why;
- explores why the language we use is so important.

1.1   What do we mean by 'law'?

Why do we have laws at all? It seems like this should be a simple question, but finding the answer is a vital stepping stone on the way to understanding why it is important for a professional, such as an architect, to know the law.

Laws are sets of rules intended to regulate human behaviour. A degree of order is a necessity in any society, if that society is to be able to sustain itself over a period of time. A 'society', an abstract concept, has no separate will or desire to sustain itself. A society is no more than the individual people that make up that society.

The imposition of law is one way of creating order and exerting social control. If the majority of the people that have the power in a society to impose and enforce laws recognise a benefit in the continued existence of the society, then laws will be created with the aim of sustaining it. If the remainder of the society similarly recognises a benefit in the imposition of those laws, or has no power to object, they will acquiesce in the imposition of those laws.

In a sophisticated, developed society, laws will develop or be created to govern all aspects of human behaviour and interaction, ranging from basic norms of personal behaviour to the rules which govern complex commercial transactions. The law of England and Wales, with which this book is concerned, is a highly developed, multifaceted system. Construction law is one aspect of this larger system.

The idea of construction law as a distinct topic, worthy of study in its own right, is a relatively recent one:

- the Building Law Reports, widely recognised as the leading authoritative law reports for construction-related disputes, first appeared in 1976 (the word 'Building' on the reports' title page was originally represented in a variation of the Moore 'Computer' font, clearly marking them as a product of the late Seventies);
- the Society of Construction Law was founded in the UK in 1983;
- the *Construction Law Journal* was first published in 1990;
- the Technology and Construction Court only acquired its current name on 9 October 1998, as a rebranding of the Official Referees' Court.

The term 'construction law' is most helpfully understood as referring not to an entirely separate entity, but rather to a broad range of general legal topics (such as contract law, tort and the supply of goods and services) specifically applied to the vast range of activities undertaken by the construction industry.

The place of construction law in the construction industry is emphasised by the way in which the development, and promotion of the understanding of, construction law has been a collaborative process, involving the interaction of construction professionals as well as lawyers. This continued interaction is vital; without the input of construction professionals, through bodies such as the Society of Construction Law, construction law would be less responsive, less relevant. Construction law both governs and serves the industry.

1.2 Why legal knowledge is valuable to architects

For the architect, construction law sets the framework within which the practice of their core skills is to be carried out. Whether developing the design, securing consents and approvals or managing the construction phase, all aspects of the architect's work require a degree of knowledge of the legal context, beginning with the decision about whether or not to tender for a project, all the way through to RIBA Stage 7, post-practical completion, and managing the risk of ongoing liability in the years after the project has finished.

European procurement law may be relevant when considering what rules must be complied with when tendering for the job. The architect will require knowledge of planning law, the law relating to party walls and the Building Regulations when applying for the relevant permissions and approvals. Knowledge of health and safety legislation will be vital for an architect in preparing their designs and administering the building contract. In their contract administration role, the architect will also need a general knowledge of the law relating to the main provisions of the major standard form construction contracts. Knowledge of the law relating to intellectual property will allow the architect to better protect their rights under any appointment with their client. What insurance is the architect obliged by law to carry? What, in law, does the wording of an insurance policy mean for the architect in practice? Will the architect be required to enter into collateral warranties with third parties? Might there also potentially be liabilities in negligence to third parties?

1.2.1 What standard of legal knowledge is required of the architect?

Underlying all of this is the architect's relationship with their client. It is important for the architect to know about their own potential rights and obligations in contract law and the law of tort. What do the words in the architect's professional appointment require them to do? What professional standard must be achieved? If there is a dispute, what are the rules for resolving it?

An architect is not expected to be a lawyer. The architect must, however, according to the 1978 case of *BL Holdings v Wood* (at page 70 of the judgment), if they are to carry out their work properly, have enough knowledge of the relevant principles of law to *'protect their client from damage and loss'*. In the *Wood* case the architect was found by the court to have failed to exercise reasonable skill and care in advising their client on the need for a particular planning permit, because the wording of the relevant Act was enough to make it plain to any competent architect engaged in planning work that an additional permit would be required to make the planning application effective.

The architect's duty to advise in relation to legal aspects extends to knowing their own limitations; if a legal question arises which is beyond the scope of the architect's knowledge, they are expected to be able to recognise that specialist advice is required. The architect should refuse to incur additional expense on their client's behalf until the client has obtained legal advice and made an informed decision.

An awareness of the boundaries of the architect's expertise is increasingly important. The scope of an architect's responsibility seems to be ever expanding, paradoxically just as the scope of an architect's authority is contracting – particularly in the area of contract administration, where shifting professional boundaries have meant that quantity surveyors, project managers and others may all have a say. Architects seem regularly to be approached by clients seeking informal advice in relation to contractor claims, looking for an opinion on the chances for success or, in extreme cases, expecting the architect to in effect run an adjudication. It can be tempting for the architect to offer advice in response to a client's request, even if the architect knows it is at or beyond the limits of their expertise.

The desire to assist the client in areas outside the scope of the architect's expertise may be entirely understandable, but it represents a very serious risk.

Professionals holding themselves out as competent to provide particular advice have an obligation to achieve a certain standard of care when giving it. A failure to attain the required standard may leave the architect open to a claim.

1.3   Where does law come from?

1.3.1   Common law

English law, of which construction law is one aspect, is made up of rules from a number of different sources (Figure 1).

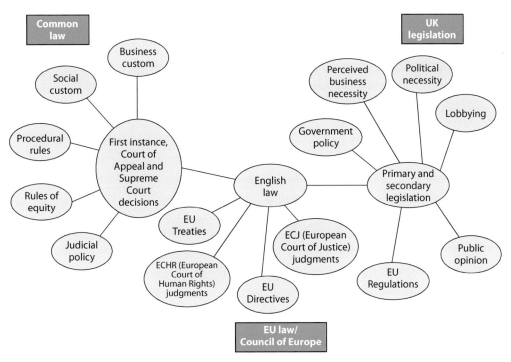

Figure 1 Sources of law

There are different legal systems even within the UK. English law subsists in England and Wales. The law of Northern Ireland is subtly different; some legislation applicable to the rest of the country does not apply there, whilst other statutes apply only to that part of the UK. The court system is also separate. Scotland also has its own courts, but the legal system as a whole is markedly different from that in England and Wales; it is based on a separate legal tradition. Scotland has a 'civil law' system dating back to the time before the Acts of Union united Scotland and England in 1707.

English law is fundamentally a 'common law' system. Originally this simply meant that it was the law that applied to (was 'common' to) all people in all parts of the country; a uniform set of rules, applied to all and enforced by the King's courts. There was no single defining moment when this system was adopted, but rather a gradual development and shaping of the law to suit the needs of the developing state.

The English system does not originate from any written collection of laws. It is based on the 'precedent' of decisions previously made by judges in individual cases. For example, in the case of *Bolam v Friern Hospital Management Committee* the court established the standard test for what amounts to 'reasonable skill and care'; if a professional, such as an architect, has acted in a way that a responsible body of their fellow professionals would have acted, then they have used reasonable skill and care and have not been negligent. After the *Bolam* case, this is now the test used by any court when considering cases where professional negligence is claimed.

There is no written set of guiding principles setting out the basis on which those judges should make their decisions. As a result, the system is extremely flexible and able to react, without governmental prompting, to the changing needs of society over time. One drawback of the common law system is that, being based upon decisions of judges in individual cases, legal development cannot take place until a suitable case arises. In practice, important issues do tend to generate 'test cases' and, where a glaring problem with the law needs to be corrected, it is open to Parliament in its legislative capacity to create a statute to change the law, as discussed further below. It is then for the judges to interpret the statute as and when required by the cases which come before them.

The common law system spread across the world on the back of the expansion of the English-speaking world, colonisation and empire. Common law principles hold sway in England, Wales and Northern Ireland, along with the Irish Republic, Australia, New Zealand, the United States, Canada, India, Pakistan, South Africa and a number of other countries.

In contrast, the system of law used in most countries throughout the world is based on the written civil codes of those countries. This system, 'civil law', relies on judges to interpret the written code and apply it to individual cases. The resulting interpretations are not binding on future courts. Judges in civil law countries do not make law through precedent. Civil law is prevalent in continental Europe as well as in Scotland, much of Africa, Asia, the Middle East and South America.

1.3.2   The courts apply the law of 'equity' too

Although the common law system we know now is remarkably adaptable and flexible, it became apparent over time that the common law was, in some instances, unable to keep up with changes in the way people conducted their business and some decisions were perceived as unfair. Over time, a parallel way of bringing claims developed; petitions were heard in the Court of Chancery, originally the court presided over by the Lord Chancellor. In contrast to the common law judges, the Chancellor and his judges were not constricted by the development of procedural rules; greater flexibility and creativity, in terms of available remedies, was therefore possible.

Since 1873, all courts have applied the rules of both common law and equity. In the event of a conflict, the rules of equity are to apply. Is the distinction between 'law' and 'equity' still relevant? The subtle differences between rules derived from common law and those derived from equity can still be important for the parties to a case. The ability to claim an equitable remedy (such as compelling a party to take a particular course of action through an injunction or an order for specific performance of a contract) is not strictly speaking a 'right', but is still considered to be subject to the discretion of the court. Whether an equitable remedy can be granted depends upon the justice of the case, the behaviour of the parties and whether an alternative common law remedy would be adequate; it depends upon whether in all the circumstances an equitable remedy would best do justice between the parties.

1.3.3   The central role of the courts in making and applying law

Because the development of common law is dependent upon the reasons given by judges for deciding individual cases, it is important that their judgments are written down. The common law is found in the reports of judgments. Not all cases make new law, but it is essential that those which do are recorded in authoritative law reports – for example the Building Law Reports, which cover construction cases – available to all courts and lawyers. Perhaps surprisingly there is no official free law-reporting service, but reports of many cases are now available on the internet. Most civil appeal cases and many High Court decisions are available for free on the website of the British and Irish Legal Information Institute (BAILII):

• www.bailii.org

The civil court system in England and Wales features two levels of 'first instance' courts (Figure 2). The county courts deal with relatively small-scale litigation, often claims for sums of money under a threshold of £5,000. These courts may be relevant to an architect, for example in the recovery of fees. Extensive guidance on making and defending small claims is available on the website of Her Majesty's Courts & Tribunals Service (HMCTS). Some claims can even be made online; details of the procedure are again available on the HMCTS pages of the Ministry of Justice website:

• www.justice.gov.uk

Even if the amounts involved are small, certain types of action are considered too important for the county courts (this guidance comes from Practice Direction [1991] 3 All ER 722). Professional negligence actions are among those types of action that are generally only suitable for the High Court. The High Court is the 'senior' court of first instance, hearing more complex cases with no financial limit. For administrative purposes, the High Court is subdivided into three divisions: the Queen's Bench

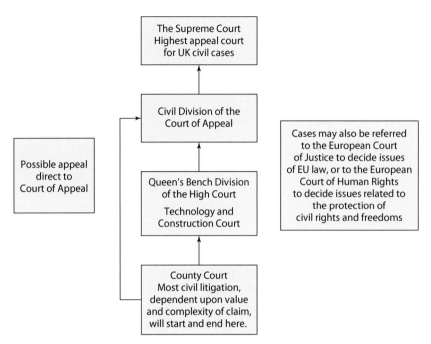

Figure 2 Civil court hierarchy in England and Wales

Division, which is the main common law court; the Family Division; and the Court of Chancery. Cases involving architects will usually be heard in the Technology and Construction Court (TCC), one of the specialist courts of the Queen's Bench Division. The HMCTS website contains numerous guidance leaflets relevant to High Court claims, as well as county court actions and appeals, and an extensive range of court forms, available to download for free.

If a party is not satisfied with the outcome of a case, there may be grounds for appeal to a higher court. Strict time limits generally apply and leave to appeal will be required, either from the trial judge or the Court of Appeal itself. Appeals against the outcome of a hearing in the county court or the High Court are mostly dealt with by the Court of Appeal Civil Division. Due to the likely time commitment and costs involved the appeal process is not something to be considered lightly.

The ultimate domestic appellate court is the Supreme Court, known until October 2009 as the Appellate Committee of the House of Lords. The Supreme Court deals almost exclusively with appeals that raise important issues of law. Leave to appeal will be required from the Court of Appeal or the Supreme Court, and is rarely given. The Court of Appeal is, for most cases that are appealed, the last word on that particular case; it hears several thousand appeals each year, of which only around one hundred go on to be heard by the Supreme Court.

1.3.4 Courts are bound by precedent

As discussed above, the basis for judicial decision-making, and consequently the basis on which lawyers advise their clients and make their arguments before judges, is not a written code, but rather the application of an unwritten principle that earlier decisions from authoritative courts should not be departed from. A decision of a judge in a particular case is a 'precedent'. Subsequent judges are said to 'apply' the decision when they 'follow' it in cases that come before them. Apart from the Supreme Court, the courts at each level in the English system are bound to follow the previous decisions of courts above them in the hierarchy, and appellate courts are bound by their own previous decisions.

Judges everywhere will tend to decide like cases alike, but the application of this principle in English law is uniquely strict, with judges in all but the highest appellate court having a positive obligation to follow previous decisions unless a case can be 'distinguished' from those decisions on its facts. The judge's obligation is to do more than simply take those previous decisions into account; sometimes it is apparent from reading a judgment that a judge disagrees with a principle of law contained in a binding precedent, but must nevertheless follow it if they cannot find a way to distinguish the current case from it.

There are rules within this rule of binding precedent. Subsequent judges are not bound by all of what has been said in a judgment, only by the essence of the reason for deciding the case in the way it was decided, known to lawyers who love jargon as the *ratio decidendi*. There is no absolute formula for identifying the ratio. One rule of thumb suggests that the ratio for a decision is that part of the legal reasoning which, if it had been reasoned differently, would have led to a different decision in the case. But cases rarely turn on just one point; sometimes the final judgment is based on layer upon layer of reasoning, and the absence of any one element could have led to a different outcome. As a result the ratio of a judgment can often be open for argument. Sometimes it is more clear cut; for example, the 'ratio' of the *Bolam* judgment described above in section 1.3.1 is: if a professional has acted in a way that a responsible body of their fellow professionals would have acted, then they have used reasonable skill and care.

For the system to work, judges employ reasoning by analogy in order to decide when a case is sufficiently similar to a previous case and therefore when a precedent applies. The facts of the current case do not have to be exactly the same as those of the precedent. For example, the *Bolam* case concerned an allegation of negligence against a medical professional, but the rule established in that case applies equally to any professionals, including architects.

Although the rule of precedent is considered to be far more strictly applied in English law than in other jurisdictions, there is in fact considerable scope for courts to exercise their own judgement. It is up to a court to decide not only whether the facts of a case fall within the scope of a previously decided case, but also what the principle of law contained in the previous decision actually is. The legal reasoning in a judgment has to be credible if the judgment is to survive, but the ratio, reasoning by analogy and applying or following a decision can all be seen as control mechanisms available to a judge to better justify adhering to a precedent or departing from it in order to do justice on the facts of the case before them.

1.3.5 Law may be created by Parliament too – 'legislation'

Legislation comprises the written law created by or under the authority of Parliament, which has supreme authority to make and unmake laws. The term 'legislation' includes Acts of the UK Parliament itself ('primary legislation') as well as the various Statutory Instruments, orders, regulations and by-laws known collectively as 'secondary legislation'. These rules are made not by Parliament but, for example, by the government of the day, government departments or local authorities, and derive their authority from Parliament.

Acts of Parliament take precedence over all other domestic sources of law. If an Act of Parliament contradicts a common law rule it is presumed that this was Parliament's deliberate intention and a court will be absolutely bound to comply with the statute.

It is important that architects keep up to date with important changes or proposed changes in legislation, primary and secondary, in areas relevant to their professional practice. An important example is the Local Democracy, Economic Development and Construction Act 2009, which finally came into force on 1 October 2011. Although this is relatively new legislation, it is not acceptable for an architect to be ignorant of the main changes to construction contracts brought about by the Act. Another obvious example would be updates to the Building Regulations.

For the most part, a full copy of all legislation, both Acts of Parliament and secondary legislation, is available free of charge on the internet:

- www.legislation.gov.uk – provides links to all published Acts of Parliament from 1988 onwards, and many other major Acts, dating back as far as 1267, along with links to all Statutory Instruments from 1987 onwards;

- www.parliament.uk – makes Bills currently before the UK Parliament freely available.

The UK Parliament website makes it possible to track the progress of relevant proposed legislation during its course through the legislative process. If an architect is in any doubt about the likely practical effect of a particular provision in an Act of Parliament, Statutory Instrument or any other piece of legislation, it is recommended that they should seek legal advice.

1.3.6 EU law

Since the UK was allowed to join the European Economic Community in 1973, that institution (now the European Union: EU) has assumed an increasingly powerful role in the creation of laws that directly affect this country.

EU law consists of several layers of legislation, some immediately directly effective in the member countries of the EU and others not. Most new legislation from the EU is in the form of either a 'Regulation' or a 'Directive'. Regulations are given force directly by virtue of the Act of Parliament under which the UK originally acceded to the European Economic Community. Directives, as the name suggests, direct individual states to achieve a particular result, but leave it up to those member states to decide on the best way to do so. In this country, that will typically involve a UK Act of Parliament to implement the Directive.

As well as the legislative bodies within the EU member states, the European Court of Justice ('ECJ') exists to interpret and implement EU law and is effectively a further rung of appeal above the UK's own Supreme Court. In the field of EU law, ECJ judgments overrule those of the national courts of EU member states.

Within the Council of Europe, which has 47 member states, including the UK, the European Court of Human Rights deals with cases relating to the European Convention on Human Rights, which has been directly applicable in the UK since the Human Rights Act 1998.

EU law takes precedence over any domestic law in the event of a direct conflict. Its influence is pervasive, covering many areas of law relevant to architects' practices and professional work: the recognition of professional qualifications, the law relating to procurement of works by public bodies, competition law, consumer protection and, particularly, health and safety.

1.4 Law is not static; it evolves

Laws, and the functions a society requires its laws to perform, will change over time as the society develops and the roles and responsibilities of the members of the society are reinterpreted. Issues that once seemed important enough to warrant making a new law may in time become irrelevant, and the law in that area will become obsolete. Laws can be created to meet a perceived need, or adapted, or repealed. The nature of law is surprisingly fluid and continually evolving. Moral, political, economic and other factors all have their influence.

The 'commercial law' of England and Wales, as broadly understood, includes construction law to the extent that it governs the actions and interactions of commercial parties. The commercial law has reached its current state following slow, often painful evolution over many hundreds of years.

Other factors have certainly played a part, but the underlying driver behind the development of all commercial law, including construction law, is economic; when parties such as architects make a contract, the law is there to give them the confidence that the deal they have made will be enforced in a predictable way. No commercial contract is risk free, but parties can manage the risks if they know that the law will implement the contract terms in the way they expect. This predictability is also good for society as a whole; removing the need for commercial parties to take unnecessary legal advice makes business more efficient and profitable, with positive consequences for the wider community through jobs and tax income.

The development of a law suitable for business users can be summarised as the result of three processes, 'facilitation', 'integration' and 'regulation'. For a more detailed discussion, in the contexts of company law and the sale of goods, see Lord Irvine of Lairg's paper *The Law: An Engine for Trade* (2001 MLR 333).

The law relating to commercial contracts, and which governs architects' professional appointments with their clients, building contracts, collateral warranties and all the types of legal agreement that architects may expect to have to deal with, facilitates trade, creating business confidence through the (generally) predictable enforcement of rules that have developed with business interests in mind. This can be seen in the way in which contract law fills in the gaps in private agreements by implying terms that the parties did not expressly include.

1.4.1 The law develops to facilitate business

Contract law allows parties the freedom to make their own business arrangements, tailored to suit their individual purposes. Some agreements may give the appearance of being a complete contract. It is rare, though, for a contract to contain every provision necessary to make clear what deal has been done and the law will imply additional terms in three situations:

- when the implied term is necessary to make sense of the contract;
- when the term reflects the 'usual' approach, and has not been excluded; or
- when statute requires the implication of a term.

Implied terms provide a safety net for parties to business contracts. If it can be shown that, even though all the components of a complete contract are in place, the contract as drafted does not make business sense, then the law will imply terms if they are necessary to make the contract reflect what it is assumed the parties must have intended.

1.4.2 The law develops by integrating existing patterns of behaviour

If there are 'usual' terms that were not expressly set out in the contract, but which the parties would, if asked, have acknowledged to be part of their bargain, again the law will imply them, so long as the contract contains no express term to the contrary. An example is the implied duty of the employer under a building contract to cooperate with the contractor to allow the contractor, all other things being equal, to carry out and complete the works. This implied term has an impact on the role of the architect; the employer will be liable for a breach of the implied term of co-operation if the architect fails to do those things required of them to allow the contractor to carry out its work. The law has in this way assumed certain rules that grew up through repeated use by and expectations of the business community.

1.4.3 The law develops to regulate behaviour that is bad for business

When it has been necessary for Parliament to regulate the construction industry through legislation, the law implements the new rules by implying additional terms into contracts to give them effect. Examples include the Housing Grants, Construction and Regeneration Act 1996 ('the 1996 Construction Act') as now amended (in terms of regulation of construction contracts) by the Local Democracy, Economic Development and Construction Act 2009 ('the 2009 Construction Act').

If a construction contract does not contain Act-compliant provisions relating to payment and the right to adjudicate, the terms of the Scheme for Construction Contracts must apply to make the contract compliant with the Construction Acts. The current relevant provision, contained in the 1996 Construction Act, section 114(4), states:

> Where any provisions of the Scheme for Construction Contracts apply by virtue of this Part in default of contractual provision agreed by the parties, they have effect as implied terms of the contract concerned.

The Construction Acts typify business-led legal development. There was extensive lobbying of Parliament in the years leading up to the creation of the 1996 Construction Act, and similar pressure leading up to the 2009 Act. The 1996 Act was focused on achieving improved cash flow within the construction industry by requiring fairer payment mechanisms in construction contracts, and by creating a statutory right to refer disputes to adjudication, a much quicker and cheaper alternative to litigation. The 2009 Act consolidates the law in relation to these two key areas.

It is understandable that business people are likely to operate to maximise their own profits, even though this may prejudice society as a whole.

Prior to the 1996 Construction Act, payment practices within the construction industry were making business life too risky for the parties lower down the payment chain – the specialist design consultants and sub-contractors that are a vital component of the industry.

Bullying clients and contractors were too often ensuring that the consultants and other specialists would take the risk that payment would not be forthcoming.

The inevitable result of the increasing risk of non-payment was that the pool of specialist talent diminished as people left the industry. The result was that prices went up. In addition, there was the problem of 'externalities', detrimental effects (other than the increase in prices) suffered by society as a whole. These effects included the discouragement of clients from instigating projects, a reduction of choice in terms of tenderers for projects and a decline in quality and innovation in a less competitive market. When Parliament created the 1996 Construction Act it did not do so out of altruism, but because better protecting the position of specialist designers and sub-contractors was a business necessity.

The facilitation and regulation of business practice, and the integration of business ideas into the law, demonstrate how, throughout its development, the law has been driven by, and has acted as a driver for, industry. As the creation of the 2009 Construction Act shows, the dialogue between law and business continues, as it must. The relationship is one of mutual dependency, with Parliament and the judiciary striking a balance between the self-interest of the business community and the interests of the public as a whole, reconciling, in Lord Irvine's phrase, 'laissez-faire and excessive regulation'.

The law of England and Wales as it affects the conduct of architects should be seen in this context. The existence of a legal framework within which architects must conduct their business encourages the business of the construction industry and is beneficial to society as a whole.

1.5 Language and law

Language is a problem. One popular misconception about the law, and one unfortunately propagated by some lawyers and politicians, is that the law can provide certainty through definition. This is not, and cannot, be the case, because of the unavoidable uncertainty associated with the use of language. All words have a core of meaning, but a word used in particular to stand for an abstract concept (for example, 'love' or 'reasonable') is always likely to have a 'penumbra' of uncertainty – possible aspects of the thing for which the word stands which some people may understand to be within the scope of the word's meaning, but others may not. In difficult cases, it is perfectly possible for two rational people to have entirely different views.

This is an issue of practical importance for architects and their lawyers. An architect should always have a written contract, their 'professional appointment', with the client. The appointment should set out as clearly as possible:

- the terms of the agreement between architect and client;
- what services will be provided;
- when fee payments will be made.

The architect may need to interpret their appointment to understand precisely the extent of their services. In the event of a dispute, the architect's lawyer will interpret the appointment, and any relevant background legislation or case law, to see if their client has a viable case. If a case comes before an adjudicator or a judge, they in turn will have to interpret the relevant documents to decide where justice lies. At each stage, someone is making a judgement about the meaning of words.

An example popular with legal theorists focuses on the word 'vehicle', which was used but not defined in the 1930 Road Traffic Act and others since. The 1930 Act made it an offence to use a trailer (which the Act defined as a 'vehicle drawn by a motor vehicle') without pneumatic tyres on a road. In the 1951 case of *Garner v Burr*, the court had to decide whether Mr Burr, who took to the road driving a tractor towing a poultry shed fitted with iron wheels, was guilty of an offence. Was a poultry shed a vehicle? This case demonstrates one very important reason why legal language is so often open to different interpretations.

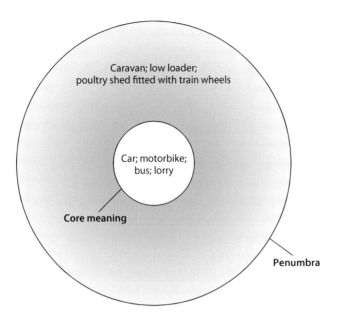

Figure 3 The 'penumbra' of meaning: 'vehicle'

Legal meaning depends upon the context in which the words are used

The court in Mr Burr's case said that the natural meaning of the word 'vehicle', which would not ordinarily bear an interpretation that included a chicken coop, had to give way to a wider meaning that was necessary to give effect to Parliament's clear intention in creating this part of the Act – the protection of tarmac road surfaces (Figure 3).

Inaccurate use of language can lead to disputes

Many disputes begin with the imperfect use of language. It is in the interests of the law and the users of it that words used for legal purposes, in contracts and statutes, should be as certain as possible, with the narrowest penumbra of uncertainty. But what does the impossibility of 'certainty' mean for an architect, practically? Is it even necessarily a bad thing? Legal certainty is important for business confidence. Commercial parties need to be able to properly assess the risks they are taking on when they make a contract; this cannot be done if it is not possible to predict how a court will interpret the words used in the contract, or the words of the relevant background legislation.

Some party or other will have lost out as a result of every development over the course of English legal history, from the very beginning; from the party who could predict how their local lord would deal with an issue in his feudal court, only to find that their case met with a different interpretation when heard before the King's travelling justices. But parties have in the past also suffered injustice due to the unyielding rigidity of procedural rules, which created an unwelcome sort of certainty. Inflexibility in procedural law and an inability of the substantive law to adapt to changing business needs could each lead to unfairness. How is the balance to be struck?

Sometimes a legal interpretation of language can, on the face of it, look illogical. In the Court of Appeal case *Tyco Fire & Integrated Solutions (UK) Ltd v Rolls-Royce Motor Cars Ltd*, which concerned a building contract insurance issue, the definition of the term 'the Contractor' became crucial. The defendant, Tyco, was named in the building contract as the Contractor, with a capital 'C'. The employer had been obliged to maintain joint names insurance to cover various parties 'including, but not limited to, contractors'. The court held that Tyco, the capital 'C' Contractor, was outside the class of parties defined as including 'contractors' with a small 'c'. At first glance this is a difficult distinction to understand and seems to be at odds with the logical interpretation that the main contractor, however described, should still be within the wider class of 'contractors' working on the project. But the court stretched the meaning of the words and favoured the less obvious interpretation because, on the facts of the case, it was the correct interpretation in order to do justice between the parties.

The absence of certainty in language allows courts room for manoeuvre to do justice between parties in hard cases, where an obvious interpretation can be made to give way to another, reasonable but less obvious, interpretation. The facilitation of justice in such cases, and the development of the law to meet changing needs, are the benefits of allowing judges to exercise their discretion when interpreting legal words. The price parties must pay is accepting the risk that the wording of a contract or statute may not mean what they had assumed it meant.

In his articles *Language and the Law* (1945/1946 LQR 61/62) Glanville Williams said:

> Since the law has to be expressed in words, and words have a penumbra of uncertainty, marginal cases are bound to occur. Certainty in law thus has to be seen to be a matter of degree.

This must be true, but it should not stop commercial parties from aiming to be as accurate as possible in the language they use to express the contracts they make. Certainty may be unattainable, and failure inevitable, but parties have to aim to 'fail' as well as they can.

The most important context for the architect is the wording of their own professional appointment. Even if we accept that the nature of language means there is always likely to be room for argument about the meaning of any particular set of words, it is still a fact that some contracts are better drafted than others. Some forms of words invite confusion; others are only likely to be the subject of dispute if the stakes are high enough to warrant innovative arguments by expensive lawyers. It is always worth recording the agreed contract terms in writing.

Chapter 2
The laws of contract and tort

This chapter:

- describes the practical differences between the two main types of civil obligation – contract and tort;

- examines how these obligations arise;

- discusses how an architect can recognise what the extent of their liability may be;

- considers what standard of performance is required of an architect;

- considers how long an architect may remain legally liable for their actions.

2.1   The civil legal obligations of an architect

This book is primarily concerned with the civil obligations that the law imposes on architects and which govern architects' relationships with their clients, fellow professionals, funders, end users of projects and members of the public. It should be borne in mind that an architect may also be subject to the criminal law in the event that their actions (or omissions) cause a harm for which the criminal law imposes a sanction. For example, if an architect designs a building so poorly that it collapses, the architect may be sued by the client for the losses the client incurs as a result; but if someone was inside the building when it collapsed and that person lost their life, the architect may also be prosecuted for manslaughter and subject to a fine or imprisonment.

2.1.1   Laws of contract and tort

The law of contract and the law of tort are the main bodies of rules in English law relating to civil, as opposed to criminal, obligations. The basis on which the law imposes an obligation in contract is conceptually different from the basis on which the law of tort imposes an obligation, and it is simpler to analyse these two areas of law separately. However, depending upon the facts of the case, English law provides that the two sets of obligations may overlap significantly. This overlap is likely to be particularly relevant in relation to professional negligence. Negligence is the most common form of tort, although there are many other types – breach of statutory duty, for example, or nuisance. Negligence is a key area of interest for architects, especially because different limitation periods will apply in relation to legal actions in contract and those in tort, as discussed below. An architect's professional appointment is likely to require them to exercise reasonable skill and care in producing their design; if the architect fails to meet that standard, they will be in breach of contract. But if the architect fails to use reasonable skill and care in their design work, they will also have acted negligently.

Both contract and tort law set down standards of behaviour with which parties must comply. Behaviour is regulated by the provision of legal remedies for the victim of a civil wrong; the award of damages for breach of contract is an example of such a remedy.

The law of contract concerns self-imposed obligations, created by an agreement between the parties which the law recognises as binding on them. In contrast, the law of tort concerns obligations that are imposed by the law on one party because of the existence of a duty of care not to harm another party, whether or not the parties have agreed that the duty of care exists and even if there is no pre-existing link between the parties at all.

2.2 The law of contract

2.2.1 What makes a contract?

A contract is an agreement recognised by law as binding on the parties to it. The parties are said to be 'privy' to the contract, and the terms of the agreement are binding on them alone and not on third parties; the contract cannot generally be enforced by or against someone who is not a party to it. This doctrine of 'privity of contract' is subject to some qualifications – for example, the effects of the Contracts (Rights of Third Parties) Act 1999, as discussed in Chapter 6 – but remains a key difference between the way contract law and tort law operate.

The history of contract law is predominantly judge-made and, as explored in Chapter 1, the modern law in this area has, to a degree, developed to create confidence within, and been informed by the practice of, the business community. It is only relatively recently that Parliament has taken a more active role in helping to shape the principles of contract law. How do the judges decide whether or not a contract exists?

There is no prescribed form for a contract. A contract may be made between two parties, or more parties may be involved. It may be written or purely oral. In practice, it can be difficult to prove before a court what was orally agreed in the event of a dispute, because it will typically be the word of one party against that of the other; but the old Samuel Goldwyn maxim that 'an oral contract is only as good as the paper it's written on' does not necessarily hold true, particularly with the English courts taking an increasingly investigative role when looking into the circumstances around a potential contract. However, certain elements must be present in the agreement to make it into a legally binding and enforceable contract.

In reality the behaviour of parties during the negotiation of a contract tends to be complex; as a result the courts have developed certain 'control mechanisms'. These are used to break down the complex interplay between the parties into simpler concepts, in order to allow the court to do justice in individual cases when the existence or meaning of a contract is in dispute:

- There must have been *agreement* between the parties.
- The parties must have *intended* that their agreement should be legally binding.

- Some *consideration* must have passed from the party receiving the benefit of the contract, in exchange for receiving that benefit (except for contracts made 'under seal').

These control mechanisms were refined in the golden age of English contract law, the 19th century, and are still used by the courts to legitimise decisions today.

2.2.2   Was there consideration and an intention to create legal relations?

The doctrine of consideration started as pure common sense; a court sought to understand why a party may have wanted to enter into a binding contract to provide particular goods or services. What bargain was made between the parties? If there was a sensible, understandable reason why the promise to provide goods or services was made, then it would be enforced. Over time a body of case law developed as to which reasons were good, enforceable reasons and which were not. Obviously the exchange of money was and remains a valid reason, so for example a collateral warranty will typically include a variation on the phrase:

> Now in consideration of the payment of £1 by the beneficiary to the architect, it is agreed as follows … .

For there to be an actionable contract binding the parties, there must also be evidence that the parties intended to create legal relations. The court in the case of *Tesco Stores Limited v Costain Construction Limited and Others* (at paragraph 152) said:

> It is … a strong strand in the policy guiding the development of the law over the years that the question whether or not a contract has been made should depend, fundamentally, upon the intention of the parties to the supposed contract, *objectively ascertained*, to make an agreement by which they intend to be legally bound.

The courts adopt an objective approach for purely practical reasons. The orderly conduct of business affairs depends upon people being taken to mean what they say, rather than being able to avoid the consequences of what they say in reliance upon unexpressed reservations. If objectively a party conducts itself in its speech, writing or behaviour in such a way as to indicate that it intends to take on by agreement legally binding obligations, then the law will enforce upon them the objective consequences of their conduct. In so doing, the law is not seeking to disregard what their actual intentions were, but only to limit the scope of the enquiry to the objective signs of their actual intentions; this was another conclusion reached by the court in the *Tesco* judgment referred to above.

2.2.3   Was there an offer? Was it accepted?

Artificial it may be – as mentioned above, the interaction between contracting parties is very often so much more complex – but the notions of 'offer' and 'acceptance' are of the highest importance in determining whether there is in fact a concluded contract.

When analysing the offer and the acceptance a court is looking at whether the parties should be taken *objectively* to have been in agreement. As with the doctrine of intention to create legal relations, the court is not concerned with the actual subjective positions of the contracting parties, to the extent that those are different from the impression given objectively. The lesson for any party, including an architect, engaging in commercial negotiations is clear – make sure that the written evidence documenting the relationship, including the written contract or appointment, properly reflects the relationship you intended to create.

For the courts, both the offer and acceptance have to be clear and unequivocal. A party cannot accept an offer by saying or doing nothing – that is not enough evidence for a court to judge objectively – and nor is it possible to accept an offer that is different from the one made. For example, if you offer to provide design services for £50,000 and the client says they accept your terms provided you reduce your fee to £40,000, there is no agreement – only a counter-offer.

To add another layer of complexity, in the event of a dispute a court must not only decide objectively whether there has been an offer and an acceptance, it must also decide precisely what has been offered and what has been accepted. How does a court decide what the substance of the agreement is?

2.2.4   How does a court interpret a contract?

What are the principles on which a court acts when trying to interpret the meaning of a contract? The general rule is that the court is limited to interpreting the expressed intention of the parties through the words actually used in the contract. If you wish to be able to rely on a particular provision, or a particular point you raised during negotiations, you must ensure it is incorporated into the final agreed contract or appointment.

The court may look at the surrounding 'factual matrix' to give colour to the words of the contract and shed light on the objective aim of the parties in making the contract; but the court cannot try to interpret the clear words of the contract as if the court were the parties acting in that factual matrix. The factual matrix that a court can take into account is basically everything apart from the things that were said by the parties during the pre-contract negotiations, so it would include, for example, evidence of the business requirements of the parties at the time of the contract, which may show why the parties would have wanted to enter into a contract on particular terms.

The court will use all the background factual information which would affect the way in which an objective, reasonable person would understand the language of the contract; but it cannot, in interpreting a contract, ordinarily use evidence of the actual stated positions of the parties in pre-contract negotiations. This is known as the 'exclusionary rule' and was reaffirmed by the House of Lords in the case of *Chartbrook Ltd v Persimmon Homes Ltd*, one of its final judgments before transforming into the Supreme Court. What the parties actually say pre-contract, and their subjective statements of intent for the contract, are not taken into account because they cannot help the court to assess the language of the contract objectively.

A court has the power to imply terms into a contract

If it is apparent to a court that, having reviewed the background factual matrix, something went wrong with the language of the contract, then the court will in such circumstances be prepared to rewrite the contract to properly reflect the terms of the offer and acceptance which the court has objectively identified. The *Chartbrook* case was tightly focused on the commercial effect of the contract as drafted. However much 'red ink' was required to make the words of the contract make commercial sense, in the context of what the parties were objectively trying to achieve as discerned from the factual background, the court was willing to make those changes – but only once the court concluded from the circumstances of the contract that the parties intended to include the additional words, but for whatever reason did not.

You should not rely on a court to make your contracts or appointments make sense – it is far better to draft the contract in the first place so that it properly reflects the deal you have made.

As discussed in Chapter 1, additional contract terms may also be implied by statute, such as those providing the right to refer disputes to adjudication under the 1996 and 2009 Construction Acts. If the parties intend that statutory implied terms are not to apply in their contract, those terms must usually be expressly deleted; however, a number of statutory provisions cannot be contracted out of, such as those in the Construction Acts.

There are limits on what the parties may agree: exclusion clauses

Parliament is also active, in certain circumstances, in protecting contracting parties from themselves, or from the adverse effects of agreeing onerous contractual provisions due to the unequal bargaining positions of the parties. Statutory provisions, enforced by the courts, do not allow certain terms to be agreed between the parties to a contract in certain circumstances. A party in a dominant bargaining position may wish to include terms in the contract which exclude or limit their liability in the event of them being in breach of contract. An architect may be affected by such concerns if their client is seeking to impose onerous terms on them; or it may be that it is the architect who has the dominant position and is seeking to limit or exclude their liability to the client, particularly to a consumer (as opposed to a commercial) client.

The two important pieces of legislation in this area are the Unfair Contract Terms Act 1977 ('UCTA 1977') and the Unfair Terms in Consumer Contracts Regulations 1999 ('UTCCR 1999'). UTCCR 1999 applies exclusively to relationships between commercial providers of goods and services and their consumer clients. As will be seen later in the context of the RIBA Standard Conditions of Appointment 2010 (2012 revision) – 'the RIBA Standard Conditions' – clauses which are potentially unfair and which have not been individually negotiated or fully explained to a consumer client will fall foul of UTCCR 1999, and the architect will not be able to rely upon them.

UCTA 1977 prevents parties from contractually excluding liability for death or personal injury resulting from negligence; and goes on to provide that liability in negligence for other loss and damage may be restricted or excluded only if the clause in question satisfies the test of 'reasonableness' in all the circumstances, as set out in the Act. Exclusions or limitations of liability for breach of contract must also satisfy the test of reasonableness, if the contract involves one party contracting as a consumer, or if the contract is made on one party's standard written terms of business. Again, this could affect an architect contracting on the basis of a standard form of appointment. For example, the 2009 case of *Langstane Housing Association v Riverside Construction Aberdeen Ltd and Others* concerned arguments by a client that a net contribution clause (a limitation of the consultant's liability which reverses the common law position and makes it harder for the client to recover its losses) was not fair and reasonable for the purposes of UCTA 1977. The court decided that in the circumstances a net contribution clause was fair and reasonable, but the credibility of this decision is undermined by the fact that the court also said that it did not consider a net contribution clause to be a restriction of liability to which

UCTA 1977 would apply. It is safest to assume that the law in this area is not settled and net contribution clauses and other limitations on liability may still be vulnerable to UCTA-based arguments raised by clients in certain circumstances.

2.2.5   Letters of appointment, letters of intent and other 'informal' contracts

An architect may come across a letter of intent on a project if they are asked to administer a building contract based on one. An architect may also be appointed on an informal basis, such as a letter of appointment, which, for want of a better description, amounts to a letter of intent. In this section any such informal contract or appointment based on a letter or an exchange of letters or e-mails will be described as a 'letter of intent'; using the term 'informal contract' would just create confusion because, as will be seen below, not every such agreement is going to amount to a legally enforceable contract.

When a new job is secured it is always tempting, especially in a difficult financial climate, to dive into the project and neglect the appointment paperwork. You might proceed on the basis of an exchange of e-mails, an oral instruction in a meeting or a letter of intent. But first things first – is it really so vital to begin work before concluding the building contract or your own professional appointment? In the majority of cases where letters of intent are used, the truth is that the perceived benefit of an early start is outweighed, in the long term, by the risks of proceeding without properly settled contract and appointment terms. In the context of a building contract, if the contractor is working on the basis of an open-ended letter of intent, and being paid, the incentive to agree a formal building contract diminishes with each passing week.

The phrase 'letter of intent' is not a term of art and does not have a fixed meaning. It covers a broad range of agreements between parties, with varying degrees of 'formality', covering a spectrum from 'definitely not a contract' at one end to 'definitely a binding contract' at the other end, and all points of 'maybe' in between. Its meaning and effects depend upon all the circumstances of each particular case. Letters of intent are not a special case; a court will use the same principles to decide whether a letter of intent is in fact a binding contract (and if so, what the binding obligations require the parties to do) as it would use for any document.

The primary disadvantage of letters of intent is their unpredictability; it is often very difficult to tell in advance what interpretation a court would give to such a document, in terms of the extent of the legal relationship (if any) it creates. It is rare for there to be such fundamental doubts about a formally agreed contract or professional appointment. Poorly thought out drafting – ambiguous wording or incomplete treatment of important issues – within a letter of intent will inevitably make it more likely that a dispute will arise about the nature and extent of the rights and obligations of the parties.

Many attempts have been made, mostly by lawyers, to identify different categories of letters of intent, but these definitions are not necessarily helpful. Every letter of intent is different, and an over-emphasis on categorisation can mask the single important issue for the parties involved: what is the legal effect of the document in question?

Interpretation of letters of intent by the courts, in theory

There is no presumption that, because the works or services required by the letter of intent have been completed or substantially completed, the letter of intent must be a binding contract between the parties. Each case will depend upon all the facts, and upon the drafting of the document in question. In the leading Supreme Court case of *RTS Flexible Systems Limited v Molkerei Alois Müller Gmbh & Company KG (UK Production)* Lord Clarke stated:

> in a case where a contract is being negotiated subject to contract and work begins
> before the formal contract is executed, it cannot be said that there will always or even
> usually be a contract on the terms that were agreed subject to contract … The court
> should not impose binding contracts on the parties which they have not reached. All
> will depend upon the circumstances.

The most common form of letter of intent describes generally the initial works or services that the employer wants carried out and sets out a maximum sum that will be paid in return for those works or services; a form of underlying contract or appointment will typically be referred to as something the parties intend to execute in due course, and payment and other terms from the 'formal' contract form may be specifically cross-referred to in the letter of intent. Such a letter of intent will also usually contain requirements for timing of the works or services.

The essential point is that the employer typically wants their letter of intent to be legally binding to some extent; there is no purpose to the exercise if the contractor or service provider is not obliged to do anything other than complete those works or services it chooses to carry out within a reasonable time. As a result, letters of intent tend to be uneasy hybrids, mini-contracts pretending to be informal agreements – too simple to cover all the important points properly, but too complex to be free of ambiguity – and often drafted with insufficient legal input, to save time and money. The majority of decided cases in this area have been concerned with this type of agreement – a mini-contract created without the care that would be taken for a 'formal' contract or appointment.

Interpretation of letters of intent in practice

In the *RTS Flexible Systems* case, the Supreme Court had to consider the principles governing the legal status of letters of intent. Müller, a food manufacturer, wished to update its packaging equipment. It entered into discussions with RTS, which over several years led to a number of quotations being received from RTS.

RTS was awarded the job on the basis of a quotation which referred to its own standard terms and conditions. Müller then issued a letter of intent setting a four-week period for the execution of a formal contract and also referring to Müller's standard terms, one of which (clause 48) stated: 'The Contract … shall not become effective until each party has executed a counterpart and exchanged it with the other'. The four-week period was repeatedly extended. After the expiry of the last period of extension, a dispute arose in relation to alleged defects in the works. Müller claimed it had no further obligation in respect of the work that had been carried out because the execution of a formal contract had still not taken place.

The case eventually reached the Supreme Court. Did the parties make a contract after the expiry of the letter of intent, and if so on what terms? The Supreme Court set out some basic principles, Lord Clarke quoting with approval, as a summary of the current position, the guidance originally expressed by the Court of Appeal in the 1987 case of *Pagnan SpA v Feed Products Ltd*. The key principles from the *Pagnan* case are:

- the existence and terms of any contract between the parties depends upon an objective reading of the correspondence, discussions and conduct between the parties as a whole;
- even if the parties have agreed all the terms of the proposed contract, there may still be no contract if, viewed objectively, the parties did not intend a contract to exist or intended that the contract should not become binding until some further condition had been fulfilled;
- conversely, the parties may be seen, objectively, to have intended the contract to be binding even though there are further terms still to be agreed or some further formality to be fulfilled;
- it is for the parties to decide whether they wish to be bound and, if so, by what terms, however objectively 'important' or 'unimportant' those terms are.

2

On the facts, the Supreme Court found it unrealistic to suppose that the parties did not intend to create legal relations. Both parties accepted that there was an agreed price, and if the price was to be accepted as a term binding on the parties the case could not, at least on conventional principles, be one of no contract. It was surely not possible that RTS would have agreed to proceed with detailed work and to complete the whole job on a non-contractual basis, subject to no terms at all. Such an approach would not make 'commercial sense'. The Supreme Court decided the basis for the contract was effectively the Müller standard terms and, on the facts, the Court was happy to infer an unequivocal agreement had also been reached between the parties to waive the problematic clause 48.

How had the contractual position been allowed to become so confused? Counsel for one of the parties before the original hearing said that 'neither party wanted the negotiations to get in the way of the project'. This is entirely understandable and at the same time extremely risky behaviour.

Any consultant or contractor should insist on the importance of settling the terms of a formal contract or appointment, rather than letting sleeping dogs lie out of a misplaced sense of being seen as 'being awkward'.

Agreeing formal terms of appointment provides a benefit for both the client and the service provider. Anything else leaves the interpretation of the relationship between the parties to the court. Using management time to settle formal terms of appointment should never be seen as a distraction from 'getting on with the job'; on the contrary, settling the terms of appointment is an essential part of the job. As Lord Clarke said in the very first paragraph of his judgment in the *RTS* case:

> The different decisions in the courts below and the arguments in this court
> demonstrate the perils of beginning work without agreeing the precise basis upon
> which it is to be done. The moral of the story is to agree first and to start work later.

Is it ever safe to use a letter of intent?

The use of letters of intent remains widespread throughout the industry. But should they have a place? Is a letter of intent better than nothing? The answer is that a letter of intent can serve a purpose, if the parties find themselves genuinely unable to agree formal terms before the works or services commence; but only if serious thought has been given to the terms of the letter so that it achieves legally that which the parties want it to achieve. Like any agreement governing the relationship between commercial parties, a letter of intent can take time and considerable skill to get right. Parties who see a letter of intent as a temporary quick fix, which can be achieved with minimal thought or legal input, will often suffer the consequences.

For very small projects an architect may be appointed on the basis of a letter contract, and the RIBA publishes *A guide to letter contracts for very small projects, surveys and reports*, which includes model letters and guidance notes. In some very exceptional cases, perhaps for a feasibility study where the final project definition remains to be determined, it may be necessary to proceed initially on the basis of an exchange of letters. The RIBA Quality Management Toolkit includes a sample 'client care letter' to cover these circumstances. Generally though the RIBA's position is that proceeding with an appointment on the basis of a letter of intent is to be avoided if at all possible.

When considering the terms of a letter of intent, ask: what do I want out of it? If it is not intended to create legally binding relations, this can be achieved by keeping the document very simple. It will not in itself be conclusive, but make explicit that the parties do not intend through the letter to create a legally binding contract. All else that needs be set out is the scope of the client's request for services, which may be accepted by the consultant. The client is indicating that if the consultant chooses to go ahead with the work, and does in fact carry out and complete the services, the client will pay what the services are reasonably worth. All other obligations that may be expected from a contract – an actual obligation to provide the work, timing for performance of that work – have no place in such an arrangement.

If the intention is to create legally binding relations, the parties need to invest management time and incur legal costs to properly set out the nature of the relationship and the extent to which they intend to be bound – just as the parties should for any contract. For example, if you do not wish to be potentially bound by the terms of a particular standard form contract or appointment, do not cross-refer to it. Refer instead, if necessary, to the specific terms with which you choose to govern your relationship. The logical conclusion to be drawn is that the time and expertise required to be invested in making a letter of intent fit for the purpose of legally binding the parties could almost always be better spent in settling formal contract or appointment terms.

If for whatever reason the agreement of a formal contract or appointment seems impossible prior to commencement of the works or services, then a letter of intent which properly sets out the scope of the work and the payment terms should be considered in preference to an oral instruction or an exchange of e-mails. But think about why the agreement of a formal contract seems impossible.

- Is it simply a question of timing?
- Is there a deep-rooted point of disagreement that no amount of time negotiating will cure?

In the former case, proceed with caution, but in the latter case, consider whether you should be proceeding at all. Consider whether it is possible to have a non-binding letter of intent; this may concentrate minds on agreeing something more formal, but are the parties willing to proceed without contractual protection in the meantime? This may simply be unrealistic on a high value or time-critical project. Sometimes a legally binding letter of intent seems like the only viable 'middle ground' between nothing and a formal contract or appointment. But viewing a binding letter of intent as a quick fix, to be taken somehow more lightly than a formal contract, is a mistake.

The parties should be no less thorough in their approach to settling a letter of intent than they would be when dealing with a full-blown contract. The letter of intent could be limited in scope, or time, or value, but if it is intended to be legally binding the terms should be no less certain than would be the terms of a formal contract.

If the letter of intent is intended to be legally binding, but important terms remain to be agreed or are ambiguous, then both parties are proceeding at risk, because there is no certainty as to how a court would interpret the relationship between the parties. In these circumstances, it is vital that the parties continue to negotiate and do not rely on the letter of intent to see them through to the end of the project. It is only safe to rely on a letter of intent through to completion if the letter sets out the parties' intentions for their respective rights and obligations as clearly as the formal contract would have done.

2.3   The law of tort

2.3.1   What is a tort?

The word 'tort' derives from archaic English for an injury, literally something twisted. It now means a civil legal wrong, as distinct from a criminal legal wrong. A party may commit a 'tort', as other parties may commit a 'crime'. Some tortious behaviour may also in fact be criminal.

In tort cases, the party that claims to have suffered a loss, and brings a claim, is called the 'claimant' and the party alleged to have inflicted the damage is the 'defendant'. The role of the law of tort is to compensate victims of tortious behaviour for their resulting losses. The objectives of criminal law, in contrast, focus on punishment and deterrence.

Tort is concerned with the allocation of legal liability for losses which will inevitably occur in any mature society. The damage may take many forms, including personal injury, physical damage to property, economic loss, damage to a party's image or reputation, and interference with rights in intellectual property. The law of tort does not provide a remedy in every case where a person suffers damage. Over the long development of the law, courts and governments have taken decisions about which interests need to be protected by the law, so we have a body of decided cases and statute law that requires people to do or refrain from doing certain things, but not others, and allows redress for an infringement of another person's rights created by those cases or statutes.

2.3.2   What is negligence?

Of the many different categories of tort recognised by law, the most important by far is the tort of negligence.

Practically, for an architect, a claim in tort will usually mean a claim for negligence.

A negligent act, or omission (a failure to do something), is one which breaches a legal duty to take care and causes damage to a claimant. So for there to be negligence, there must be:

- a legal *duty of care* on the part of the defendant not to cause damage to the claimant;
- a *breach of that duty*; and
- *damage* suffered by the claimant as a consequence of the defendant's breach of duty.

The separation of these elements is sometimes not realistic when a court reviews the facts of a case, but nevertheless the courts have developed tests to decide whether each of these elements is present in any particular set of circumstances. Arguably, these are simply three ways of assessing the underlying issue of 'foreseeability'. Could the defendant have foreseen that the specific claimant could be affected by its conduct? Could the defendant have foreseen that its conduct would cause harm? Could the defendant have foreseen that its breach of duty would cause the damage suffered? One complicating factor is that, although the principles of tort law have general application, and the duties concerned are duties owed to people generally, the courts decide cases on individual sets of facts. There are therefore two key questions for the court:

- Does the defendant owe a duty of care to *this* claimant not to cause *this* type of damage?
- Has the defendant breached its duty to *this* claimant?

Foreseeability in practice – the case of *Acrecrest Ltd v Hattrell & Partners*

The architect in this case had been engaged by a developer to design a block of flats. The architect's specifications required the foundations to be built to a depth of 3 feet 6 inches; during a subsequent examination of the foundation trenches, a local authority building inspector found tree roots in part of the site and instructed that the foundations in that area should be dug to a depth of 5 feet. The architect complied, but the foundation design was still not in accordance with the Building Regulations then current, which required foundations to be specified and constructed to a depth sufficient to safeguard the building against damage by swelling or sinking of the subsoil.

The offending trees and tree roots were removed from site before construction commenced. Unfortunately, when the block of flats was complete, cracks began to appear in the structure; the removal of the trees had resulted in swelling of the subsoil, which caused the foundations to 'heave' which, in turn, caused the cracks in the structure. The foundations had not been specified or constructed to a sufficient depth to counteract the heave; if the foundations had been specified to a uniform depth of 5 feet over the entire site, the problem could have been prevented.

The court held that the architect's foundation design should have been based on adequate knowledge of the subsoil conditions and the then current Building Regulations. The heaving and cracking were entirely foreseeable consequences of failing to specify foundations to a sufficient uniform depth. The architect was liable to the client for the full extent of the damage caused by heave, because it was foreseeable that damage of that type would be caused. It did not matter that it was not foreseeable that the damage would be quite as extensive as it turned out to be.

2.3.3 When does a party owe a duty of care?

The concept of the duty of care is used by courts to define when a party should be considered to be obliged to take care not to harm the interests of another party through their negligent behaviour. An act or omission may be negligent, and may even cause damage, but it is not in every case that the law decides the negligent party should be held legally responsible.

The duty of care is the key control mechanism used by the courts to maintain the scope of negligent liability within the limits that they think wider society, and the court system, can bear. The courts have regularly exercised their considerable discretion, finding the existence of a duty in some cases, and the absence of a duty in other cases, based on policy considerations such as, for example, what would be considered 'fair' in all the circumstances, or to what extent a duty can be allowed to exist without opening the floodgates and swamping the courts with claims. So how do the courts decide when a duty of care is owed?

The neighbour principle

The modern law of negligence began less than 100 years ago with the case of a Mrs Donoghue, who suffered illness after drinking a bottle of ginger beer that had been bought for her by a friend. She was prevented by the doctrine of privity from making a claim in contract – she had not purchased the drink herself. Even so, the House of Lords in the case of *Donoghue v Stevenson* found that the manufacturer did owe her a duty of care to make sure that the contents of the bottle would not cause her physical harm.

The court started from the biblical passage requiring believers to 'love thy neighbour' and derived from this the legal principle that people 'must not injure' their neighbour. The 'neighbour principle' means that a person must take reasonable care to avoid acts or omissions which a reasonable person could foresee would be likely to cause harm to their neighbours. For these purposes 'neighbours' was defined to include those people so closely affected by the acts or omissions that a reasonable person could have foreseen them suffering harm.

There was a period of significant expansion in the law of negligence during the years 1978 to 1990, beginning with the House of Lords case *Anns v London Borough of Merton*, when the floodgates were opened and the courts showed a willingness to consider the neighbour principle as generally applicable unless there was a good reason of public policy for it to be excluded. Since then the tests for duty of care have become more restrictive, as set out below, but it is worth knowing the historical context in this fluid area of law, to understand the potential unpredictability of the courts.

Development of the current, more restrictive tests for a duty of care

The courts do not now recognise a general principle of liability in negligence. In *Caparo Industries v Dickman*, the court identified a three-stage test to decide the presence of a duty of care:

1   Was it reasonably foreseeable that the defendant's conduct would cause damage to the claimant?

2   Was there a sufficient relationship of 'proximity' between the claimant and the defendant, so that the defendant should have had the claimant in mind when carrying out its actions?

3   Overall, was the situation one in which the court considers it fair, just and reasonable that the law should impose a duty of a given scope on one party for the benefit of the other?

This remains good law but has been refined further by subsequent House of Lords cases.

In 1995, the House of Lords in the *Henderson v Merrett Syndicates* case focused on 'assumption of responsibility' by the party committing the tort as the basis for the claimant to recover damages. This approach has been adopted in many important cases, sometimes in tandem with the *Caparo* three-stage test, though sometimes the court has considered assumption of responsibility to be a sufficient test on its own. In 2008 the House of Lords took a chisel to their sculpture once again in the *Transfield Shipping* case and this time emphasised the need for a court to decide whether the defendant ought fairly and reasonably in all the circumstances to be seen as having accepted responsibility to the claimant to guard against the type of loss which occurred. That is where we currently are.

The concept of a duty of care is discussed further below in the context of economic loss, which was the focus of many of the cases mentioned in this section.

2.3.4   What amounts to a breach of duty?

Architecture is a profession, and the legal duty of any professional architect in carrying out their work is to exercise the reasonable skill and care that would be expected of the ordinarily skilled architect. This is an entirely objective test and the particular special skills or inadequacies of the individual architect compared with other members of their profession are not generally taken into account. The largest international practice and the smallest one-man band are subject to the same test for breach of duty, in tort.

Most professionals will aspire to perfection, but they do not ordinarily have to achieve perfection. It is possible for an architect to make a mistake without being negligent. Some errors are not substantial enough to amount to negligence; others may be substantial, but if the architect can show that a responsible body of members of their profession would have done the same thing, they will not ordinarily be said to have acted negligently.

For example, if an architect has designed a building with an access ramp for wheelchair access from the street up to the doorway, the architect will be negligent if on their elevation drawings they misstate the existing site levels so that the ramp gradient when built is outside the tolerances allowed by Part M of the Building Regulations. However, if the site levels shown on the architect's elevations are incorrect but the access ramp when built on the basis of the drawings remains within the allowable tolerances, this is just an error, not a negligent error, and the architect has been fortunate.

Whether an architect's actions amount to a breach of duty is judged on the basis of the state of knowledge within the profession at the time the architect acted. There is no place for hindsight in this judgement and no scope for an architect to be retrospectively punished for acting in a way that was accepted at the time but subsequently came to be seen as negligent.

Ultimately, though, it is not always possible or desirable to keep separate the questions of breach of duty and the existence of a duty in the first place, and the question of whether the damage caused was too remote a possibility to foresee. Reasonable foreseeability is at the heart of all this; if a reasonable person can foresee that damage is likely to result from their actions, this both creates the duty and sets the parameters for what will amount to a breach of that duty.

2.3.5 What do we mean by 'damage'?

For there to be negligence, the claimant must establish that the defendant's breach of duty caused actual damage. Generally, damage must mean physical damage to persons or property in order for there to be a viable claim in tort.

To prove causation, the claimant must not only show that there is a factual material connection between the defendant's actions and the damage, but must also show 'causation in law' by establishing that the damage which occurred was a reasonably foreseeable consequence of the defendant's actions.

Once again, foreseeability is the key ingredient. Even where there is a duty of care not to cause a particular type of damage but that type of damage occurs and the damage was factually caused by the actions of the defendant, this is not in itself proof of negligence without the missing ingredient – there must be proof that the damage was a reasonably foreseeable consequence of the defendant's actions.

2.3.6   Can an architect be liable in negligence for pure economic losses?

The existence of a duty of care in cases of physical damage, to persons or property, is generally not problematic. It is difficult to argue against a duty to take care to avoid physical harm being caused to other people or their property.

The real battleground, for the past 30 years if not longer, has been in the field of pure economic loss:

- pure economic loss resulting from negligent conduct is generally not recoverable;
- pure economic loss resulting from negligent misstatements, in contrast, has long been considered recoverable in appropriate circumstances.

Pure economic loss means loss suffered by a claimant which is not an immediate consequence of physical damage caused by the actions of the defendant. The word 'pure' is used to distinguish such losses, generally not recoverable, from economic losses which are a consequence of physical damage and can be recovered in tort. This can sometimes be a hard distinction to make, but the case of *Spartan Steel and Alloys Ltd v Martin & Co (Contractors)* shows how the courts define which losses are 'truly consequential' on the material damage.

The production of metal in the claimant's factory was brought to a standstill when the defendant, a contractor, negligently damaged an electricity cable and cut off the claimant's power supply. The price for the metal went down during the period the electricity was cut off. The claimant lost profit on the melt that had been in production at the time; they also claimed for the loss of profit on four other melts that would have taken place had the electricity not been cut off. The majority decision of the Court of Appeal was that the lost profit on the metal in production at the time of the power cut was recoverable, but the lost profit on the other four melts was pure economic loss, not recoverable because it could not be shown to be an immediate consequence of the physical damage the contractor had caused.

Pure economic loss is an area of the highest importance for architects, because of the potentially huge increase in the scope of the architect's liability if they assume responsibility for pure economic losses. So it is unfortunate that some of the fine legal distinctions in the decided cases can be so difficult to understand. Was the lost profit on the melt that was in progress really any different from the loss of profit on the hypothetical 'lost' melts? The delay in production as a whole did, after all, flow from the physical damage to the electricity cable. Part of the problem is that the courts are not trying to say there is a logical distinction. Instead, the courts are expressing a reluctance to recognise a duty of care to guard against pure economic loss, on policy grounds. Partly the courts are wary that they would be swamped with claims for economic losses if their approach ever again became less restrictive, and partly the courts consider it unfair to hold a defendant liable for all of the consequences of their actions, however remote and unforeseeable those consequences might be. There have to be cut-off points somewhere, and pure economic loss is one of them. But caution is still required – even pure economic loss can be recovered in certain circumstances.

The starting point for the current restrictive approach was the case of *Murphy v Brentwood* which decided that the infliction of a purely economic loss on a party does not universally require to be justified, in contrast to the approach to be taken in cases of physical injury to people or property:

> If [pure economic loss] is to be characterised as wrongful it is necessary to find some
> factor beyond the mere occurrence of the loss and the fact that its occurrence could
> be foreseen.

This doctrine does leave the door slightly ajar; if there is some additional factor, some special circumstance, that justifies the imposition of a duty to avoid causing pure economic loss, a successful claim can be made. Looked at in this way, the *Murphy* case does not provide the comprehensive protection against claims for pure economic loss that some construction professionals had hoped it did.

In the years since *Murphy,* whilst the overall trend has been restrictive, the courts have also explored a potential line of authority in support of economic loss claims, discussed below, based on the concept of an 'assumption of responsibility' on the part of consultants and contractors to carry out their services using reasonable skill and care not to cause pure economic loss.

2.3.7 In what circumstances does an assumption of responsibility arise?

Since the post-*Murphy* clamp-down, what has essentially happened is this. The courts have taken the rule made in a 1964 case, *Hedley Byrne v Heller & Partners*, which said that pure economic loss could be recovered in tort in certain circumstances if it resulted from a negligent misstatement, and expanded it to allow such claims, in restricted circumstances only, even if the loss is caused by negligent conduct.

The *Hedley Byrne* case involved a negligent financial reference; the claimant, in reliance on the negligent advice it received, suffered a financial loss following the insolvency of a client. The House of Lords decided that the defendant must be liable for pure economic losses resulting from negligent misstatements if there was in existence a special relationship between the parties based on a voluntary assumption of responsibility, and if the claimant had reasonably relied on the defendant's statement.

The House of Lords, again in the case of *Henderson v Merrett Syndicates Ltd*, took the logical step of saying that if a person assumes responsibility to another in respect of certain services, there is no reason why they should not be liable to that other person in damages in respect of any pure economic loss that flows from the negligent performance of those services. There was no reason for the principle to relate only to liability for statements but not actions; any professional task or service, by word or deed, is now covered by the principle.

A contractual relationship may establish an assumption of responsibility

It will be obvious that the most common way of assuming responsibility to another in a business context is through a contract. So the law is now that an architect, or any other construction professional, including a contractor without design responsibility, may be potentially liable in tort for pure economic losses to a party if there is a contract between the parties requiring the professional to exercise reasonable skill and care. The current position is summed up neatly in the case of *Robinson v PE Jones (Contractors) Limited*. Importantly, the *Robinson* case also makes clear that the terms of the contract can be drafted so as to prevent a concurrent duty of care in tort from arising at all; just such a term was included in Mr Robinson's contract and as a result he was unsuccessful in his claim. Both points of principle were later upheld by the Court of Appeal.

Mr Robinson had signed a contract with the house builder PE Jones in 1992; when a significant defect in the chimney flue of the completed property emerged over 12 years later, an action for breach of contract was not possible because the relevant contractual limitation period had expired. Only a claim in tort would do – for latent defects, the long-stop limitation period is 15 years. Mr Robinson had suffered pure economic loss only – his house was worth less because of the building defects. Was there enough to establish a duty of care in tort?

The Court held that there was. If there is a contractual relationship obliging the professional to exercise reasonable skill and care in the performance of the services, this in itself may be enough (note, not necessarily *will* be enough) to establish an 'assumption of responsibility'; therefore there may be a duty of care in tort to avoid pure economic losses which is concurrent with the duty of care under the contract. This concurrent duty in tort may arise from a contractual relationship in circumstances where:

- one party has a special 'skill', broadly understood to include special knowledge;
- that party agrees to perform services (not limited to the provision of information and advice, or to the performance of professional services), in circumstances where there is an express or implied obligation to exercise reasonable care and skill while providing those services;
- considered objectively, those circumstances disclose both an assumption of responsibility by that party to the other for the performance of those services and reliance by the other party; and
- the contractual relationship is not inconsistent with the existence of that duty in tort.

As expressed by the High Court in *Robinson*, there is effectively a presumption (in relation to professional consultants) that there has been an assumption of responsibility in cases where there is a contract between the parties requiring reasonable skill and care. In the absence of circumstances pointing to a different conclusion, all the necessary ingredients to establish a tortious duty of care are present. The Court of Appeal was more measured in its decision and focused on the entirety of the relationship between the parties, of which the contract was just one element, as being indicative of whether or not there was an assumption of responsibility. But the principle is beyond doubt:

liability for economic loss in tort can exist alongside a contractual duty of care, if all the evidence points to an assumption of responsibility.

2.3.8   Pure economic loss and the Defective Premises Act 1972

Parliament has made provision by statute through the Defective Premises Act 1972 ('the DPA') for the recovery of pure economic loss. The DPA imposes a number of specified obligations in relation to those involved in the construction of dwelling houses. In fact, the *Robinson* case, and those others which can be interpreted as equating an assumption of responsibility in tort with a contractual relationship, do not go as far as the DPA. The DPA provides that any person taking on work for the provision of a dwelling owes a duty not only to the original owner (the *Robinson* situation), but also to every person acquiring an interest in the dwelling – any subsequent owners.

This duty requires that the work is carried out in a workmanlike or professional manner such that the dwelling will be fit for habitation when completed. The DPA applies to all building professionals, including architects. The duty cannot be excluded by contract.

The remedy for breach of the DPA is damages, and pure economic loss (the diminution in value of the property itself caused by negligence) is recoverable. The potentially onerous nature of the DPA obligations was highlighted in the case of *Bole v Huntsbuild*, which concerned cracking to a building structure caused by heave due to inadequate foundation depth – facts very similar to the *Acrecrest* case discussed above. The Court of Appeal strongly upheld the consumer protection spirit of the DPA, both in the strictness with which it defined 'suitability for purpose' and 'fitness for habitation' and the apparent generosity with which it established the correct measure of damages.

It is possible that an increasing number of claims for pure economic loss could be brought against architects under the DPA, particularly bearing in mind the current restrictive approach to pure economic loss favoured by the courts. However, the limitation period for actions under the DPA is just 6 years from completion of the work concerned, which may limit the scope for a significant increase in claims. For subsequent owners with no prospect of a contractual or assumption of responsibility-based claim, though, the DPA is a potentially useful tool and one of which architects should be aware.

2.3.9 Summary of practical effects for architects

When is a duty of care owed? When may an architect be liable for pure economic loss?

The numerous attempts to define and refine the scope of the tort of negligence, and in particular the duty of care, seem when taken individually to be sensible, useful, applicable tests for lawyers and judges. But for an overview, it is instructive to go back to the *Caparo* case, where the House of Lords denied that any such practical application was possible, commenting that:

> a series of decisions [in the House of Lords] have emphasised the inability of any single general principle to provide a practical test which can be applied to every situation to determine whether a duty of care is owed and, if so, what is its scope

and that proximity, fairness and assumption of responsibility are:

> little more than convenient labels to attach to the features of different specific situations which, on a detailed examination of all the circumstances, the law recognises pragmatically as giving rise to a duty of care of a given scope.

What does all the legal theory mean, practically, for architects? Liability for negligence is an intensely practical issue for architects; every statement made, every drawing produced, every certificate issued, in a professional capacity, is an expression of the architect's skill and potentially creates a duty of care for parties relying on the quality of the architect's performance, whether or not they have a contract with the architect.

The numerous tests for establishing a duty of care are arguably just so many ways of saying the same thing. Is an assumption of responsibility really any different from saying that the parties have a relationship of proximity? The overall lesson for an architect is that the closer the relationship with another party, the more likely it is that a duty of care in tort will be found to exist and, if the relationship is contractual, the scope of the duty of care may be wide enough to include a duty to avoid causing pure economic losses.

Some key principles are apparent:

- An architect will be liable in negligence for loss which is the direct result of physical damage to persons or property, if duty, breach and causation are established.
- An architect is likely to owe their client the same duty in negligence in relation to pure economic loss as they owe under any contract the parties have made ('concurrent liability'), unless there are any circumstances which would lead the court to a different conclusion.
- The architect and the client can by the terms of their contract prevent such a concurrent duty of care in negligence from arising.
- An architect may be liable in negligence for pure economic loss caused to non-client third parties by negligent misstatements under the principle in *Hedley Byrne*, if there has been an assumption of responsibility coupled with reliance.
- An architect's liability in negligence for pure economic loss caused to non-client third parties by negligent conduct is restricted, but not eliminated, and the courts have left open the possibility of there being an assumption of responsibility for pure economic loss caused in this way – a contractual relationship is not necessarily the only way for there to be an assumption of responsibility.
- An architect may be liable under the 1972 DPA for pure economic loss caused to non-client third parties by negligence.

2.4   Limitation periods

2.4.1   Why are limitation periods important?

With the passage of time, it becomes increasingly difficult for the courts to do justice between the parties to a civil claim. The memories of witnesses may become more unreliable and important documents may be mislaid.

As a matter of public policy, the law imposes limitation periods within which an action in tort or for a breach of contract must be commenced. 'Commencing' an action means issuing a claim form to begin the litigation process before the courts. The limitation periods are imposed by statute, primarily the Limitation Act 1980 as amended by the Latent Damage Act 1986.

With any new claim, but particularly for claims relating to latent defects (discussed below in section 2.4.3) or projects that were completed some years ago, it is important that an architect seeks specialist legal advice so as not to miss out on the possibility of a limitation defence. If the limitation period has expired, the defendant will generally have an absolute defence to any action which the claimant tries to instigate. The claim is described as being 'statute-barred'.

The limitation periods for actions based on contract and tort are different, with time beginning to run from different starting points:

- in a negligence claim, time will usually run from the date when the negligent act or omission caused damage to occur;
- in a contract claim, the limitation period runs from the date when the contract was breached.

The time limits also differ according to the type of contract and, in tort, according to the cause of action.

Because of these differences, the question of whether a claimant has the option of pursuing a claim in either contract or tort can become extremely important. If the limitation period for an action under the contract has expired, the claimant may have no option but to explore the possibility of making a claim in tort on the same facts.

By way of example, the 2010 case *Robinson v PE Jones (Contractors) Limited*, discussed above in section 2.3.7 in the context of economic loss, required the court to consider whether a builder could in principle owe a duty in contract and at the same time owe a duty to their client in tort not to cause the client to suffer economic loss. The motivation for the client in trying to make a claim in tort was that their ability to bring a claim in contract had expired. Mr Robinson entered into a contract with Jones to purchase a property in 1992; serious defects to the chimney flues were only discovered in 2004 and Mr Robinson issued proceedings in 2006, 14 years after the last work was done at the property by Jones. Even if it had been executed as a deed, the limitation period for an action in contract had long since lapsed; Mr Robinson sought the benefit of the extended limitation period for an action in tort for latent defects resulting from negligence.

The *Robinson* case also highlights one further important limitation issue; limitation periods may be varied or even excluded by agreement.

A client with a strong negotiating position may seek to effectively extend the contractual limitation period in an architect's appointment, for example by insisting upon time running from the issue of the certificate of making good defects. But the architect's involvement in the project may have ended long before that; or indeed, making good of defects may never happen, potentially leaving the limitation period open-ended.

Architects should always resist any attempt to extend the limitation periods for actions under their appointments. The Limitation Act periods were decided upon for a reason; after an extended period of time, it becomes harder to guarantee a sufficiently high quality of justice. An architect coming under pressure to agree an extended limitation period should remind their client of this practical reason for the statutory rules, and also remind the client that an extension of the statutory duration of liability may not be covered by the architect's professional indemnity insurance (PII). PII policies typically provide that performance warranties in contracts are only covered to the extent that they would have existed anyway, without the specific wording of the contract in question. An extension beyond the statutory periods discussed in section 2.4.2 would not, therefore, usually be covered.

In contrast, a contractor or consultant whose work on a project incorporates products using cutting-edge technology may seek to drastically reduce the limitation period for actions under their contract because of the inherent risk that the working life of innovative technology can be difficult to gauge.

In *Robinson*, the court rejected the building owner's claim in tort, even though it found that in principle a builder could owe a concurrent duty in contract and in tort, because the terms of the contract agreed between the parties were not consistent with the concurrent duty. The builder had gone to the trouble of negotiating a provision in the original contract that excluded any duty to the employer in respect of 'any defect, error or omission in the execution of the work' save for the 10-year period covered by the National House-Building Council's (NHBC) standard agreement, 'on which alone his rights and remedies are founded'. Unfortunately for Mr Robinson, the 10-year period of the NHBC agreement had expired, and it cut across any other longer limitation period for actions that may otherwise have been available to him.

2.4.2   The limitation period in contract

In a claim based on a 'simple' contract, one executed under hand or otherwise not as a deed, the limitation period is 6 years, running from the date when the contract was breached. The period is extended to 12 years if the contract was executed as a deed.

The date of breach of the contract may, especially for an architect or other design professional, occur before any physical damage becomes apparent. If there has been a negligent design of a building element, it may be possible to show that physical damage will ultimately be caused to the building. The breach of contract occurs when the negligent design is produced, and so the client will be entitled to claim for the diminution in value of the property before the physical manifestation of the damage. This has positive and negative implications for an architect. If a negligent design is spotted early, the architect can be sued for breach there and then. But if the problem is not identified until the physical manifestation of damage, it may be that the contractual limitation period has expired, and the client will be left at best with a claim in tort – always a slightly more problematic prospect evidentially for a claimant, because the first thing the claimant would have to do is establish that the architect owed them a duty of care at all.

The limitation rules relating to indemnity provisions

One issue which may have significant practical implications for an architect is the limitation period for liability under indemnity clauses. Bespoke forms of professional appointment and collateral warranty drafted by clients will often feature indemnity provisions. For example, the consultant may be obliged to indemnify the client in relation to third party claims for breach of intellectual property rights, claims relating to death or personal injury or claims arising from a breach of confidentiality provisions. Some may even go so far as to seek a general indemnity in relation to any losses arising from the performance of the architect's services. Architects should always resist the incorporation of indemnities. One important reason for doing so is that the limitation period associated with claims under an indemnity runs only from the date when the indemnified liability or loss is actually suffered. This could be significantly after the expiry of the ordinary period for contractual claims, which starts to run from the date of the breach of contract that caused the loss. Claims based on indemnity clauses are also unlikely to be covered by most PII policy wordings.

2.4.3   The limitation period in negligence

According to the Limitation Act 1980, an action founded on tort must be brought within 6 years of the date when the cause of action 'accrued' (Figure 4). No further explanation is given, but the common law rule is that the cause of action in negligence accrues when damage is caused. If the damage is physical damage, the courts will generally say that the cause of action accrues when the physical damage first becomes manifest – although there is some conflicting authority for the proposition that in the case of a defective building the cause of action in negligence accrues at the time when the value of the property in the market falls as a consequence of the relevant defects. The issue can be of great importance, particularly in relation to defects which have remained undiscovered for a long period of time; clarification from the courts is overdue.

Of particular relevance to building cases is the potential for 'latent damage', damage which was not reasonably discoverable before the expiry of the basic 6-year limitation period. It is possible to bring a claim outside the 6-year limitation period in such circumstances thanks to section 14A of the Limitation Act 1980, which was included following amendment by the Latent Damage Act in 1986. In such circumstances, the limitation period will be 3 years from the date when the claimant had 'the knowledge required for bringing an action for damages in respect of the relevant damage', or 3 years from the date they could reasonably have been expected to know that they could bring such a claim. In either case,

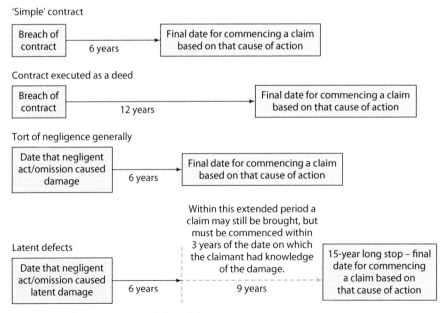

Figure 4 Limitation periods for claims

claims are subject to a long-stop limitation period of 15 years from the date of the defendant's original negligent act or omission.

The latent defects limitation period highlights two important practical issues for architects. It is vital that proper provision is made for the retention of documents relating to any project for 15 years after completion (16 years to be on the safe side) because, even though it may be unlikely that a claim will be made at such distance from the date of the project, it will be impossible to properly defend yourself against a claim if you do not have the relevant written records relating to the project. For the same reason, it is also vital that PII is maintained in relation to projects for the same period.

2.5   Working overseas

2.5.1   The same rules will not apply

The potential benefits of expanding your practice to include work on projects outside the UK come with certain risks attached. Different legal considerations apply in relation to work in foreign jurisdictions. You should always seek legal advice before entering into an appointment to provide services overseas and this advice should include, as appropriate, advice from a local lawyer based in the relevant jurisdiction.

2.5.2   Particular problems in relation to foreign work

Foreign laws may be more onerous

The local laws relating to your duty of care and the interpretation of your professional appointment may be expected to be different from those which you would expect in the UK, but some local laws are particularly onerous. For example, when carrying out work under an appointment governed by the laws of the United Arab Emirates, architects should be wary of the provisions of the local code that impose strict liability – that is, obligations that require more than the exercise of reasonable skill and care. Emirati law provides that both contractors and consultants may have to compensate their employer for the collapse of, or a defect which threatens the stability of, a building.

This liability may apply even if the contractor or consultants are not at fault and, for example, the fault is found to be with the land being built upon. This strict liability provision is known as 'decennial liability', because contractors and consultants are subject to such liability for a period of 10 years after handover of the building. The Emirati code is not unique and decennial liability is a feature of the laws of many jurisdictions in the

Middle East and elsewhere. Take local legal advice; it is also vital to clarify with your insurers whether accepting terms of appointment governed by foreign laws may create a coverage issue under your PII policy.

Your PII cover may not apply to the overseas job you have secured

Check with your broker – does your policy provide cover for projects worldwide? There is also the question of the extent to which local laws will create policy coverage issues. Decennial liability is an example; under such 'strict liability' provisions it is not necessary to prove negligence or breach of a professional duty of care in order for a claim to be made. But most PII policies cover only negligent acts and omissions and breaches of contract, so may not respond to a claim where there is no accusation of negligence. Check with your broker and insurer to see whether specific endorsements to your policy may be required to cover you adequately for work on overseas projects.

You will need to comply with local standards/building regulations

As well as the laws governing your own appointment, and the contractual relationships with the rest of the project team, you should bear in mind that the project will need to be designed and constructed in compliance with the local equivalents of our procurement laws, planning law, health and safety legislation and Building Regulations. Do you have this local knowledge? If not, it is vital that you work in conjunction with a local architect who does have this knowledge and expertise.

You may be required to enter into an association with a local architect

Some clients in foreign jurisdictions will require you to work in association with a local architect in any case. One reason for this is that it is common sense – the client wants to ensure that the local building laws are complied with, but knows there is a risk that, however knowledgeable a foreign architect may be, their knowledge of the local law and practice may never be as intimate as that of a local architect. Another reason is that many foreign governments want to ensure work for local consultants. You should be wary of working with a local architect whose work you have no experience of. You must ensure that your appointment terms make very clear that, to the extent that the local architect is responsible for ensuring compliance with local building laws, this responsibility is entirely that of the local architect and you cannot be held liable for any errors or omissions in their work. It is vital that you see and approve the local architect's appointment and the schedule of the services that they are going to be providing.

Finding a satisfactory dispute resolution mechanism may be problematic

Arbitration may be the safest course in the event of a dispute because it can be harder to enforce a judgment of a UK court in a foreign jurisdiction than it is to enforce an arbitrator's award. The architect may not be given a choice though. If the client selects a local court of arbitration, what can the architect do to attempt to ensure fairness? Insisting upon a three-person arbitration panel is always sensible; agreeing to abide by the judgment of a single arbitrator is a leap of faith if the architect has no prior experience of that individual's competence or fairness.

Getting paid can be more problematic

Getting paid can be problematic with any client with whom you have not worked extensively. Different clients have different approaches to the timing of payments and the niceties of withholding sums you think are due; some clients are just less scrupulous than others. When working in a foreign jurisdiction the risk is increased because of the potentially less effective dispute resolution options; there is no right to launch a quick Construction Act adjudication in Emirati law if you think a fee payment has been unfairly withheld.

The possibility of not being paid in full is a commercial risk. The options available to you to reduce that risk depend largely upon the strength of your bargaining position before you enter into your professional appointment. The safest option is to get money up front, but clients are often unwilling to take such a leap of faith. You could consider requesting that an 'escrow account' is set up – a bank account into which the client must deposit sums in advance to pay forthcoming fee invoices, and which is administered by an independent third party. Alternatively you could request that the client provides a payment guarantee bond; depending upon the precise wording, you would be entitled to 'call' on the bond if the client fails to pay a sum properly due to you under your appointment. Finally, if your foreign client has a UK holding company, you may request that the UK parent provides a parent company guarantee.

Chapter 3

Professional appointments generally

This chapter:

- examines why it is essential for an architect to have a written appointment;

- provides an overview of the professional regulatory requirements for architects' appointments;

- describes the formalities for correct execution of a professional appointment.

3.1 The need for a written appointment

The contract that you make with the client on a job is described in this book as your 'professional appointment', or just simply the 'appointment'. For professionals, as opposed to contractors or sub-contractors, it is traditional to refer to the binding agreement made with the client in this way. It is helpful in that it avoids any confusion that might arise when referring to the 'contract' with the main contractor on a project. But simply put, the architect's appointment is their contract with the client.

Some publications refer to 'the fee agreement' when meaning the professional appointment, but this is potentially misleading. The appointment is not just about recording your level of fees. A good appointment will set out, in some detail, your fees, your services (the 'what you have to do' part) and your terms and conditions of appointment – the part that records the standard of care you must achieve when performing those services.

There is nothing that prescribes the form of appointment that an architect must have, and nothing to tell you how to recognise an appointment or what is should look like. In theory, the contract may be simple or complex, made by e-mail or exchange of letters, or as a 'deed', in a standard form, or a bespoke form, or even through an oral agreement not recorded in writing. This is just the theory though. In practice, there is every good reason to have a properly thought-out contract in writing, every time. The Architects Registration Board (ARB) and RIBA Codes of Conduct both require the architect to have a written appointment agreement.

Some architects are wary of pushing for the agreement of a formal appointment, particularly on smaller projects, with domestic (not commercial) clients or at times in the economic cycle when competition for work is intense. The perception is that clients may be put off by large amounts of paperwork, or that a client will see an architect presenting proposed appointment terms as having an unhealthy interest in protecting their own position or entitlement to fees. Alternatively, architects can get caught up in the whirlwind of a fast moving job, where there always seems to be something more important or urgent to do than settle the appointment terms, or sometimes an architect will want to concentrate on 'being an architect' rather than acting like a pseudo-lawyer. These are all dangerous positions to take.

Well-thought-out written appointment terms provide vitally important benefits and protection to both you and your client, especially in the situations where it is most likely that appointment terms will not be properly addressed – for example with a naïve domestic client, with a client who does not want to engage with the detail, or on a fast-moving commercial project. Agreeing the appointment terms, and taking the initiative to ensure that the issue is not forgotten even if the client is reluctant to address it, is not self-interest, it is 'being an architect'.

3.1.1 What are the applicable professional standards?

The ARB, created by the Architects Act 1997, is the UK's statutory regulator of architects. It maintains a public register, searchable online, of around 33,000 architects. The RIBA, founded in 1834, is a non-statutory body and receives no government funding, but acts on behalf of its 40,000 members for the general advancement of civil architecture through the promotion of its three guiding principles: integrity, competence and respect for the rights of others.

Both the ARB and the RIBA have written codes of professional conduct and, as discussed further in Chapter 10, each has investigative and disciplinary powers in relation to breaches of their code. Although only the ARB, operating under the Architects Act, has the power to impose fines for breaches of its code, both bodies have the power to suspend or erase an architect's name from their list. A suspension imposed by the ARB would effectively prevent an architect from describing themselves as an architect during the period of suspension, and a suspension imposed by the RIBA would prevent the architect from using the RIBA title; either of which may be expected to have a potentially serious effect on the architect's ability to practise until reinstated. The ARB and RIBA disciplinary procedures are considered in detail in Chapter 10 of this book.

Both the ARB Code and the RIBA Code set out detailed requirements for certain elements making up the agreement with the client to be set out in writing.

The terms of the RIBA Code (RIBA Code of Professional Conduct, Guidance Note 4) focus on the obligation of members to provide to their client, at the outset of any project, their terms and conditions of appointment. Guidance Note 4.2 provides that the terms of appointment should include:

- ☐ a clear statement of the client's requirements;
- ☐ a clear definition of the services required;
- ☐ an obligation to perform the services with due skill and care;
- ☐ an obligation to keep the client informed of progress;
- ☐ the roles of other parties who will provide services to the project;
- ☐ the name of any persons with authority to act on behalf of the client;
- ☐ procedures for calculation and payment of fees and expenses;
- ☐ any limitation of liability and insurance;

☐ provisions for protection of copyright and confidential information;
☐ provisions for suspension and determination; and
☐ provisions for dispute resolution.

The ARB Code (Architects Code: Standards of Conduct and Practice 2010 Version; published in September 2009) is, if anything, more strict. Instead of merely 'providing' terms of appointment, a requirement which could be complied with by, for example, cross-referring to a standard form of appointment in correspondence, the ARB Code provides in Standard 4.4 that *before* undertaking any professional work an architect must actually enter into a written agreement with their client, and the agreement must adequately cover:

☐ the contracting parties;
☐ the scope of work;
☐ the fee or method of calculating it;
☐ who will be responsible for what;
☐ the extent to which any of the architectural services will be sub-contracted;
☐ any constraints or limitations on the responsibilities of the parties;
☐ the provisions for suspension or termination of the agreement;
☐ a statement that the architect meets ARB insurance cover requirements;
☐ a statement that the architect is ARB registered and subject to the ARB Code;
☐ the architect's complaints-handling procedure;
☐ the ability of the client to refer complaints to the ARB;
☐ details of any special arrangements for resolving disputes.

In order not to fall foul of the professional standards, therefore, agreeing a written appointment prior to beginning work is not merely an option but a necessity.

3.1.2   Avoiding disputes over fees and the scope of work

The two go hand in hand. Inadequate or ambiguous terms of appointment may not always be the root cause of a dispute, but the failure of the parties to properly describe the essentials – who is doing what, when and for how much – can easily exacerbate a dispute which has arisen for other reasons.

Unless it is set out unambiguously in writing, there will always be scope for disagreement about what constitutes a 'basic' service, on the basis of which the basic fee is paid, and what is 'additional'. Why allow the potential for a dispute? An architect's fee should be based on an expectation of what it is they will be asked to do, so it is common sense to set out, clearly, a list of basic services and a list of potential additional services (ideally based on the RIBA Standard Conditions of Appointment 2010 (2012 revision) Schedules booklet, with as much additional detail about the services as possible), along with a mechanism for calculating the basic fee and a statement of what it is, and a mechanism for calculating the additional fees.

Without these basics, there may be scope for payments to be delayed as a result because it is unclear what sum is 'due' or what documentation the architect must present to the client when issuing accounts for payment. Cross-referring to the fee payment mechanism in another document, for example a standard form appointment, is never adequate. You should set out the fee payment provisions in the appointment document, in the context in which they will be operated.

3.1.3 Professional indemnity insurance requirements

A professional indemnity insurer can be expected to take a keen interest in the terms of any professional appointment, framework agreement, collateral warranty or other contract that the architect enters into in relation to their professional work. There may be a possibility of significant benefits for the architect insured if the insurer is given the opportunity to comment on the legal terms and conditions and the architect agrees to comply with the legal advice given by the insurer or on the insurer's behalf. There is conversely likely to be the risk of an increased insurance premium if the insurer becomes aware that its insured does not have a procedure for reviewing or negotiating the terms of its professional appointments and does not typically seek to negotiate out contractual liability provisions that are more onerous than the market standard.

3.2 Execution of documents

3.2.1 What is execution?

There are a number of different ways to validly 'execute' (signify your intention to be bound by) an appointment. All forms of execution involve marking the appointment document on its face in some way, either through the signature of relevant parties who are capable of binding the practice (for example, the partners) or by using a company seal, a stamp purchased from a law stationers that marks documents with a 'seal' incorporating the name of the company. The way in which an appointment is executed will depend partly on the nature of the document being agreed – is it to be a simple contract, or a deed? How you execute the appointment will also partly depend upon the legal capacity in which you are executing the document – are you executing the appointment in your capacity as an individual, a partnership, a limited liability partnership, a company?

3.2.2   Simple contract or deed?

There is no hard and fast rule, but typically the bigger the project and the more sophisticated the client, the more likely it is that you will be required to execute your appointment as a deed. A high contract value, a complex build, the involvement of large numbers of contractors and consultants and the use by the client of third party funding are all factors that would tend to lead to an architect being appointed by deed. In contrast, an appointment on a small-scale project such as a domestic refurbishment may often be executed as a simple contract, or 'under hand', terminology referring to the way in which parties execute a simple contract by their 'hands' (signature) and dating back to the days when a signature was not enough on its own to execute a document as a deed.

Why the difference? It all comes down to the respective contractual limitation periods. As discussed before in this book (see section 2.4.2), the limitation period for actions under a deed is 12 years and for actions under a simple contract the period is 6 years. A large project may take up a significant part of that 6 years before it is completed. If clients and funders are spending a lot of money on a project, they will want to protect their investment as effectively as possible for as long as possible. The way they typically achieve this is by having all the project documents, including the appointment of (or collateral warranties from) any professional, executed as deeds.

There is no requirement for the actual working content – the terms and conditions – of an appointment to be different if it is going to be executed as a deed as opposed to being executed as a simple contract. Most standard form appointments and building contracts contain signature blocks (formally known as 'execution' or 'attestation' clauses, but simply the section in a contract where the parties sign and/or attach their company seal) suitable for either. In practice, though, it is common for a deed of appointment to be longer and more detailed and for appointments executed under hand to be shorter, usually covering the same issues but in a less comprehensive way.

3.2.3   Execution as a deed

A number of formalities must be complied with in terms of the description and signing of an agreement in order to make it a deed. The agreement must:

- be in writing;
- make clear on its face that the parties making it intended it to be a deed; for example, by describing itself on its front sheet as a 'deed of appointment', and also by stating 'This deed is dated [   ]';
- be validly executed as a deed by the parties, so the signature block must explicitly say 'Executed as a deed …'; and
- be delivered.

'Delivered' in this context is a term with a long history, dating back to an age when parties were required to physically hand over the executed deed. Its meaning now is more conceptual; a deed is delivered by a party when they signify their intention to be irrevocably bound by its terms, so for many purposes the act of executing a deed in itself incorporates delivery.

There are in fact numerous ways for parties to execute an appointment as a deed, depending on their legal capacity, but a signature block for a practice set up as a partnership would typically provide as follows:

3

SIGNED AND DELIVERED AS A DEED BY [NAME OF PARTNERSHIP]

———————————————

Partner

———————————————

Witness

———————————————

Partner

———————————————

Witness

Each partner will sign, then the witness of each partner's signature; the client will sign in the way appropriate for them.

3.2.4 Execution under hand

No special formalities are required on the face of the appointment for execution under hand. The signature block for an appointment being executed in this way will typically provide as follows:

```
AS WITNESS THE HANDS OF THE PARTIES


_____          _____

Architect              Client



_____          _____

Witness                Witness
```

3.2.5 Execution by an individual

An architect who practises as a sole trader is able, as an individual, to execute contracts both under hand and as a deed, by signing the document in question in the presence of a witness, who also signs. To indicate that the witness has been present during signing it is generally sufficient after the architect's signature for the contract to read 'in the presence of' and be followed by the signature of the witness. It is a good habit to get into to ask the witness to also print their name, address and occupation. If there is any subsequent dispute about the circumstances in which the contract was witnessed, this will make it easier for the witness to be identified and located, if required to give evidence.

In order for the contract to be executed as a deed by an individual, the document must in addition comply with the usual formalities required for a deed, as described above.

3.2.6 Execution by a partnership

For reasons of tradition, and convenience, many group practices are in the form of a partnership. A partnership is described as a 'firm', never a company. Also in contrast with a company, a partnership does not have legal capacity in its own right – the partnership is simply the individuals who comprise it. It is best practice for the partners involved to execute a partnership deed, a contract setting out their respective rights and obligations. Although a number of profitable businesses over the years have operated without this degree of formality, it is strongly recommended that the nature of the working relationship is clarified whenever two or more architects act together. The question of whether a partnership exists or not can be very important in the context of collective liability, for example, and intellectual property rights.

The way in which a partnership executes deeds and other contracts is highly dependent upon the provisions of any partnership deed, which will, amongst other things, shed light on the question of who has authority to commit the partnership to a contract (to 'bind' the partnership). Generally, under the Partnership Act 1890, every partner is an agent of the firm and their other partners for the purpose of the partnership's business, and the acts of every partner will bind the firm and their partners. For the execution of contracts under hand, the signature of one partner will suffice to bind the partnership, provided the partner had authority to act for the firm. A partner's authority is based on the principle of 'agency' – the Partnership Act provides that each partner is the agent of the partnership for the partnership's business purposes.

The position is different for execution as a deed. Generally, one or more partners do not have implied authority to execute a deed that will bind the firm. Authority to execute a deed on behalf of a partnership must itself be conferred by a deed – usually in the form of the partnership deed, or a separate 'power of attorney' which must be executed by all the partners. If this authority is given, and the deed explicitly states that the partnership is executing the deed by a single partner as its agent, then a single partner may execute a deed so as to bind the partnership.

If no delegated authority is given in this way, a deed can only be validly executed by all the partners.

3.2.7   Execution by a limited liability partnership

The Limited Liability Partnerships Act 2000 created this new way of organising a business. The aim of a limited liability partnership (LLP) is to combine the benefits of limited liability that are conferred by company status with the other beneficial attributes of a traditional partnership structure. The LLP concept has proved very popular in some fields – the overwhelming majority of large law firms are now LLPs.

One important difference from the traditional partnership model is that an LLP has a legal personality separate from that of its members (the LLP equivalent of partners in a partnership). A Statutory Instrument (the Limited Liability Partnerships (Application of Companies Act 2006)

Regulations 2009, SI 2009/1804) allows LLPs to execute deeds and documents in the same way as companies, so execution of a deed requires two members to sign the deed on behalf of the LLP, or the use of the common seal of the LLP witnessed (and signed) by two members, or (this was the key change to execution of documents rendered by the Companies Act 2006) the signature of a single member acting on behalf of the LLP in the presence of a witness.

3.2.8   Execution by a company

An appointment may be executed by a company in a number of ways. It can be signed by a director in the presence of a witness who also signs (the new procedure allowed by the Companies Act 2006), or by two directors, or by a director and the company secretary, but as long as the document also states that it is duly executed by the company then any of these forms of execution will be valid and will have the same effect as execution using the common seal of the company (this rule comes from the Companies Act 2006 section 44(4)). In order for a company to execute an appointment as a deed, the formalities for a deed as set out above must also be complied with.

3.2.9   Dating a contract or deed

The date when the appointment, or any other contract, is executed by all parties and delivered should be made clear on the face of the document. The primary purpose of this is to show when the parties intended unequivocally to be bound by the terms of the agreement. The dating of the document will be done by hand, often by the lawyers for the originator of the document. In a standard form appointment there will always be a space for adding the date of execution; with a bespoke appointment, the date will often be added in a space on the front sheet. If the date is not written in, this will not generally invalidate the contract or deed; it simply means that any party seeking to rely on the date when the document took effect (the date of delivery, which in turn is generally the date it is executed) will have to prove what that date was.

The date of the contract or appointment is not relevant to the liability limitation period.

It is rare nowadays for all parties to be present and sign at the same time, so the date of an appointment will be the date when the last party executed it. It is bad practice to backdate any contract, especially a deed. Sometimes, usually in the context of a bespoke appointment, a contract will contain a clause setting out its 'effective date'. This may be earlier than the date when the document is executed, and will be intended by the client to ensure that all the work provided by the consultant or other service provider is viewed as being provided under and subject to the appointment, even if the first services were provided some time before execution of the appointment.

There are risks for an architect in agreeing to such an arrangement. If there is any question that any of the early services may have been provided in a way which does not meet the standards imposed by the subsequent appointment then either the 'effective date' should be rejected altogether or it should be agreed that the effective date does not apply to any specified services which do not comply with the appointment. A client will always push hard to ensure that *all* of the services provided by an architect, whether before or after the date of the appointment, are covered by its terms.

How would it work in practice if an architect knows that some of their early services are not in compliance with the form of appointment they are subsequently asked to sign? The client cannot force the architect to sign, but if the client insists that all of the services must be covered by the appointment, both parties are faced with a choice. For the architect, is the likely consequence of signing an appointment, knowing that they are in breach of its terms, a more serious risk than the consequences of not having a signed appointment at all? Can the architect do anything to bring the non-compliant early services into line with the appointment terms? Can the client be persuaded to compromise? After all, there are distinct disadvantages for the client in not having a signed appointment; without a signed contract, each party is taking a chance on what a court will decide has been agreed between the parties.

3.2.10   Do not take shortcuts

The approach to finalising and executing deeds and documents in the construction industry can sometimes be overly 'relaxed', sometimes at least in part because of the scale of the task involved; with a large number of documents involved in large construction projects, and with these regularly requiring last-minute amendments, standards can slip. There is no reason at all for an architect to get drawn into this culture. The general rule must be for an architect to exercise caution at all times when it comes to the execution of documents, whether this means the architect's own appointment or collateral warranties, or the execution of any other construction documentation, for example the building contract, that the architect is required to organise. Because the execution of a contract is the only way for a party to show a court unequivocally what it intended to agree, the courts have tended to take a strict line when it comes to defective execution, especially of deeds.

By way of example, the case of *R (on the application of Mercury Tax Group and another) v HMRC* ('the *Mercury* case') involved the dubious practice of 'recycling' a signature page, where the party organising the signing of documents by a number of parties took a signature from a superseded draft and attached it to a revised final contract to convey agreement of its terms by the signing party. This practice no doubt takes place regularly in the business world to avoid the potential inconvenience or embarrassment caused when an amendment is required to documents that have already been signed by all parties. The court confirmed that a signature on an incomplete draft contract or deed cannot be transferred and used to validly execute an amended final version of the document. This is common sense; the law and practice around the execution of contracts and deeds exists to protect commercial parties against the effects of fraud and mistake.

What if an amendment has to be made to a contract or deed after execution by all parties?

If the agreement has been executed by all the parties and contains a specified procedure for making amendments, this procedure must be complied with. For example, there may be a clause providing that:

> 'No additions, amendments or variations to this agreement shall be binding unless in writing and signed by the duly authorised representatives of the parties.'

If there is no specified procedure, it depends whether the document is a deed, and also whether the proposed changes are 'material' – whether the amendments alter the legal effect of the document on the respective parties, in terms of their rights and obligations under it. In short, if a document is not a deed the formalities for amending it post-execution are more relaxed, as long as the amendments are shown to be agreed by all of the parties.

With a deed, the position is more complicated. A non-material amendment, such as adding the date to the face of the deed, or filling in a blank – for example, adding the name of the structural engineer in a list of consultants – will not affect the validity of the deed, even if there is nothing to show that both parties agreed to the information being completed; this guidance comes from the case of *Raiffeisen Zentralbank Osterreich AG v Crossseas Shipping Ltd*. For a material alteration, both parties must consent, and demonstrate their consent, if the deed is not to be rendered void. An agreement to vary the material terms of a deed must in itself possess the attributes of a contract, but does not necessarily have to be a deed.

It is possible to amend a deed without executing a deed of amendment or variation, as long as both parties signify their agreement to the changes and there is valuable consideration (see section 2.2.2); this could be done by a simple contract, by letter, by an exchange of e-mails, or even orally, though the latter approach would store up trouble for the future in the event of a dispute about what amendments were agreed. What often happens in practice is that the parties agree to amend a document and arrange for amendments to be made 'in manuscript' (with handwritten additions or crossing out on the face of the document) by the lawyers for the party who originated the document. But bearing in mind the strictness with which the courts have applied the rules relating to the validity of execution of deeds, as in the *Mercury* case, proceeding with caution, even if it results in an increased administrative burden and takes up more management time, is sensible. The safest approach, for all but the most minor material amendments to a deed, is to record the agreement of the parties to the amendments in a separate document that is itself executed as a deed.

3.3 Who writes the written appointment?

What are the options for a written form of appointment? There are various standard form appointments drafted by industry bodies. The RIBA form has traditionally been the most popular standard form of appointment for an architect and would seem the obvious place to start. The current suite of appointments, the RIBA Agreements 2010 (2012 revision), has standard appointments in booklet form appropriate to a number of scenarios:

- a general appointment appropriate for medium- or large-scale projects;
- a concise, less detailed agreement for smaller projects;
- a domestic agreement; and
- a sub-consultant's appointment.

Unfortunately, certain clients, particularly commercial clients, may not want to accept the appointment of an architect on the basis of a RIBA standard form without amending its terms to, as they would see it, achieve a better balance of risk between the parties.

A standard form is produced by the Association of Consultant Architects ('ACA') the current version is known as ACA SFA 2012 Edition, which was updated to take into account the 2009 Construction Act and the 2010 Bribery Act. Again, a sophisticated client may not agree to use the ACA form as drafted.

It is open to an architect to take the initiative by proposing their own bespoke form of appointment, typically a document worked up by a lawyer, which can be adapted to suit the needs of an individual project. Because of the expense of obtaining professional legal input, these are usually the preserve of major architectural practices taking on large-scale commercial work. Smaller practices may have 'home-made' standard terms or engagement letters; however, it is generally not wise to use a document which has not been commented on by a lawyer. Commercially savvy clients will again often be reluctant to agree a bespoke form of appointment proposed by an architect, but a less sophisticated client engaging in a one-off project may welcome this approach.

Large-scale commercial clients who regularly engage in construction work will often have their own bespoke forms, or they will instruct firms of solicitors who will issue their own bespoke form of appointment to the architect for agreement. Any such document can be expected to favour the client's interests at the expense of the consultant, and should not be entered into without comment from legal advisors and insurers.

Whatever the nature of the document used as a starting point, each appointment on each project should be fully negotiated by the architect to ensure that the final signed version is appropriately tailored to the project in question and properly records all the terms of agreement between the parties.

Different projects will involve different balances of bargaining power between the architect and the client. A first-time domestic client may welcome an architect taking the initiative and issuing appointment terms, for example through a standard form booklet, for approval. In these circumstances, the architect should recommend in writing that the client seeks independent legal advice, but should in any case highlight any important or potentially onerous terms, such as limitations on their liability. Consumer clients are protected by the Unfair Terms in Consumer Contracts Regulations 1999, which require contract terms to be individually negotiated in this way – failure to do so could lead to certain terms of the appointment being invalidated.

When the terms are agreed, it will be for the architect to tailor the standard form to the project by completing the blanks in the booklet – the names of the parties, the fee and so on. It is good practice to issue two copies for signing, so that each party may keep an original for their records. Ideally, signing should be at a face-to-face meeting with the client to allow them to ask any last-minute questions and talk through the terms again as necessary.

In contrast, an experienced commercial client will not usually seek the advice of the architect in relation to the architect's own appointment, but will have its own legal advisors. Such a client will be used to getting its own way, particularly if negotiating through its solicitors with an architecture practice that is looking to take a step up in terms of the size and complexity of work it is involved in. In these circumstances, typically, a bespoke form of appointment will be issued by the client's solicitors for comment. After negotiation, those solicitors will issue the agreed form to the architect to sign; this may be called an 'engrossment', a technical legal term which means a document in its final form (and in practice means it may be bound, printed on slightly better paper and have a plastic cover), which will be subject to no further amendments and is ready for signature. The consultant will be expected to sign first, and then return the document to the client, usually via their solicitors to check that signing has been carried out properly. It is recommended that an architect takes a copy of any document they sign, even if the client has not signed it at that point. A final, 'completed' copy (one signed by both parties and dated) may, for whatever reason, not be forthcoming.

3

Chapter 4
Standard forms of professional appointment

This chapter:

- reviews in detail the RIBA Standard Conditions of Appointment for an Architect 2010 (2012 revision);
- contains hints and tips for negotiation with clients;
- contains an overview of the main alternative standard forms of appointment.

4.1   RIBA Standard Conditions of Appointment for an Architect 2010 (2012 revision)

4.1.1   Form and content of the RIBA Standard Conditions 2010 (2012 revision)

The RIBA Standard Conditions of Appointment for an Architect 2010 (2012 revision) ('the RIBA Standard Conditions') contain four elements: a memorandum of agreement (essentially the signing block; an alternative way for the parties to agree to be bound is by each signing a form of covering letter cross-referring to the RIBA Standard Conditions, and a sample letter is provided in the RIBA Standard Conditions pack); a set of schedules including options for the services to be performed and the fees and project data (project-specific information such as the level of insurance required); a set of notes on how to complete the appointment and a sample letter of appointment; and the terms and conditions of appointment themselves.

It is strongly recommended that a standard form, ideally the RIBA Standard Conditions, is used by an architect as the basis for any appointment. As discussed above, however, commercial clients in particular might not want to accept, in whole or in part, the RIBA Standard Conditions. In contrast there has in the past been almost universal acceptance of the RIBA stages as setting out a generic outline plan of work for a project. The schedule of services contained in the RIBA Standard Conditions schedules booklet follows the RIBA stages, as now fundamentally amended by the RIBA Plan of Work 2013. The *RIBA Job Book* (2013, RIBA Publishing) is an invaluable tool for expanding upon and explaining in detail the services required of the architect to adequately complete each stage. A good rule of thumb is that if you are not using the standard RIBA schedule then the more specific you can be about the services you are providing, the better.

4.1.2   Obligations and authority of the architect (Clause 2 RIBA Standard Conditions)

The architect's duty of care, set out in clause 2.1, is expressed as an obligation to exercise reasonable skill, care and diligence in accordance with the normal standards of the architect's profession. This is the fundamental standard of performance that has to be achieved, and clause 2.1 provides that this standard applies both to the performance of the services and to all of the architect's other obligations under clause 2. This standard of care, that of the ordinary skilled professional, is the one which would be implied at common law in the absence of an express contractual provision; the case of *Bolam v Friern Hospital Management Committee* established this as the standard. A term to the effect that the architect will carry out their services with reasonable skill and care is also implied, where the architect is supplying services in the course of their business, by Part 2, section 13 of the Supply of Goods and Services Act 1982. An experienced client will often seek an enhanced standard of care referring to the architect's specific expertise – there is a detailed discussion of this issue in section 5.2.6. In either case though, the architect's liability is not absolute and, as discussed in section 2.3.4, if a loss is suffered by the client as a result of the acts or omissions of the architect, the architect will not necessarily be liable. It must be shown by the claimant that the architect's performance fell below the required standard of care.

4.1.3   Obligations and authority of the client (Clause 3 RIBA Standard Conditions)

Under the RIBA Standard Conditions, the architect's work is to an extent collaborative and the client cannot, by appointing an architect, excuse themselves from all responsibility for those areas of a project covered by the appointment. The client's obligations set out in clause 3 are extensive, more so than many commercial clients would want.

Clauses 3.2, 3.3 and 3.4 in particular require the client to provide certain information, decisions and approvals in order for the architect to be able to perform the services effectively and meet any programme requirements. It is explicit that the architect is reliant upon the input received from the client and this may in practice be a useful way for an architect to defend themselves against a claim for negligent performance. Clause 3.2 imposes a potentially difficult obligation on the client to advise the relative priorities of the client's requirements, their brief, the construction cost and the timetable. Most clients would presumably say that all are equally important and any statement of priority of one over another may be felt to limit the client's scope to object if a lower priority area suffers slippage. These provisions could also be read as a way of tying the client into a definitive approval of these elements, limiting their scope to claim later that the architect's input was negligent.

Clauses 3.3 and 3.4 are also, as a client would see it, potentially onerous. Clause 3.3 requires the client to effectively assess what information (obtainable by it or in its possession) is necessary for the 'proper and timely' performance of the architect's services – there is no scope for the client to rely on the architect's expertise in requesting information that the architect considers relevant; the client has to make this judgement. Clause 3.4 obliges the client to give decisions and approvals 'and take such actions necessary' for the proper and timely performance of the services; what these actions might be is not expressed, but the obligation could be widely drawn on the basis of the wording used.

Clause 3.6 is an important provision consolidating the architect's ability to control the flow of instructions to the project team. This can become a particular issue on some projects, for example domestic projects where the family continues to live in or visit the site regularly; the temptation to directly instruct additions or changes to the work carried out by the contractor or other designers can be hard to resist. Under clause 3.6, the architect is not responsible for instructions other than those issued through them, if they have responsibility for directing and co-ordinating the work.

Clause 3.8 is a potentially useful limitation on the architect's liability. The clause provides that the client acknowledges the architect does not warrant the competence, performance, work, services or solvency of any other contractor or consultant appointed by the client. Although not expressed explicitly as such, the practical effect of this clause may be to limit the architect's liability to their own defaults only – effectively a net contribution clause. Net contribution is dealt with below in the context of clause 7.3 (see section 4.1.7), but put simply a net contribution clause reverses the common law position of 'joint and several' liability and would prevent a client from pursuing the architect for the whole of their losses in cases where one or more other parties are also arguably responsible.

Clause 3.9 is also effectively a net contribution clause, specifically relating to the contractor, and obliging the client to hold the contractor (and not the architect) responsible for the management and operational methods necessary for the proper carrying out and completion of the works in accordance with the building contract. This is another useful limitation on the potential scope of the architect's liability, as it may often be the case that both the contractor's workmanship and the architect's design could be the cause of the problem. This clause would seem to make it incumbent on the client to only claim against the architect for their part in the fault.

Clause 3.10 is another limitation on liability, this time providing that the architect does not 'warrant' (here meaning an explicit commitment to achieve a particular outcome) the granting of planning permission, other third party approvals, or their timing, and does not warrant compliance with the client's stated construction cost or timetable. For some clients, these concessions may be hard to accept.

4.1.4   Assignment and sub-contracting (Clause 4 RIBA Standard Conditions)

Clause 4.1 prevents assignment of the benefit of the appointment by either party without the prior written consent of the other. This is important because, generally, unless there is something in a contract preventing or restricting assignment, the benefit is freely assignable. What is the benefit of the appointment? For the architect it is the right to payment of fees; for the client it is the right to receive the services contracted for. A commercial client will often want to have the ability to assign the benefit of the appointment, for example to a funder or another group company, and may be unwilling to accept that it must seek the architect's written consent.

Clause 4.1 does not refer to assignment of the 'burden' (the obligations) under the appointment because strictly speaking this is not legally possible. The burden of a contract can be transferred, but only by agreement between the original parties and the incoming party accepting the burden. This is known as novation, which is discussed in more detail in Chapter 6.

4.1.5   Fees and expenses (Clause 5 RIBA Standard Conditions)

The basic payment structure

Setting the correct fee for a project, whether it be a percentage of the construction cost, a resource-based lump sum or on the basis of time charges (all of which are options under clause 5) is crucial for an architect, as is cash flow, governed by the timing of fee payments. The basic fee, calculated in accordance with clause 5.2.1, relates to the performance of the services; under any appointment there should always be scope for payment of additional sums for expenses and disbursements and, importantly, 'additional' services.

The RIBA Standard Conditions go further than this and allow for adjustment and additions to the basic fee in a number of circumstances. Clause 5.8 allows for adjustment, including the allowance of loss and expense, in the event of material changes to the brief, the construction cost or the timetable, or if the services are varied by agreement. Clause 5.9 allows additional fees, if not already covered by any other provision of the appointment, if the architect for reasons beyond their reasonable control does extra work or otherwise incurs loss and expense. Reasons given may include the architect being required to vary work, provide a new design or develop an approved design, or the performance of the services being delayed, disrupted or prolonged. Change control issues are dealt with

4

in detail in Chapter 5 of *Leading the Team: An architect's guide to design management.*

Clause 5.16 prevents the client from exercising rights it would generally have at common law to 'set-off' sums against the fees claimed by the architect. Knowledgeable clients will be aware of the potential benefit of being able to say 'I would be obliged to pay you, but because I have a counterclaim against you for defective or incomplete work I am entitled to hold onto a sum equivalent in value and set this off against your claim'. Such clients will be reluctant to give up their rights to set-off.

Clause 5.17 allows the architect to issue an account for payment for work carried out to date in the event of suspension or termination of performance under the appointment, even if as a result of the architect's default. Again, a sophisticated commercial client might be unwilling to agree to payment in such circumstances until completion of the services. It may be that the client considers they are owed money in the final outcome if they have been put to the trouble of engaging a different architect to complete the services and their costs have as a consequence gone up. Similarly, a commercial client might seek to resist the principle of paying loss and damages resultant on the termination or suspension, in any circumstances, and is also likely to resist the principle of paying loss of profit.

Clause 5.19 is another useful tool for the architect, obliging any party making late payment of a sum due under the appointment (so, almost always the client) to pay interest on the outstanding sum at 8% above the Bank of England base rate at the time. This is the rate required by order under the Late Payment of Commercial Debts (Interest) Act 1998 (the 'Interest Act 1998'), but many commercial clients would seek to reduce this rate while still complying with the Act – often to as low as 2% over base. Clients who are 'consumers' would not ordinarily be subject to the Interest Act 1998. Special care is required if an architect wishes to include such a provision in their appointment with a non-business client.

Payment and payment notices (Clauses 5.14 and 5.15 RIBA Standard Conditions)

These clauses set out the provisions on timing and withholding of payment necessary to comply with the 1996 Construction Act as amended by the 2009 Construction Act, which came into force on 1 October 2011 and applies to all 'construction contracts' entered into on or after that date.

The process begins under clause 5.14 as payment becomes due to the architect on the date of issue of their account, which counts as the architect's 'payment notice'. So if you have done the work, issue your invoice. Chase it up persistently if it is not paid on time. The final date for payment of the sum due to the architect is 14 days from the date of issue of the account in question. The amount of the payment notice will be the 'notified sum' as described in the 2009 Construction Act.

Clause 5.14 provides for the architect to issue payment notices (their invoices) at the intervals specified in the schedule of fees and expenses; this will typically be at least once every month, although there is the option to agree a different interval in the schedule of fees to be completed with the terms and conditions; this is a judgement to be made on a project-by-project basis. It can be useful to break the fee up into particular percentages for each stage of work – this limits the scope for the client to dispute that a sum is payable. But in any case, submitting a monthly fee account, based on a schedule of fee instalments (included in the appointment, describing the percentage due at each fee stage) and a detailed record of work carried out, is a useful habit to get into.

Clause 5.15 sets out the mechanism, required by the 1996 Construction Act and amended by the 2009 Construction Act, by which the client must give notices of the amount they will pay and the amount they propose to withhold, in response to the architect's application for payment. Under clause 5.15, if the client intends to pay less than the notified sum they must give a written notice to the architect not later than 5 days before the final date for payment (which you will recall is the date 14 days after the date on which the architect issues their account), specifying the amount that the client considers to be due on the date the notice is served, the basis on which such sum is calculated, and if any sum is intended to be withheld, the ground for doing so or, if there is more than one ground, each ground and the amount attributable to it.

If no such notice is given, the amount due to the architect shall be the amount stated as due in the architect's account and the client shall not delay payment of any undisputed part of the architect's account.

Failure to serve a withholding notice leaves the client liable to pay the full amount contained in the architect's application by the final date for payment. If no pay less notice is served and payment is not made by the final date, the architect has a statutory right under the 1996 and 2009 Construction Acts to suspend performance of the services on giving 7 days' notice to the client; this right cannot be contracted out of, and is in fact repeated in clause 8.1.2 of the RIBA Standard Conditions. Suspension is a powerful tool; many architects would, if faced with a continuing failure to pay, chase payment informally at first in order to preserve

4

good relations with the client, but the threat of suspension and the ability to serve a formal notice of intention to suspend performance are available from the moment the final date for payment is missed. Beyond suspension, the ultimate sanction would be to instigate the formal dispute resolution procedures under the appointment to recover the outstanding sums, either before or after exercising any contractual right to terminate the appointment. Consulting a solicitor before taking such measures is strongly recommended.

Bearing in mind the consequences for the client if they fail to comply with the pay less notice procedure, is it incumbent on the architect to explain how the mechanism works – to tell the client how to properly withhold the architect's fees? The answer must be yes, although the degree of explanation required will depend upon the nature of the client; as will be discussed below, the architect has particular obligations in relation to clients who are in the position of a 'consumer', defined by the Unfair Terms in Consumer Contracts Regulations ('UTCCR 1999', SI 1999/2083) as a natural person (not a company or partnership) who makes a contract for purposes which can be regarded as outside their trade, business or profession.

4.1.6 Copyright and use of information (Clause 6 RIBA Standard Conditions)

The common law position on copyright is restated in clause 6.1 – the architect owns the copyright in the original work produced in the performance of the services. This encompasses any designs and the drawings representing them; all other things being equal, the architect is free to reproduce their design on another project, and free to sue the client or anyone else if they attempt to do the same without permission. This is fair; an architect's designs are a fundamental part of their business.

The client is granted, by clause 6.3, a licence to copy and use the drawings and other material produced by the architect, and the designs contained in them, for the purposes only of the project in question. Use of the designs for any extension of the project, or on any other project that the client might be involved in, is forbidden without the agreement of the architect. Such use is also subject to the payment of an additional fee; this fee may either be specified in the appointment or subsequently agreed. It may seem sensible to negotiate this fee at the outset; however, one argument against doing this is that the true value of the design to the client may only become apparent when they need to use it, so a better fee for the licence may be realised at the time of the subsequent work.

Clause 6.3.2 links the basic copyright licence granted by clause 6.3 to the payment of all fees due to the architect. If the client is in default, the architect may suspend further use of the licence on giving 7 days' notice of their intention to suspend. In practice this may be of limited value for the architect against a client who is habitually late in paying. In the event of a more fundamental breakdown in the client/architect relationship, however, it can help to concentrate the client's mind if, as well as a claim for outstanding fees, there is also a claim for breach of copyright.

Clients, particularly commercial clients, regularly reject in principle the linking of the copyright licence with the ongoing payment of fees. Many clients are wary of the possibility of an injunction to prevent work continuing, reasoning that the potential liability for breach of copyright if the licence is suspended could lead to the project being held up each time there is a payment dispute with the architect. However, no court would grant an injunction to halt a project half way through in response to a breach of copyright claim. An injunction is a remedy that is available to prevent a breach of copyright and is by definition only available before the breach has taken place. So what is really at stake is the potential for the architect to sue to recover the amount they should reasonably have been paid for the licence to use the copyrighted material – another monetary claim.

One client, presumably thinking about the prospect of an injunction bringing their project to a standstill, described the fee/licence link during negotiations as 'being held to ransom', which somewhat misses the point that the client can avoid any copyright licence issues, even under the RIBA wording, by paying the architect's fees on time.

For further discussion on copyright issues, see section 5.2.15.

4.1.7 Liability and insurance (Clause 7 RIBA Standard Conditions)

Time limit on actions (Clause 7.1 RIBA Standard Conditions)

A time limit on actions in connection with the appointment (not just 'under' the appointment, but expressly covering claims in negligence as well as breach of contract) is provided by clause 7.1. The limit is to be included in the project data booklet forming part of the appointment, so may, for example, be agreed as 6 years for a simple contract or 12 years for a deed. A number of alternatives are given for the date when the period starts to run, those being the date of the last service performed by the architect under the appointment, the date of practical completion, or the statutory limitation period if it expires earlier. This clause may protect an architect against claims in negligence for latent defects, where you will

4

recall from Chapter 2 that the limitation period can be longer than 12 years, but of course the appointment terms only bind the architect and the client and would not prevent third parties from bringing claims in negligence after the agreed period has expired.

Limit on liability to the level of insurance (Clause 7.2 RIBA Standard Conditions)

Clause 7.2 contains an even more significant limitation on the architect's liability. It provides that the architect's liability for loss or damage shall not exceed the amount of the architect's professional indemnity insurance (PII) required for the project, as set out by the parties in the project data booklet. This may of course be an amount less than the architect's actual total PII cover. This is an absolute cap on the architect's potential liability for any individual claim by the client, and if it is agreed in the appointment the architect can be certain of the potential extent of their exposure in the event of a claim by the client.

Clients are not always receptive to such limits, reasoning that there is no such artificial limit on their potential losses if something goes drastically wrong. However, there is something appealingly pragmatic about a claim-by-claim overall cap on liability set at the level of PII maintained by the architect. The cap provides certainty for the client as well as the architect. The client could not realistically hope to recover more from the architect than the level of their insurance, without time-consuming and costly litigation to get at the assets of the firm; and in fact clause 7.2.2 operates to prevent claims against individual directors or partners within the architect firm, so there is no scope to try and pursue such individuals for their houses or other possessions.

Although a sensible provision, clause 7.2.1 does not provide absolute protection for the architect. First, the architect must actually have maintained the level of PII agreed and included in the project data. Second, the clause refers simply to the level of PII, not to the amount which the architect may actually recover from their insurer in relation to any claim. If the insurance covers only part of a claim (because for example, the amount claimed exceeds the headline level of PII cover), the architect is left to bear the shortfall from their own assets. Finally, the cap is only effective in relation to claims from the client, as only the client and the architect are ordinarily bound by the terms of their appointment. So if a claim is received from a third party in negligence or under a collateral warranty, and the PII pot has been used up, the architect will again be left with a gap in their cover. Third party claims might not be a particularly remote possibility on a large project. An architect may have been required to provide numerous collateral warranties in favour of purchasers, tenants and funders, who may all suffer a loss as a result of the same default. A single 'claim' as defined by the architect's PII policy may include any individual action resulting from the same negligent cause, and may not treat the individual actions as 'claims'; in such circumstances the single limit of indemnity could be exhausted very quickly.

Net contribution (Clause 7.3 RIBA Standard Conditions)

Clause 7.3 contains a potentially controversial limitation on liability. The clause provides that the architect's liability shall not exceed such sum as it would be just and equitable for the architect to pay. The calculation of what is just and equitable is expressly based on the assumption that all other consultants and contractors providing work and services for the project have paid to the client their just and equitable share of the client's losses, along with the assumptions that all those parties owe similar contractual undertakings to the client and there are no limitations or exclusions of liability or joint insurance provisions between any of those parties and the client.

In other words, in the event of a claim, the architect can only ever be liable for their fair share of the losses incurred.

A net contribution clause, like this, reverses the common law presumption of joint and several liability. If the client suffers a loss as a result of a default caused by more than one party, they are ordinarily entitled to sue any one of those parties to recover the whole of their loss. The unfortunate culpable party is then left to seek contributions from anyone else who may arguably have been responsible for the client's loss; a cause of action is available to the culpable party, who has had to bear the brunt of the client's claim, under the Civil Liability (Contribution) Act 1978 ('the 1978 Contribution Act').

The principle of joint and several liability is very useful for clients, and sophisticated clients who are aware of the advantage that the common law position gives them will often be very reluctant to give it up. In situations where more than one party is arguably liable for their loss, the client can simply sue the culpable party with the deepest pockets and avoid expensive multiparty litigation (adjudication, the quickest and most cost-effective form of adversarial dispute resolution, is not suitable for pursuing multiple parties), and the expense of obtaining expert evidence to prove which party was liable for which part of the loss. Joint and several liability also means that the client does not bear the risk of one of the culpable parties becoming insolvent. If the contractor and

4

the architect are both partly responsible for the loss, and the contractor has become insolvent, the client is free to recover 100% of their losses from the architect. After the contractor's insolvency, the architect in this example may have no other avenues for recovering contributions towards the damages they have had to pay. If the architect had included a net contribution clause in their appointment, it would be for the client to bear the insolvency risk.

Is it reasonable for an architect to have a net contribution clause in their appointment?

The common law position may seem counter-intuitive. How can it be right for an architect to foot the bill for losses that were caused by other parties; for the law to allow an architect to be 100% liable for the damages, even though their share of the blame might be 10% or lower? But many clients will take a different view. The project, and hence the work for the architect, would not exist without them. Why should the client bear the risk in the culpable parties becoming insolvent, and the risk of paying potentially huge legal costs to sue multiple parties, when the client has done nothing wrong? Clients are particularly wary of including design and build contractors in the net contribution equation; if the contractor is responsible for the whole of the design and build of a project, what is the architect's fair and reasonable share of any loss? Arguably, nothing at all.

The balance of power between commercial clients and architects is such that it remains unusual for a net contribution clause to be agreed in a professional appointment, although clients are often more relaxed about agreeing net contribution in collateral warranties, particularly for tenants and purchasers, if not for funders. Failure to obtain a net contribution clause in a professional appointment leaves the architect facing a number of risks. Their ability to obtain contributions from other culpable parties can be undermined by various factors, including the insolvency problem outlined above. Under the 1978 Contribution Act, the party from whom a contribution is sought (in our example, by the architect) must be liable to the client for the same loss or damage as the architect. This may not be the case if, for example, there is no contract between the client and that other party; or if the other party has a contract with the client, but liability for the loss or damage in question is excluded under the terms of the contract.

Professional indemnity insurance (Clause 7.4 RIBA Standard Conditions)

Clause 7.4 sets out the architect's obligation to maintain a PII policy. It is extremely important that the obligation mirrors precisely the level of cover the architect actually maintains. The architect can include appropriate wording in the relevant section of the project data to ensure that the obligation matches the reality, not just in terms of the headline level of cover, but also any aggregate or reduced aggregate limits, or even exclusions, the policy may contain. Aggregate limits and exclusions often apply to claims in relation to pollution, contamination, date recognition or asbestos.

The obligation to maintain PII is subject to such insurance being available to the architect on commercially reasonable terms; so, in the RIBA Standard Conditions at least, this is not an absolute obligation. The ARB's Architects Code is more strict; Standard 8 of the code requires that architects have 'adequate and appropriate insurance cover', adequate to meet a claim whenever it may be made.

The wording of clause 7.4 is nevertheless advantageous for the architect. The obligation is subject to insurance being available to the architect on commercially reasonable terms. It does not matter whether other architects might be able to obtain such cover. In this way, the RIBA Standard Conditions allow the architect's own claims record, which may be the reason why they cannot obtain insurance at a reasonable premium, to be used as a reason for not maintaining insurance. How much of an issue this is in practice is questionable – no sensible client would engage an uninsured architect and no sensible architect would continue to practise without PII cover, high premium or not. Some clients do not like this subjectivity, and will insist upon an insurance obligation that allows derogation only if such insurance is not available to the market generally at commercially reasonable rates. It can be hard to argue against this, although an architect might justifiably say that the position of the market in general is irrelevant; if PII is not available to me, personally, I cannot enter into an obligation to obtain it.

Collateral warranties and third party rights (Clause 7.7 RIBA Standard Conditions)

This clause obliges the architect, if requested, to enter into collateral warranties, or provide third party rights, to funders, purchasers or first tenants. Collateral warranties and third party rights are discussed in detail in section 5.2.13 and Chapter 6. The main issue for an architect is whether the job in question is sufficiently important for it to be appropriate to consider extending the scope of their contractual liability out to third parties. If it is, the form of collateral warranty or schedule of third party rights is key; an agreed form should be attached to the appointment, so that there is no question of the architect being asked to provide something different, and potentially more onerous, at a later stage. It is also important

4

for the client to attach the desired form of collateral warranty, because a contractual obligation to provide a collateral warranty in a form 'to be agreed' is unlikely to be enforceable at all. It is not generally possible as a matter of contract law to enforce an agreement to agree something later.

4.1.8   Suspension and termination (Clause 8 RIBA Standard Conditions)

Not every client is happy to give an express right for the architect to terminate their appointment, even for material breaches of contract by the client. The market norm seems to be that both the architect and the client have the right to terminate the appointment, but these rights are asymmetrical; the circumstances in which the architect may exercise their right to terminate are more restricted than those in which the client may terminate. This is not reflected in clause 8 of the RIBA Standard Conditions. Commercial clients may often want the right to terminate the architect's appointment on notice, without any fault on the part of the architect. This may seem unfair, but if for whatever reason funding for the project falls through, or the project is no longer wanted, it would be unreasonable to tie the client in to an appointment with an architect to provide services that the client cannot afford or does not want. The flipside of this is that most commercial clients would be unwilling to accept an appointment that would allow the architect to simply walk away from the project on notice without any fault on the part of the client. Finding a replacement could be costly and the process could delay the project. Clause 8.2.1 gives the parties equal rights to terminate the appointment on notice, stating the reasons for doing so.

Clause 8.1 enhances the architect's statutory right to suspend performance for non-payment of fees, originally conferred by the 1996 Construction Act and amended by the 2009 Construction Act. Clause 8.1.2(c) allows the architect to suspend performance if prevented from or impeded in performing the services for reasons beyond their reasonable control or (clause 8.1.2(d)) a 'force majeure' event. Force majeure means literally 'greater force', implying the intervention of some higher power, and is typically understood to include events such as flood, earthquake or volcanic eruption. Such clauses, especially clause 8.1.2(c), are again generally not popular with commercial clients. An event that to an architect is 'beyond its control' may look to a client more like a failure to anticipate an event that was reasonably foreseeable.

4.1.9   Dispute resolution (Clause 9 RIBA Standard Conditions)

A number of procedures are contemplated by this clause. It is for the parties to set out in the project data whether they agree to mediation as an option, whether adjudication will be available (statutory adjudication under the 1996 and 2009 Construction Acts is not available in a dispute with a residential occupier, although the parties are free to expressly agree to its application in their contract) and whether arbitration or litigation applies. The RIBA has its own adjudication scheme for 'consumer' contracts, but it should be borne in mind that any adjudication provision must be explained and individually negotiated with a consumer client, as discussed in more detail in section 4.1.11.

4.1.10 The consumer's right to cancel (Clause 10 RIBA Standard Conditions)

Clause 10 enhances the consumer client's rights conferred under the Cancellation of Contracts etc. Regulations 2008. Footnote 7 of the RIBA Standard Conditions says that the clause applies where the project relates to work to the client's home or second home, including a new home, and the client is a consumer. A consumer is defined by UTCCR 1999 regulation 3(1) as a natural person, not a company, partnership, club or society, who, in making a contract, is acting for purposes which are outside their trade, business or profession. Clause 10 protects consumers by allowing them to cancel the appointment on notice for any reason within 7 days starting from the date when the contract was made. The architect is entitled in these circumstances to recover fees properly due for work instructed or confirmed in writing and carried out prior to the notice of cancellation.

4.1.11 The position of the consumer generally

Architects must exercise caution when entering into an appointment with a consumer client. A company may also be a consumer, for the purposes of the Unfair Contract Terms Act 1977 ('UCTA 1977') if not UTCCR 1999. This will be the case if the contract is not one of a type that it regularly enters into and if the project covered is incidental to, and not the primary focus of, its business activity. It is recommended in the notes to the RIBA Standard Conditions that such companies or organisations, which may include charities, educational institutions or healthcare trusts, should be dealt with as if UTCCR 1999 does apply.

There is a risk that certain terms of the RIBA Standard Conditions (or any standard terms and conditions of agreement, including industry standard forms such as the ACA and NEC3 appointments, as well as any architect's own 'standard' terms and conditions) will be invalidated and ineffective against a consumer client if the architect has proposed the form of agreement and its terms have not been individually negotiated. A term will, according to UTCCR 1999, always be regarded as not having been individually negotiated where it was drafted in advance of agreement and the consumer was as a result unable to exert any influence over its substance.

Ideally with a consumer client the architect should go through each term in turn in the context of the consumer's rights and record in writing that this process has taken place. The notes to the RIBA Standard Conditions, and the RIBA Conditions for a Domestic Project, provide advice on negotiating terms with consumers. An architect is not going to be able to discharge their duty to a consumer client by simply providing the notes for the client to read without giving any further input.

A contractual term will not be upheld by a court against a consumer if it is unfair. UTCCR 1999 regulation 5(1) emphasises the need to individually negotiate terms with a consumer. If not, a term will be regarded as unfair if it 'causes a significant imbalance in the parties' rights and obligations arising under the contract, to the detriment of the consumer'. Such a term will be contrary to the requirements of good faith, which in this context means simply that the parties making the contract should not deceive each other. If you know that a consumer client has taken no legal advice and you propose terms of appointment that contain significant limitations on your liability, such as the RIBA Standard Conditions, without explaining to the client how these terms may prevent them from recovering the full extent of their losses in the event of a claim, then you are perceived in law to be taking an unfair advantage.

The risk of behaving in this way is that you would not in practice be allowed to rely on such limitations on your liability. This is a genuine risk; as the RIBA Standard Conditions notes suggest, it is surprising how often consumer clients maintain in the event of a claim that the full implications of a contractual provision were not explained to them, to their disadvantage.

UTCCR 1999 helpfully, in its Schedule 2, provides an indicative (but not exhaustive) list of the types of term that may be considered unfair. They are not automatically unfair – it is for the consumer to prove that the application of a particular term is unfair – but an architect should be particularly wary of proceeding to enter into the RIBA Standard Conditions with a consumer client without explaining the full implications of the following clauses in particular:

- the contractual embodiment of statutory provisions that would not ordinarily apply to consumers: clauses 5.15 (payment notices under the 2009 Construction Act), 5.17 and 5.18 (suspension under the 1996 and 2009 Construction Acts), 5.19 (charging interest under the 1998 Interest

Act) and clause 9 (dispute resolution options – generally a consumer has a right to refer any dispute to the courts);
- provisions limiting sums that may be recovered: clauses 5.16 (no set-off) and 7.2 (cap on liability);
- provisions potentially increasing costs liability, such as clause 5.20; and
- exclusions of liability: clause 7.1 (limit on actions in time) and clause 7.3 (net contribution).

Unless a project is large or complex, the RIBA generally recommends the RIBA Conditions for a Domestic Project for use when the appointment is by a consumer client.

4.1.12 Will my client agree to use the RIBA Standard Conditions?

Inexperienced domestic consumer clients will often be happy to use the RIBA Standard Conditions, or the RIBA Conditions of Appointment for an Architect for a Domestic Project. Very many projects every year use a RIBA standard form; not every project involves a major international developer and funders investing millions of pounds. The RIBA forms have the benefit of familiarity and, if not always drafted in language a layman can easily understand, they are comprehensive, come with helpful notes and have the right 'feel' for many clients; it often just seems appropriate to use a RIBA document. Clients of this nature tend to be wary of the time and legal costs that are likely to result from trying to negotiate something bespoke, but they know they should get something formal in place. If the architect has something like the RIBA Standard Conditions that they can propose to get the ball rolling, all the better.

Commercial clients may agree to use the RIBA Standard Conditions, but it is likely to remain unusual for a commercial client, with the benefit of legal advice, to agree to use an unamended standard form, RIBA or otherwise, unless they are particularly hassle-averse. Like domestic clients, some commercial clients may be swayed by the convenience of agreeing the RIBA Standard Conditions if the client either does not have its own bespoke form of appointment or does not want to pay a lawyer to draft one. They may in addition be unwilling to spend legal fees negotiating amendments, or may be unhappy with the possible increased fee an architect might seek to cover the additional risk of signing up to a bespoke appointment. The RIBA Standard Conditions also have the advantage of being, and being known to be, insurable by architects' PII providers.

Sometimes events may conspire. An architect could begin work with a limited scope and fee on the basis of the RIBA Standard Conditions; the work may later expand, but the issue of a new appointment to fit the additional risks to the client may never be addressed. If an architect has the opportunity to take the initiative and propose a form of appointment, the RIBA Standard Conditions are a safe option.

4.2 Association of Consultant Architects Standard Form of Agreement for the Appointment of an Architect 2012 (ACA SFA 2012 Edition)

The ACA form is intended to be suitable for the full range of commercial and consumer projects and includes various elements – memorandum of agreement, schedule of services, schedule of fees, a form of collateral warranty, notes, forms of initial letter to the client, and the terms and conditions of appointment. The SFA 2012 Edition effectively updates the ACA standard forms SFA/08 and SFA/10 to take into account the 2009 Construction Act and the 2010 Bribery Act. But the form also suffers from the same problem as the RIBA forms, and every other industry standard form, including NEC; would a commercial client be happy to use it without significant amendments?

The ACA is less widely used than the RIBA forms and does not have the advantage of familiarity to many. The ACA form offers no advantages to the client over the RIBA Standard Conditions, containing similar provisions for an overall cap on liability and a net contribution clause. If anything the ACA is slightly less realistic about what a commercial client might be expected to accept. Arguably, there is nothing in the ACA form that would immediately justify an architect choosing it over the RIBA Standard Conditions, if the architect is able to propose their own preferred form of appointment.

4.3 NEC3 Professional Services Contract

This standard form of consultant's appointment is being used more and more, and increasingly on high-profile projects. As well as being the preferred form of appointment used by the Olympic Delivery Authority for work in relation to the 2012 Games, it is widely used by influential clients in the Middle East, and by major clients in the utilities, energy, transport and education sectors in this country. Its popularity with major clients may be the result of its inherent flexibility; in a sense, the NEC3 Professional Services Contract (PSC) is not really an industry standard form at all.

PSC consists of a number of core clauses, which are read in conjunction with selected 'optional' clauses, ready drafted, to cater for issues such as the provision of collateral warranties and an overall limitation on the consultant's liability. Inherent in this scheme is that the client and the consultant may also agree to include additional conditions of contract – 'Z clauses' in the terminology of PSC – which are bespoke, generally client-led, amendments to the standard clauses. This entails more than simply completing the project-specific contract data, as in the RIBA Standard Conditions, as these bespoke additional terms and conditions may alter the balance of liability under the appointment. PSC is unique as a standard form in the way it, if not encourages, realistically accepts that clients will wish to use additional bespoke clauses to shift the burden of liability under the appointment further towards the consultant.

At its heart, PSC contains a duty to use the 'skill and care normally used by professionals' providing similar services. However, PII policies normally cover only 'reasonable' skill and care. This is just one example of a core clause within PSC that appears unnecessarily onerous. In any case, none of the major clients who use PSC do so without incorporating a schedule of bespoke Z clauses. For this reason, detailed analysis of the standard core and optional clauses is somewhat redundant. An architect is unlikely to be presented with the plain PSC as a proposed basis for an appointment; the real interest will usually be in the Z clauses, and they may significantly change the picture.

Also at its heart, PSC is really a sophisticated project management tool. It requires a sophisticated and experienced client to get the best out of it, and an experienced consultant to manage its side of the bargain. A party can suffer if it is not used to keeping the paper trail going. For example, core clause 61.3 imposes a condition precedent such that if the consultant wants to claim for additional fees or time as a result of a 'compensation event' (one of a list of possible events beyond the consultant's control, such as the client giving an instruction changing the scope), then it has to notify the client that it wishes to make a claim within 8 weeks of becoming aware of the event. Without notification before the deadline, there is no entitlement.

Architects presented with PSC should proceed with caution and take legal advice, irrespective of whether the proposed appointment contains a significant number of Z clauses. There is much that an architect could find objectionable, in addition to the basic failure to subject the duty of skill and care to the usual reasonableness standard.

4.4 FIDIC Client/Consultant Model Services Agreement, Fourth Edition 2006

The International Federation of Consulting Engineers (FIDIC) professional services agreement is widely used on international projects in Europe, the Middle East and Asia. The basic duty of care required by the FIDIC standard form is reasonable and insurable, being simply the consultant's reasonable skill, care and diligence. The consultant is only liable to pay compensation to the client arising out of or in connection with the FIDIC standard form's terms if a breach of that duty of care is established. Any compensation is limited to the reasonably foreseeable loss and damage suffered as a result of such breach, and not otherwise. There is also an option to include an overall cap on liability.

Even better for architects, the client is obliged by the FIDIC standard form to indemnify the consultant in relation to any third party claims arising out of or in connection with the agreement.

This all sounds good in theory, but the FIDIC form is almost never used for consultant appointments on UK-based projects, is rarely used unamended and is almost always subject to the law of a foreign jurisdiction required by the client.

Chapter 5

Bespoke professional appointment wording

This chapter:

- explains what a bespoke form of appointment is and why clients may want to use one;

- provides a detailed review of typical bespoke wording, clause by clause;

- highlights forms of wording to avoid and suggests alternative wording;

- provides hints and tips for negotiation with clients.

5.1   Overview of bespoke forms

5.1.1   Why would a client propose a bespoke form of appointment?

If a client has sufficient resources to do so, they may propose to use a bespoke form of professional appointment. The expense to the client comes not only from the fact that a professional legal advisor will have been required to put the document together initially, but also from the likelihood that an architect will not be willing to accept bespoke terms as drafted without proposing amendments, whether the amendments suggested come from the architect's own experience or from their legal advisors or insurers. The client's legal team will be required to conduct any negotiations to settle an agreed form.

Because of the potential additional expense, the client will need to have a good reason to use a bespoke form; if the client is a regular user of architectural services, or a job is particularly complex or high value, the client may consider that the standard forms on offer, including the RIBA Standard Conditions, do not provide sufficient protection.

It almost goes without saying that the use of a bespoke form of appointment is likely to increase costs for the architect too. Agreeing a non-standard form, without taking legal advice and seeking insurer approval, is not sensible practice. The cost of obtaining legal advice can be significant, although some insurers and insurance brokers provide a 'contract review' service as part of the overall PII package, under which they will arrange for solicitors to provide comments on a draft appointment form for free. Discuss this with your broker. Typically, this advice will be limited to issues that may affect cover under the architect's insurance policy; this is a different focus from the 'full commercial review' that an independent solicitor would provide if instructed to review a draft appointment. If an architect does have to seek advice from an independent solicitor, the client may be willing to pay or contribute to these costs; in other cases, the architect might factor their legal costs into the fee in another way.

There may be occasions when architects, particularly large and international practices, have and propose their own bespoke forms. However, this chapter concentrates on bespoke forms put forward by clients, where the reasoning behind the terms being proposed, and their effects in practice if accepted, can be obscure.

Client bespoke forms will be drafted to shift the balance of risk in favour of the client in many, often subtle, ways. This chapter sets out areas where bespoke appointments are likely to be more onerous than the industry standard forms. Not all of these points are going to be worth fighting over every time; it is for the architect and their legal advisor to decide what is important on a project-by-project basis, and to assess the relative strength of the bargaining positions of the architect and the client in each case. It is rare that a legal argument is so persuasive on its own that it will convince the other party to agree an amendment. Each negotiation is a mixture of legal argument and commercial pragmatism to achieve an overall compromise.

5.1.2 How does a negotiation progress? How do I express my preferred amendments?

If the bespoke form is proposed by the client, the client's solicitor will usually get the ball rolling by sending out an initial draft. The draft should have been properly tailored to the nature of the project, but this is not always the case and you may need to spend some time striking out obviously inappropriate provisions.

How should the architect indicate the areas they cannot accept? There are three main options:

- Manuscript mark-up of the appointment (handwritten amendments). This is not best practice because of the potential confusion that may result from having to decipher an individual's handwriting squeezed onto a page.
- Electronic mark-up, tracking the changes proposed by the parties at each stage in the negotiations (often shown in different colours depending upon the software used). Electronic mark-ups are very useful tools, but can themselves create confusion if, for example, the clause numbering changes when individual provisions are deleted or if, when a dispute arises, only a black and white hardcopy of the mark-up remains.
- Electronic schedule of comments in the format: 'clause number – comment'. This is arguably the clearest way to record proposed amendments and track the negotiation, although it is also potentially the most time consuming.

The architect should always insist upon seeing a final draft for review, in both clean and 'track changes' versions, before a document is sent out by the client for signing ('execution').

What if the client says there will be no amendments?

Some clients profess to be unwilling to consider any amendments to their proposed form, particularly clients with an effective monopoly in their respective areas, such as major transport or utilities companies. But in a commercial world it is usually possible to achieve a fairer balance in the appointment document, even if 'no amendments' is the client's opening position. The architect may have particular concerns which are potential 'deal-breakers', issues that may either make it not commercially viable for them to take the job on or which may compromise coverage under their PII policy. An architect should always raise at least these points with the client, however strongly the client has stated that they will not accept any amendments. Your insurer may be willing to agree a specific one-off endorsement to your PII policy if the client is unwilling to compromise on a particular provision that may create a coverage issue.

If everything else is favourable – the architect's proposed design, their approach, the fee, the personalities – then a client will generally be open to a compromise on particular terms of the appointment. But no appointment is risk free.

5.2   Discussion of particular forms of words used in bespoke appointments

5.2.1   Defined terms

A bespoke appointment will usually have a clause setting out the meaning of certain terms which appear elsewhere in the appointment, signified by beginning with capital letters. A client may wish these meanings to be wider (or narrower, as in the example of 'Additional Services' below) than the architect had anticipated. For the architect to understand how the definition may work to their disadvantage, they must cross-refer to the other parts of the appointment where the defined terms appear. Examples are given below.

'Additional Services'

'any substantial additional services which are not foreseeable by the Architect at the date of this Agreement, provided that design changes made in discussion with the Client and the preparation of alternatives before such design is finally agreed by the Client shall not constitute Additional Services.'

The intention of this wording is to restrict the architect's ability to claim additional fees even though they have a legitimate claim because they have carried out additional work over and above their basic services. There is no reason for an architect to accept such a restricted definition of what is additional; this does not represent the market norm.

The use of the wording 'not foreseeable' is harsh because it is not subject to a standard of reasonableness. The client will argue that the architect should have foreseen that the additional services provided were going to be required and therefore the client should not pay for them. A similar effect is created by wording requiring the architect to provide the basic services and in addition do all things that 'may be reasonably implied by them or are reasonably incidental to them'. But the architect needs to know with certainty what their basic services are and, from that, what will be additional; it is impossible to provide an accurate fee estimate without this information, something which is not helpful to the client or the architect.

The wording relating to design changes is indicative of a growing trend for clients to seek redesign for free as part of a 'value engineering' exercise or series of such exercises on a project. This is a misuse of the term value engineering, which when used correctly is about innovation through design to reduce cost. The risk being considered in this section is where the client seeks to oblige the architect to redesign down to cost.

This could involve significant redesign by the architect, but the likelihood is that the need for designing down will not be, or not be exclusively, the fault of the architect. It is for the quantity surveyor, usually, to keep track of likely expenditure. If the quantity surveyor only realises late on in the design process that a project is over budget, and that cost savings can only be made if the design is changed, the amount of work thrown away and work which must be redone can be huge. It is unreasonable to expect the architect to bear their own costs of the redesign in these circumstances, and such work should be treated as an additional service. Ideally the architect's right to additional fees for such work should be expressly stated in the appointment. Ideally the architect should also be allowed some input in agreeing cost changes, and should ensure that the quantity surveyor's appointment requires the quantity surveyor to seek the architect's input before changes are made.

'Brief'

'The initial statement of the Client's requirements as the same may be developed or varied from time to time.'

If the brief does change significantly, and the architect finds that the building they are designing is substantially different from the one which they originally agreed to design, any additional work required must be paid for as an addition to the basic fee. This is normally not controversial, but it is vital that the architect keeps track of changes from the initial brief. Development of the brief may be inevitable, but a wholesale change in the scope of the design is something that should be notified to the client,

5

an instruction sought, and an increased fee agreed, before the additional work takes place. It is so important to keep on top of these changes; lots of little adjustments can cumulatively amount to a significant deviation from the initial brief.

'Documents'

'All drawings, models, plans, elevations, sections, perspectives, specifications, schedules and any other works and documentation produced or to be produced by or on behalf of the Architect as part of the Services including any designs contained in them'

This definition will link in with a 'copyright' clause in the main body of the appointment. A client will expect to receive a copyright licence in relation to all of the documents, as defined, or in the worst case may even expect copyright in the documents to be assigned to them. The use of the words 'by or on behalf of' require the architect to secure the right to grant a copyright licence from any other party whose copyrighted material the architect has incorporated into the work they have produced. This can be extremely difficult to achieve in practice, so at the very least the obligation in relation to third party copyright should be subject to a 'reasonable endeavours' obligation – an obligation to do only such things as are commercially reasonable, rather than everything possible, to achieve a copyright licence for the client from such third parties.

In addition there should be an express exclusion in relation to proprietary products, such as computer software, whose originators are unlikely to be willing to grant copyright licences without a formal fee arrangement, if at all.

'BIM': building information modelling/management

The architect may be required by their appointment to collaborate with all of the other designing contractors and consultants on the project through BIM. BIM is described in detail in section 12.3 of the RIBA *Architect's Handbook of Practice Management* (eighth edition). As the authors note:

> BIM is not just the software that facilitates the team's delivering a single-project model, or the way that model is stored and accessed; it is the process through which the whole team collaborates and co-ordinates the design towards a common output.

The perceived advantages of BIM include the promotion of more efficient team working, enhanced clash detection, easing the integration of architectural design with mechanical and electrical services, structure and programming, and providing a focus for design meetings.

It is vital that, in the context of BIM, the architect's appointment makes very clear that they shall not be liable for the work, acts or omissions of others. BIM dates back to the 1990s, but the potential advantages and pitfalls are still being discovered; the following questions remain to be resolved:

- Who owns the copyright in the design if all consultants and specialists have collaborated on a single common output?
- Can BIM create liability between designing parties? How does this sit with the legal doctrine that contractual liability is generally only possible between parties to a contract?
- What is the best way to audit design changes and track who has done what and who is meant to do what?

The RIBA Plan of Work 2013 has been developed to embrace the use of BIM and the design management processes and leadership issues referred to in the 2012 BIM Overlay to the Outline Plan of Work 2007 are embedded in the new Plan of Work, specifically in the Key Support Tasks bar and the references to the need for a project execution plan and a technology strategy.

'Losses'

'All losses, costs, claims, demands, actions, damages … and liabilities, including legal expenses.'

If the main body of the appointment makes the architect liable for the client's losses as a result of particular breaches of contract, you should check whether 'losses' has been defined. The intention may be to create an 'indemnity' under which the architect is liable to the client for a far more broadly defined range of losses than would ordinarily be recoverable for breach of contract. This should not be accepted. This is an important issue for architects, because PII policies are generally based on the more restrictive common law definition of the losses that can be recovered.

'Third Party Agreements'

'Each and every agreement relating to or affecting the Project which has been or shall be entered into by the Client from time to time and disclosed to the Architect.'

A definition such as this will usually be linked to a clause in the main body of the appointment obliging the architect to perform their services so as not to cause or contribute to any breach of such agreements by the client. This should generally not be accepted without qualification.

The architect's primary duty is to carry out their services for the client, exercising reasonable skill and care. There is no reason why this should

5

necessarily be compatible with the client's obligations under agreements with third parties. For example, the client may enter into an agreement for lease with a potential tenant that includes a penalty if the building is not completed by a strict deadline. But the architect's duty is to use reasonable skill and care, not to guarantee completion of the building on a particular date.

If the client is insistent, then additional wording may be proposed providing that the architect's obligation to carry out their services in compliance with any third party agreement is subject to the terms of the appointment itself taking precedence in the event of any discrepancy or conflict between the terms of the third party agreement and the appointment. Failing that, the architect should insist on an additional fee to cover the potential risk that any services provided under the appointment may cause or contribute to a breach of the third party agreement; or add wording such that only a breach of the appointment or negligence would fall within the scope of the obligation – not the simple fact of performance of the architect's services.

Finally, the architect must ensure that their obligation in relation to third party agreements is only effective to the extent that the architect has received a copy of any such agreement prior to commencing their services; the architect cannot reasonably be expected to carry out their services in compliance with a document they have not seen. The architect should be entitled to recover the additional costs of re-doing any services that need to be amended to comply with a third party agreement that the architect had not seen at the time they carried out the services in question.

5.2.2   Entire agreement

'This Agreement supersedes any previous agreements or arrangements between the parties in respect of the Services and represents their entire understanding in relation thereto.'

This 'entire agreement' provision is intended to prevent the architect from seeking to rely on any promises or agreements made during the course of negotiations – for example, a promise by the client to pay an additional fee if the architect's services are not required beyond the planning stage. This is not necessarily a problem for the architect, but it does mean that if there is something that was agreed during the pre-contract negotiations, or some assurance given, on the basis of which the architect was persuaded to enter into the appointment (and on which the architect may later want to rely) then the architect must ensure that the agreement or assurance is included in the written terms of the formal appointment.

5.2.3 Effective date

'The appointment of the Architect shall be deemed to have commenced with effect from the date of this Agreement or, if earlier, the date upon which the Architect shall have begun to perform the Services.'

If significant services have been carried out prior to the date of the appointment, such an 'effective date' clause can create problems for the architect. This is particularly true if the appointment imposes additional conditions or standards of performance – such as the requirement to comply with the terms of a third party agreement – that the architect was not aware of at the time they began performing the services. If there is any question of the architect's prior performance being in breach of the appointment terms subsequently proposed, the architect must insist that the appointment commences on the date it is executed and no earlier. Failing that, the architect could propose that if any work carried out prior to the date of the appointment needs to be revisited in order to ensure compliance with the terms of the appointment then this additional work will be paid for by the client.

5.2.4 Pre-existing work by others

'any architectural design services carried out by or on behalf of the Client prior to the date hereof shall be treated as forming part of the Services and the Architect hereby assumes responsibility for the same.'

Assuming responsibility for the work of others is a high-risk venture and should not generally be considered. There is usually no need for the client to have this protection – the client will generally have a contract with, and therefore a contractual right to sue, any previous architect or other designer for defaults – but it is advantageous for the client to have a single point of responsibility for the internal coherence of the design.

If you assume responsibility for previous work, you must use reasonable skill and care to check it, including the design assumptions on which it is based, or you are acting negligently. Consider the nature of the previous work and ask the following questions:

- Is the work extensive and fundamental to the design going forward?
- Are you being given the opportunity to properly assess the quality of the existing work?
- Are you being paid an enhanced fee for accepting the risk of integrating the existing work into your overall design?
- Why is the previous designer no longer involved?
- Do you trust their work?
- What does your insurer say?

5

5.2.5   Additional services and instructions

'The Architect shall not perform any Additional Services unless the Client has instructed their performance in writing.'

In practice an instruction will often be given orally, but the architect should always wait for, and chase if necessary, written instructions, and written agreement of any consequent cost and programme adjustments. This is a project management issue; it is entirely within the architect's control to keep the paperwork ticking over and make sure there is a written record of any changes to the scope of services, the fee or the programme.

There must be scope under the appointment for the architect to notify the client when they reasonably consider that additional services are required. Any such variations to the services should again be recorded in writing and only carried out if agreed in writing by the client. If the architect considers that additional services are required, and the client disagrees, the architect should consider whether further correspondence is necessary. If the failure to instruct additional services is, in the architect's reasonable opinion, likely to compromise the project in some way, this advice has to be set out in detail in writing to the client.

The architect should expect, under their appointment, to be obliged to comply with the reasonable instructions of the client. But if the architect receives an instruction which, in the architect's reasonable opinion, conflicts with the terms of the appointment, or any statutory or other legal or regulatory requirements, the architect should be able, under the appointment, to reject the instruction.

In addition, if for any other reason the architect considers in the reasonable exercise of their professional judgement that the client should not proceed with such instruction, they should be expressly entitled to advise the client in writing of their opinion and the appointment should clearly say that to the extent, if at all, the client proceeds with the instruction against the advice of the architect, the client proceeds at their own risk.

5.2.6   Duty of care

As mentioned in section 4.1.2 in the context of the RIBA Standard Conditions, knowledgeable commercial clients will usually expect an enhanced duty of care, over and above the standard of the ordinary skilled professional that is implied by law.

'The Architect warrants that in respect of the Services they have and will continue to exercise all the reasonable skill, care and diligence to be expected of a properly qualified professional architect holding itself out as competent

and experienced to perform such Services having due regard to the size, scope, nature, complexity and value of the Project.'

It can be hard to argue against this enhanced duty – it is effectively the market norm in a bespoke appointment – and it is easy to see why a client who has selected an architect on the basis of their reputation and past experience expects to be able to rely on the architect achieving a special, subjective level of skill, not merely the ordinary standard of skill that the client could expect to get from any other architect. If the architect in question does actually possess the enhanced degree of skill and care, the practical consequences of accepting the enhanced duty may be limited.

Even so, no architect should feel compelled to agree the enhanced standard without exploring whether the client will accept instead the standard of the ordinary skilled professional. As a compromise, an architect could seek to add wording to the effect that:

'Notwithstanding any other provision of the Appointment, the Architect shall not be construed as owing any greater duty to the Client than to exercise the level of reasonable skill, care and diligence required by this clause.'

Incorporating this wording should be enough to cut across any more onerous standards of care or obligations (such as indemnities) that may otherwise be expressed in or implied by the appointment.

Many PII policies are based on the ordinary standard of care, so agreeing the enhanced standard in an appointment could potentially be a reason for the insurer under such a policy to deny cover. It would be rare for an insurer to take this point in isolation – most would tend to be more pragmatic, because this enhanced standard of care crops up very regularly in bespoke appointments, and it is still not as onerous as an indemnity – but if there are other factors that count against the insured consultant, such as a failure to operate the PII policy notification procedures properly, an insured may find their agreement to the enhanced standard of care is held against them.

Reasonable skill and care or *all* reasonable skill and care?

In the absence of any express terms to the contrary, in any contract entered into by an architect for the provision of services, there will be an implied term that the professional should undertake their duties with reasonable skill and care. Most contracts for professional services do in fact contain express wording to this effect, rather than relying on the implication by law of the term.

It is difficult to see any practical difference between 'reasonable skill and care' and 'all reasonable skill and care'. There is no real parallel with the

5

concepts of reasonable and all reasonable endeavours, considered in a number of recent cases and discussed below; 'endeavours' means a set of actions that can be taken, whereas 'skill and care' is a standard in itself. You can use your reasonable endeavours, and if you need to do more you can use 'all' reasonable endeavours; but reasonable skill and care is an objective standard and adding 'all' to the beginning cannot impose a requirement for more skilfulness, or more care. It is still reasonable skill and care.

Reasonable endeavours, all reasonable endeavours, and best endeavours

The use of the term 'reasonable endeavours' in a professional appointment or contract is usually linked to the achievement by a professional of a particular end result.

In the case of *Rhodia v Huntsman*, the High Court decided that 'reasonable endeavours' imposes no obligation on a party to sacrifice its own commercial interests. The Court in that case went on to say that 'all reasonable endeavours' was probably equivalent to 'best endeavours'. However, in another case from 2007, *Yewbelle v London Green*, the Court of Appeal decided that 'all reasonable endeavours' does not require a party to lay out significant funds to do, or achieve, the particular thing in question. The case of *CPC Group v Qatari Diar* concerned a clause within a contract that required the defendant to use 'all reasonable but commercially prudent endeavours' to obtain planning permission. The Court made clear that 'all reasonable endeavours' does not always require the party subject to the obligation to put the achievement of the stated objective before its own commercial interests. In the *CPC* case the Court took into account the impact of the additional words 'commercially prudent', which seemed intended to allow the party subject to the obligation to weigh its own commercial interests against its obligation to achieve the stated objective.

'Best endeavours' wording creates the most demanding obligation, short of an absolute obligation. To satisfy the obligation to use best endeavours, a party must take all reasonable courses of action to achieve the stated purpose. Best endeavours may require the expenditure of significant sums by the professional to achieve the required end and may, where necessary, imply an obligation to litigate or appeal against a decision given under a formal dispute resolution process. In April 2012 the Court of Appeal, in the case of *Jet2 v Blackpool Airport*, confirmed that an obligation on the part of an airport operator to use best endeavours to promote Jet2's interests extended to keeping the airport open outside normal operating hours to allow for Jet2 arrivals and departures – even though this created significant extra costs for the airport operator.

Both for commercial and PII policy compliance reasons, professionals should be wary of agreeing any obligation beyond 'reasonable endeavours'. In practice, this will require the professional, using reasonable endeavours to achieve an aim, to take only one reasonable course, not all of them. An architect should also be wary of agreeing to carry out certain specific steps or activities as part of an obligation to use reasonable endeavours. Where the contract does specify that certain steps have to be taken in order to exercise reasonable endeavours, those steps will actually have to be taken, even if they may involve the sacrificing of that party's commercial interests.

Skill and care or skill, care and *diligence*?

The common sense meaning of diligence seems to imply attentive working – making an effort – and careful attention to the task in hand. These attributes are surely aspects of 'care' and so the addition of diligence to reasonable skill and care makes no practical difference.

Good faith

A bespoke appointment may, in addition to the requirement for the exercise of reasonable skill and care, contain an express obligation on the parties to perform their respective sides of the contract in good faith. In some specialist contexts, such as insurance contracts, a failure to act in utmost good faith can have practical legal consequences; but in an ordinary commercial contract, such as an architect's appointment, can you really be liable to a claim for damages for not acting with sufficient good faith? In all but the most extreme cases, the answer is almost certainly not. The High Court has provided guidance in the case of *Gold Group Properties v BDW Trading Ltd*. A good faith obligation does not require either party to give up a freely negotiated commercial advantage clearly embedded in the contract; such an obligation does not require a party to subordinate its own interests to those of the other party, but merely to have due regard to the reasonable interests of both parties in enjoying the benefit of the contract.

A good faith obligation can be given legal meaning by a court in exceptional circumstances. For example in the March 2012 case of *Medirest v Mid Essex Hospital*, the court found that an employer, subject to an obligation to act in good faith, had acted in breach of contract by exercising its contractual rights to make deductions from sums due to a catering contractor in an entirely arbitrary and 'patently absurd' way, to the severe detriment of the contractor. The NHS Trust's behaviour led to the breakdown of the relationship between the parties and the termination of the contract.

5

A mutual obligation to act in good faith can provide a significant benefit to both the architect and the client in terms of an atmosphere of collaborative working, while not imposing onerous legally enforceable obligations with which an architect may struggle to comply.

'Warrants', 'guarantees', 'undertakes' or 'ensures'

A professional appointment may contain wording to the effect that the architect 'warrants' that a particular statement is true or a particular event has taken or will take place. This is a warranty, as opposed to a collateral warranty. It is a particular type of contractual obligation. The wording may also provide that the architect 'warrants and undertakes' to do or ensure a particular thing. The strict legal effect of the warranty wording taken on its own is that the architect is giving an absolute guarantee in relation to the thing warranted.

Generally, such wording should not be accepted. If the happening of an event is beyond the architect's control, they cannot absolutely guarantee that it will happen; likewise if the background to a particular statement is outside the scope of the architect's actual knowledge, they cannot guarantee that it is true.

There are alternatives that an architect may suggest. Instead of:

'The Architect warrants that it has not specified prohibited materials.'

the architect could suggest:

'The Architect agrees that it has not specified prohibited materials.'

replacing a word that carries with it a known legal effect with one that is more ambiguous. Some employers will accept this compromise; others will say, not unreasonably, 'what do you mean when you say you agree with that statement?' Alternatively, the architect could simply leave out the linking word altogether, so in the example given the warranty becomes a simple statement:

'The Architect has not specified prohibited materials.'

One other option would be to add a specific cross reference to a standard of reasonable skill and care, to get:

'The Architect warrants, using reasonable skill and care, that it has not specified prohibited materials.'

Finally, the architect could add wording relating the warranty to the degree of control the architect has over the warranted outcome, for example:

'The Architect warrants that, to the extent it is within its reasonable control to do so, it has not specified prohibited materials.'

How strictly a court would read these alternative wordings is open to debate, but they each serve to dilute, to some extent, the absolute nature of the warranty.

If a client is unwilling to compromise on a contract warranty, consider the potential practical effect. Is there a general duty to exercise reasonable skill and care? If so, this obligation may cut across the warranty and the practical effect will be that the architect has to use reasonable skill and care to warrant the particular statement or event. What are the potential losses if the warranted thing does not occur? How much control does the architect have over the matter which is subject to the warranty? If the event is entirely within the architect's control, and the architect's duty in any case is to exercise reasonable skill and care, it may not be worth an argument.

PII policies typically exclude claims arising from contractual performance warranties or guarantees (including fitness for purpose provisions, covered in section 5.2.24), penalty clauses, or liquidated damages provisions. The RIBA Insurance Agency, with the RIBA Practice Department, has produced a useful short guide to reviewing appointment contract documentation from a liability perspective, which is freely available on its website:

- www.architectspi.com/Pages/RiskManagement.aspx

5.2.7 Compliance with other standards and documents

'In performing the Services, the Architect shall … adhere to the Programmes and … comply with any Act of Parliament, regulation, by-law …'

Generally, these types of clause only require the architect to carry out their services in compliance with the background rules and regulations, such as planning law, Building Regulations and the Construction, Design and Management (CDM) Regulations, which the architect must be aware of in any case if they are to carry out their services competently. The difficulty with such a clause is when it pushes these boundaries, for example requiring compliance with a programme or budget. Any such requirement should not be absolute, but should be subject to the exercise of reasonable skill and care, because any programme or budget will be subject to change and the architect may fail to comply with them through no fault of their own; for example, the architect might be prevented from complying with a programme because they receive information late from the client.

In relation to the usual statutory requirements, the client will expect the architect to carry out their services in compliance with Acts of Parliament and other legislation and regulations that are current at the time the architect is providing the services – not necessarily the same as those that were in place at the time the appointment was agreed. An architect

5

is expected to keep up to date with changes in statutory requirements and other background rules, by reading journals, discussing issues with their peers, taking advice and keeping up their continuing professional development hours. Changes in legislation rarely come out of the blue and are often trailed years in advance.

It is, however, arguably unfair to expect an architect to take the risk in extensive redesign resulting from unforeseen changes in the background law and regulations. You should include wording such that any additional work resulting from a change in the statutory requirements that was not reasonably foreseeable at the time the appointment was made should be subject to an additional fee and additional time for performance of the services as necessary.

5.2.8   Redesign to cost

'In the event that the Construction Budget is or is likely to be exceeded, the Architect shall carry out such redesign at its own cost as necessary to achieve compliance with the Construction Budget.'

Such 'Additional Services' are also discussed in section 5.2.1 of this chapter. Sometimes mistakenly presented as 'value engineering', this is a potentially extremely onerous obligation and should not be accepted. There are a number of ways in which a client may try to impose an obligation on the architect to carry out redesign at no cost in order to maintain an overall project budget; defining 'Additional Services' to exclude such redesign is one way; this express provision is another. The unfairness comes from the absence of any necessary link between the architect's performance and the fact of the budget being exceeded. It is possible that the loss of cost control may in any particular case be the architect's fault; but equally possible it is not.

If the client is unwilling to compromise it will be necessary for the architect to build a substantial sum into its fee to cover the risk that any such redesign proves to be extensive. Ideally, an appointment should recognise an obligation on the part of the architect to take such reasonable action if it becomes aware that the project budget is or is likely to be exceeded, while at the same time recognising the architect's right to be paid for any substantial redesign required for budgetary reasons that are not the fault of the architect.

5.2.9   Review and comment on designs by others

'The Architect shall, exercising the degree of skill, care and diligence required … review and comment on all designs submitted to it by the main contractor and the other consultants.'

A clause of this type is fair in principle, if review of others' designs is a service the architect is being paid to provide. It is sensible to add that, for the avoidance of doubt, the architect shall not be responsible for the designs provided by others. The architect should delete any provision that requires them to 'approve' the designs of others, which amounts to an overt assumption of responsibility for the work.

5.2.10   Prohibited materials

'The Architect shall not recommend or specify for use or knowingly allow to be used in the Project any materials generally known at the time of recommendation, specification or use to be deleterious to the health and safety or durability of the Project.'

In former times such clauses were known as 'deleterious materials' clauses. This terminology has now fallen out of use, so the apocryphal story goes, because of the threat of lawsuits in the United States from disgruntled manufacturers who objected to the pejorative description of their products as 'deleterious'. Sometimes a clause will refer to the general state of knowledge in the industry, as here; alternatively, it may refer to a long list of prohibited materials; to materials not in accordance with British Standards; or to materials not in accordance with the 1997 Ove Arup guidelines (*'Good Practice in the Selection of Construction Materials'*, Ove Arup & Partners 1997) or the long awaited *Good Practice in the Selection of Construction Materials 2011* published by the British Council for Offices ('BCO'), which updates it. Sometimes a prohibited materials clause will refer to all four.

In general, lists of prohibited materials should not be accepted. They do no favours to the architect (unnecessarily restricting creative use of materials in designs) or to the client (limiting choice so increasing costs; also, lists are always just out of date so offer inadequate protection) and are fundamentally too simplistic. The focus should be on the context in which a material is specified, and a simple list does not address this issue. Asbestos, for example, is prohibited for use across large parts of the 'developed' world, but it had a role to play until recently, insulating the solid rocket boosters on the space shuttle fleet. Context is important.

There is unlikely to be any material which has the potential to harm the health and safety or durability of a project in particular circumstances that is not covered by either the British Standards or the Ove Arup guidelines (as updated by the BCO in 2011) or both. A prohibited materials clause should be based on compliance with these as updated from time to time, allied to an overall obligation to exercise reasonable skill and care in the selection of materials.

5

Any obligation on an architect in relation to materials should be limited to the context of the architect's specification role. The architect will usually have no opportunity to closely monitor the use of materials. Unless the architect has agreed a general site monitoring role, any reference to 'knowingly allowing' the use of such materials should be deleted; how would an architect be expected to police the use of materials in any case? They usually have no contractual relationship with the contractor or sub-contractors. In addition, the requirement for compliance with the British Standards and the Ove Arup or 2011 BCO guidelines must be limited to the time of specification by the architect; the architect usually has no say over the timing of the use of a material on site.

An obligation to pass on information about the use of prohibited materials on site, if the architect becomes aware of such use, is acceptable; provided that the clause goes on to say that no additional site monitoring role is implied as a consequence.

5.2.11   Keeping the client informed

'The Architect shall keep the Client informed on all matters within the Architect's responsibility in relation to the Project which are of interest to a prudent Client.'

This is too wide a remit. A prudent client will want to know about anything in relation to the project that has the potential to compromise or delay delivery or increase costs. That could include almost anything. The architect's obligation should be to keep the client informed in respect of all matters reasonably relating to the performance of the architect's services. This does not mean that the architect should be unhelpful. The architect is a pivotal member of the professional team and so it is inevitable and beneficial that the wider project should be discussed at site meetings and in other meetings with the client. However, an express obligation to keep the client informed about all aspects of the project may imply a degree of knowledge that the architect does not have the contractual ability to acquire if the other parties involved in the project do not want to give it freely.

5.2.12   Key personnel

'The Architect shall not change any of the key personnel without the prior written approval of the Client.'

Clients often want this or similar protection to ensure a degree of continuity in the service they receive. This is usually acceptable, provided there is an exception to the requirement for approval in cases where an individual retires, resigns, is sacked or dies.

A commercial client will usually also want the right to approve any replacement. This is generally acceptable as long as approval cannot be unreasonably delayed or withheld. A client may want the right to require the removal of a particular individual from its project. This should usually not be accepted, unless the client's right is subject to a reasonableness standard.

5.2.13 Collateral warranties and third party rights

'The Architect shall, within 10 days of each request made by the Client, execute and deliver to the Client a deed or deeds of collateral warranty in the form set out in Appendix [ ], or will agree that the schedule of third party rights set out in Appendix [   ] shall apply, in favour of:

(i)   any funder providing finance in relation to the whole or any part of the Project;
(ii) any Purchaser or Tenant taking an interest in the whole or any part of the Project;
(iii) any Group Company or Affiliate of the Client; and
(iv) any Freeholder.'

Rights of third parties in general

The nature of the obligation to provide contractual rights to third parties, either through collateral warranties or third party rights (TPRs), is discussed in detail in Chapter 6. The main point for the architect is to consider whether the job is one which warrants an obligation to provide contractual rights to third parties at all. Is the architect's fee sufficient compensation for the risk? Is the job high value, complex, strategically important to the client and the architect? Even if it is appropriate to give a collateral warranty, is it appropriate that it should be executed as a deed?

The next question to deal with is the nature and extent of the likely beneficiaries. On a large retail development, it may be fair enough to provide collateral warranties or TPRs in favour of key anchor tenants, but not for every news kiosk and shoe repair stand. The enabling clause must adequately set out the limitations of the architect's obligation to provide contractual protection for third parties.

How realistic is it to propose restrictions?

If there is no limit on the overall number of collateral warranties that may be required (or TPRs; the phrase collateral warranties is used in this section for ease of reference, but the points considered apply generally to both), this obligation can soon become very onerous, not just in terms of the extension of contractual liability to many parties over and above the architect's immediate client, but also (particularly in relation to collateral warranties) because of the amount of management time required to deal with them. There is also a temptation for clients to propose particular amendments to suit individual beneficiaries if the enabling clause allows for reasonable amendments to be proposed; most architects will be willing to consider changes. The time outlay and potential costs of taking legal advice can mount up over the course of 10 or 20 individual collateral warranties.

It is most sensible to seek certain limitations on the overall obligation to provide collateral warranties. But this is an intensely commercial area where legal arguments carry little weight. A commercial developer client is interested solely in the marketability of their project and will have a fixed idea about the strength and comprehensiveness of the collateral warranty package they want to be able to offer to incoming tenants and purchasers; negotiating a less strict obligation in these circumstances can be unrealistic unless the architect's insurer has made clear that a particular aspect of the obligation to provide collateral warranties will not be insurable.

'Reasonable' requests

If the architect has a strong bargaining position, they may argue for the inclusion of an obligation to provide collateral warranties in response to a 'reasonable' request; the implication of this wording would be that some requests may be unreasonable. A client will find this hard to accept, but this wording would protect the architect from the possibility of providing a collateral warranty to, for example, a beneficiary with a track record of making nuisance claims. As an alternative to address this issue, the architect may propose a specific exclusion of the obligation to provide collateral warranties if the parties are in dispute over fees, or a right for the architect to reasonably object to providing a collateral warranty in particular circumstances. It would be unusual for a client to accept such limitations; but if it is apparent that the client's own obligation to procure collateral warranties under a sale agreement or agreement for lease is subject to the use of the client's reasonable endeavours (rather than being an absolute obligation), there is arguably no reason why the architect's obligation to provide collateral warranties should not also be subject to certain exceptions.

Limitation to first purchaser or first tenant

It is arguably the market norm for collateral warranties in favour of purchasers, tenants and funders to be limited to the 'first' such beneficiary in that category. This would mean in practice that if the project is sold to a purchaser, the architect would provide a collateral warranty in their favour; but if the project was subsequently sold again to a second purchaser, the architect would not have to provide a collateral warranty. Even though clients do not like any such restrictions on their ability to procure collateral warranties, an architect can make a strong argument for the inclusion of 'first' wording, because collateral warranties generally allow for the beneficiary to assign the benefit. Rather than requiring the architect to provide a new collateral warranty, it is not unreasonable to expect the first purchaser, in this example, to assign the benefit of their collateral warranty to the party purchasing their interest.

A client may object to the inclusion of a 'first' limitation particularly in respect of funder collateral warranties. In these circumstances an architect can press the issue by querying the need for an unlimited ability to call for funder collateral warranties; how many funders, realistically, are likely to be involved? Any limit, or any wording that can provide more certainty about the likely extent of the architect's collateral warranty obligations, is a benefit worth arguing for.

Limit by extent of interest

An architect with a strong bargaining position may be able to limit the collateral warranties obligation not only to the 'first' of any category (tenant or purchaser for example), but also to a first beneficiary taking that particular interest in the *whole* of the project. Most clients will have drafted the clause to refer to, for example:

'any tenant of the whole or any part of the Project.'

The architect could propose limiting this, as a compromise, to the:

'whole or any <u>substantial</u> part of the Project.'

The architect could propose more definite limitations by setting specific parameters based on, for example, a monetary value of the interest taken, or a minimum floor area.

Limit in number

'The Architect shall on request provide collateral warranties … up to a maximum number of 10.'

The use of this wording provides a degree of certainty for the architect and the client, but it is a blunt instrument and potentially unhelpful to both. Once the collateral warranties are all used up, the client has no legal right to require any more, no matter how important the incoming third

5

party is; conversely, the architect will still be obliged to provide collateral warranties in response to each of the first ten requests, whether or not there is an ongoing fee.

Amending the form of collateral warranty

An enabling clause will often require the architect to provide collateral warranties:

'generally in the form attached but incorporating such reasonable amendments as may be required by the Beneficiary.'

An architect could argue that this amounts to an agreement to agree a collateral warranty form – an obligation not usually enforceable in law – and that it is too uncertain to create a viable legal obligation to accept amendments; it is in any case best practice to eliminate the scope for amending the form attached to the appointment. This does potentially limit the marketability of the collateral warranty package – the client can largely, but not entirely, predict what an incoming third party will need – but it provides a degree of certainty that the obligation is enforceable. There is nothing to stop the parties agreeing amended terms, subject to a possible additional fee to cover the risk to the architect, if a potential beneficiary is adamant that they require something other than the agreed form.

Limit to either collateral warranties or TPRs

An architect may want to limit their obligation to provide either collateral warranties or TPRs. Depending upon their PII position, this may not make much practical difference to the architect, but there is some commercial advantage in limiting the scope of the obligation to collateral warranties only and excluding the possibility of TPRs, and the obligation may be less complex to manage if the architect only has to consider one type of document.

'Penalties' for failure to provide

The architect should delete any proposed withholding of fees for failure to provide on request collateral warranties. The client will argue that the clause will only affect the architect to the extent it is in breach of contract, and that the provision by the architect of collateral warranties (as opposed to sub-consultant collateral warranties, arguably) is entirely within the architect's control. But many such provisions are likely to be ineffective anyway. How can the parties realistically judge the potential worth of a collateral warranty at the time the appointment is signed?

And if the clause requiring compensation is not a genuine pre-estimate of the client's potential losses as a result of the failure to provide the collateral warranty, then the provision is likely to be struck out by a court as an unenforceable penalty. Any clause to the effect that the provision of collateral warranties shall be a pre-condition to the payment of fees as a whole is similarly very likely to be unenforceable.

Powers of attorney

'The Architect appoints the Client as its true and lawful attorney in the name of and on behalf of the Architect to complete any deed of collateral warranty and to execute and perfect any such collateral warranty … and the Architect agrees to ratify and confirm whatsoever the Client shall do or purport to do by virtue of this power of attorney.'

The collateral warranty enabling clause in a bespoke appointment may require that the architect agrees to the client being its lawful attorney for the purposes of executing collateral warranties in the event of the architect's failure to do so. The client will argue that there is no reason for the architect to be concerned about this clause, because it will only ever become relevant if the architect is in breach of contract and has not provided a collateral warranty they are obliged to give. But there is likely to be a good reason why the architect has not provided the collateral warranty in question. An architect should never accept a power of attorney provision; it is extremely important that the architect maintains control over the contracts they enter into. The architect's PII policy may not cover the architect for obligations under a contract entered into in this way. The imposition of such an obligation at the outset also creates a poor impression – the client only needs to include such a clause if, at the outset, they do not think that the architect will comply with their contractual obligations.

Execution of collateral warranties in escrow

'The Architect shall execute [   ] deeds of collateral warranty to be provided pursuant to this clause immediately on execution of this Agreement, provided that where at the time of execution of the deeds of collateral warranty by the Architect the identity of the beneficiaries is not known, the details of any such beneficiary shall be left blank and shall be inserted by the Client once such details are known'.

There is no good reason why an architect should provide collateral warranties executed 'in escrow'. Without knowing their identity, an architect cannot judge the potential risk of the beneficiary making a

5

claim. Such obligations appear in draft appointments relatively rarely, largely because there is no sensible argument in support.

Sub-consultant collateral warranties

The architect may also be obliged under the enabling clause to procure collateral warranties from some or all of their sub-consultants. This should always be subject to the architect's 'reasonable endeavours'. The client will argue that procuring such collateral warranties is entirely within the architect's control – the architect after all will generally have chosen their own sub-consultants – and will say that if the architect had not chosen to engage sub-consultants, the additional collateral warranties would not be required. However, the architect can make the point that, even if there is a strict obligation to provide collateral warranties in a sub-consultant's appointment, this is still not a guarantee that the collateral warranty will in fact be provided – the sub-consultant may breach their obligation. Also, it is not realistic to expect some sub-consultants to provide collateral warranties, particularly if their services are not extensive or are low value. Finally, the architect can point out that their own collateral warranty covers all of their services, whether or not they were sub-consulted out.

5.2.14 **Indemnities**

'The Architect shall be liable for and shall indemnify the Client against any and all claims, actions, liabilities, losses, damages and expenses (including legal expenses) incurred by the Client which arise out of or in connection with, directly or indirectly, the Architect's performance under this Agreement.'

General comments on indemnities

This type of general indemnity, which may feature particularly in a bespoke sub-consultancy appointment, should never be accepted.

Most PII policies are based on negligence. Cover is activated when a party establishes that the insured has breached their professional duty of care by acting negligently. But an indemnity obligation does not work in this way.

There is a real risk that, under a typical PII policy, the architect will not be covered to the extent that a claim is based on an indemnity.

Some PII policies contain express exclusions of cover for obligations in the nature of indemnities.

Any use of the word 'indemnity' or 'indemnify' should set alarm bells ringing, but a clause can amount to an indemnity even without explicitly using the word; any obligation to 'hold the client harmless' in relation to or 'be liable for' an extended definition of 'direct' losses (potentially covering losses, costs, claims, demands, actions, damages, expenses, compensation and liabilities, including legal expenses) may amount to an indemnity, if a court decides the intention of the parties was that it should.

Specific disadvantages for an architect in agreeing an indemnity

Liability for sums not ordinarily recoverable
If the client is able to rely on an indemnity then, depending upon the precise wording of the clause, there may be no obligation for them to 'mitigate' their losses; they will be able to recover the full extent of their losses without the need to take any positive action to keep their losses to a minimum. The definition of what constitutes a recoverable loss is also expanded. There is potentially no issue of remoteness of damage; everything may be recovered if the client can establish a causal link between the breach and the loss. There is also potentially no issue of contributory negligence; the client is entitled to give up all responsibility for self-preservation.

Liability without negligence
The possibility that a claim under an indemnity may not be covered by the architect's PII cover stems from this aspect of the nature of an indemnity. The client does not have to prove that the architect was negligent in order to successfully claim under an indemnity. Negligence is not required at all; only that the client has suffered a loss for which the architect has provided an indemnity. In the example wording given above, the indemnity relates to any and all losses which arise out of or in connection with the architect's performance under the appointment. The indemnity does not relate only to negligent performance; it is any performance, including performance by the architect of their obligations entirely as required by the appointment.

Say, for example, the architect, exercising reasonable skill and care, properly refuses to grant an extension of time; if the contractor goes to adjudication claiming an extension of time and prolongation costs, and the adjudicator takes a different view from the architect and makes an award in favour of the contractor, the client is entitled to sue the architect under the indemnity to recover all their resulting losses and expenses, even though the architect's original decision was not negligent.

Extended limitation on actions in time
The limitation period for an action under a contractual indemnity will be 6 or 12 years, depending upon whether the appointment is executed

5

under hand or as a deed. However, in contrast to an ordinary action for breach of contract, where the limitation period starts to run from the date of breach, the period for an action under an indemnity starts to run only when the client suffers a loss, which could be years after the contractual limitation period expired.

Arguments against accepting an indemnity

The most potent argument against accepting any indemnity in a professional appointment or collateral warranty is that the obligation is unlikely to be covered by the architect's PII policy. Unless an obligation is insured, it is generally of limited value to the client. Not all PII policies exclude cover for indemnities, however. The architect should check this point as part of the overall request to the insurer for comments that should follow any proposal to sign a bespoke form of professional appointment.

If the client is not convinced by the PII argument, it is worth requesting that the client should explain why they require an indemnity instead of a potential claim for breach of contract in the usual way. The market does not dictate that an indemnity is required for any particular aspect of the architect's obligations. The wording does regularly appear in the context of breach of copyright and liability for personal injury, death and damage to property, but there is no convincing argument why an indemnity should be more appropriate in these contexts than others. If the client cannot explain or does not understand why they require the more onerous obligation, this is a good argument against including it.

If an architect finds that their arguments against an indemnity provision in principle are not persuasive, there are ways of considerably limiting its scope. For example, an architect could seek general wording to the effect that, notwithstanding any other provision of the appointment, they shall owe no greater duty than to exercise reasonable skill, care and diligence. This would ordinarily cut across any indemnity provision.

Alternatively:

- a limitation on actions in time could be expressly included, such that no actions under the appointment (implicitly including an action under an indemnity) could be commenced after the expiry of 12 years (6 years if the appointment is not a deed) after completion of the architect's services;
- the architect could limit the definition of losses to those which are 'reasonably foreseeable, legally enforceable and fully mitigated';
- the architect could propose wording to limit the application of the indemnity to their 'negligent acts or omissions or breach of contract'.

Incorporating this wording would mean that the clause is no longer an indemnity at all.

However, a knowledgeable client, anxious to preserve an indemnity, would be unlikely to accept such limitations.

More limited indemnities

More specific indemnities with a limited scope may also be proposed by a client; for example, in the context of breach of copyright claims and claims relating to personal injury or death. Although the nature of the indemnity remains the same and there remains the risk of uninsurability, some architects choose to accept these more limited indemnities as acceptable commercial risks.

5.2.15 Copyright

Copyright is also discussed in Chapter 4, section 4.1.6.

Who owns the copyright in a piece of work?

An architect's intellectual property rights are extremely important to their business. By law the copyright in any designs, through the drawings and the finished building representing the designs, is owned by the architect, and the architect is generally free, unless they make an express or implied agreement to the contrary, to recycle their work on other projects. Copyright law is subject to the Copyright, Designs and Patents Act 1988 ('the CDPA 1988'). Copyright subsists in the physical expression of ideas, rather than the ideas themselves – drawings, plans, sketches and specifications will all attract copyright protection as 'literary works' – and gives the owner the right to prevent others from using their material in particular ways, primarily from copying it. As well as the documents produced by the architect, works of architecture are protected, coming within the definition of 'artistic works' for the purposes of the CDPA 1988 (section 4(1)(b)), and a work of architecture in this context can mean architectural models as well as the building itself. Copyright in an artistic or literary work will usually subsist for a period of 70 years from the end of the calendar year in which the author died.

An architect's drawings and other documents will typically be issued marked with an assertion of copyright, along the lines of:

'© 20[   ]. [   ] is the author of this document and owns the copyright in it. This document may not be reproduced in any form in whole or in part without the prior written permission of the copyright owner.'

5

This is good practice, as it eliminates any ambiguity about the source of a document, although such an assertion alone cannot conclusively establish authorship or copyright ownership.

Implied copyright licences
Although the architect will generally own the copyright in any material they produce during the course of carrying out the services, it is usual in the market for the client to be granted a licence to use any such copyrighted material for the purposes of the immediate project. This licence may be granted expressly under the terms of the architect's appointment, or implied by law – if the architect has been engaged to provide drawings for a building project, the client cannot be prevented from using the design in those drawings as the basis for construction, provided that the client has paid the architect for the work they carried out. This is the case whether the original appointment was to obtain planning permission only or to provide a full service, and whether or not the architect is subsequently retained to provide construction phase services. There are conflicting decided cases – the *Blair* case discussed below (yes to a licence) and the case of *Stovin-Bradford v Volpoint* (no licence) – but there appears to be a clear principle that the client does receive an implied licence to use the designs through to completion of the project without paying any further fee, even though the original architect has no further involvement in the project.

The principle seems to be strongly linked in the perception of the courts to the receipt by the original architect of a fee adequate to take into account the use of their design through to completion of the project, rather than just for the limited use of obtaining planning permission. In the case of *Blair v Osborne*, the court found that there had been no breach of the original architect's copyright because the architect had received reasonable compensation for their work; payment was based on the then current RIBA fee scales for partial services, which were deliberately front-end weighted to provide an in-built compensation for the use of designs created to achieve planning permission but which are then used, without any further involvement of (or payment to) the original architect, to complete the project.

This reflects the traditional approach to an architect's payment structure, allowing for significant front-end weighting in the fees up to completion of the scheme design stage, reflecting the importance of the architect's creative skill in achieving a solution to the client's brief. The architect's efforts in creating a design that obtains planning permission have conventionally been seen as justifying a reward beyond that which would be payable on the basis of time costs.

Can subsequent site owners use the architect's design?

What if the original architect is engaged to produce designs with a view to achieving planning approval, and does so, but the client then sells their interest in the site and passes on those designs to the purchaser, who uses them to complete the project? The position seems to be the same; if the architect has received adequate compensation, there is an implied licence which can be transferred by the first owner and relied upon by the new owner to build out the project using the original designs.

It is for the architect to make sure in these circumstances that the compensation they receive really is commensurate with the value of the work carried out to achieve planning approval for the first owner. Additional wording can be proposed which would require the payment of an additional fee in the event that the architect is not retained but their design is used to complete the project, whether by the client or by a party to whom the client sells the site; this is in fact the mechanism used in the RIBA standard form appointments, in which payment of a copyright licence fee for subsequent use of a design is required. Alternatively, the architect could simply ensure that their fee for the initial design to the end of RIBA Stage 3 is appropriately weighted. If there is any hint that the client is in financial difficulties, the architect has a far stronger case for insisting upon wording in their appointment that expressly denies a copyright licence in the event that their fees are not paid.

Sometimes use of a very similar design does not amount to breach of copyright

There may sometimes be special circumstances which mean that the original architect cannot successfully claim for breach of copyright even if they have not been properly paid and the design used to complete the project is very similar to that which they originally produced. One case in particular highlights the risk. *Jones v London Borough of Tower Hamlets* concerned an architect who had been engaged by a client to design a housing development, shortly before the client went into liquidation. The architect produced a scheme design but was not paid. A subsequent owner of the site went on to obtain planning permission based on a scheme design ostensibly provided by their own team, but the architect, Jones, claimed that his designs had been copied. The new developer's defence to the claim for breach of copyright was that the similarities between the two designs were not the result of copying, but were unavoidable; the physical constraints of the site would not allow an alternative design solution. The court agreed; the new developer's scheme design would have been arrived at by any competent designer operating within the constraints of that particular site and project brief.

5

Express copyright licences

'The Architect hereby grants with full title guarantee to the Client an unconditional, irrevocable, royalty-free and non-exclusive licence to use, copy and adapt any and all of the Documents and the designs contained in them for any purpose whatsoever connected with the Project or the Site, including without limitation the design, completion, execution, repair, maintenance, modification, extension, promotion funding, reinstatement, letting or sale thereof. Such licence shall carry the right to grant sub-licences …

The Architect shall indemnify and keep the Client indemnified in connection with any claim … relating to the infringement of any third party intellectual property rights'.

It is entirely standard for a professional appointment to contain wording obliging the architect to grant a copyright licence to the client to use the architect's copyrighted material generated during the course of the project. The details of the licence will vary from appointment to appointment; bespoke appointments often push the boundaries of what the architect should accept and what is considered appropriate in the market, and an example is given above.

The architect should seek to include a provision linking the copyright licence to the payment of their fees. Commercial clients in particular are often unwilling to agree to this, but if there is any question about the strength of the client's financial covenant, the architect has a stronger position from which to argue this point; if the client is based overseas, or is a new developer with no proven track record, these are good reasons for arguing that there should be a link between the licence and the payment of fees.

The use of the wording 'grants with full title guarantee' should generally be removed; the extent of the additional covenants implied is not clear, and not many clients will be able to honestly say what they are hoping to achieve by using such wording. References to an 'unconditional, royalty-free, irrevocable' licence should also be removed if the architect has the bargaining strength to insist upon linking the licence to payment of their fee, in which case the licence is subject to conditions and may be revoked.

Clients will typically want the right to create sub-licences in favour of third parties, generally other members of the project team, or to assign the benefit of the licence – hence the use of the wording 'non-exclusive' (the licence is not just for the client). If the architect's bargaining position is strong enough, they may insist upon the client indemnifying them in relation to any claims relating to use by such third parties. At the very least, the architect should insist that any such right is subject to an exclusion of liability in relation to any use by these third parties of the copyrighted material for any purposes other than those for which the material was originally provided; this exclusion should also apply to the client's own use and is entirely standard wording.

This limitation can have unanticipated consequences for the client if the scope of the architect's initial engagement was limited; for example, clause 6.3 of the RIBA Standard Conditions allows a licence to use the copyrighted material only for the specific purposes for which it was prepared.

If the material was prepared under an instruction to achieve planning permission only, this would not give the client the right to use the designs to build out the project without the architect's permission and, most likely, payment of an additional fee.

It is usual for the architect to object to the copyright licence allowing reproduction of the design for any extension of the project, or for use on any other project that the client may become involved in. Any such use should be subject to an additional fee.

The architect should not accept an obligation to indemnify the client in relation to third party claims for breach of copyright. There is no logical reason why the client should not rely on their ability to sue for breach of contract in the usual way if there is any question of the architect failing to comply with their obligations under the copyright clause.

The client will usually require that the architect procures similar copyright licences from their sub-consultants and in relation to all other copyrighted material used in the performance of the services but not owned by the architect. As discussed above in the context of the definition of 'Documents' (see section 5.2.1), any such obligation should be subject to the use of reasonable endeavours, rather than a strict obligation, and should expressly exclude proprietary products.

Transfer to the client of copyright ownership
An architect should generally not accept an obligation to assign the ownership of their copyright material generated in carrying out their services in relation to the project. There is rarely a good reason for the client to require an assignment, as opposed to the more usual licence, and if pressed on the issue a client will often be unable to say why they have asked for it.

Occasionally a client does have a genuine need to own the copyright; for example, if the client is developing a statement project that they wish to

5

form the basis of a distinctive brand, they will not want the architect to reproduce the same designs for their next client. However, insisting upon an assignment of copyright is counterproductive; such an approach stifles design innovation. There is little incentive for the architect to produce unique features or develop groundbreaking techniques if they know that they will never be able to make use of them again.

Any agreement by the architect to transfer copyright ownership should only be made if it is an absolute requirement of the client and subject to adequate compensation for the architect.

Remedies for breach of copyright

In reality, it is going to be rare for a court (because of the disproportionate nature of the remedy in comparison to the wrong) to stop a project proceeding because of an alleged infringement of an architect's copyright, even supposing the original architect was able to bring their case quickly enough to allow the court to consider this remedy as a possibility.

Seeking an injunction is expensive because of the degree of legal input required in a restricted timescale. It is also a high-risk strategy, because if a court subsequently decides, on hearing the evidence in full, that there was no breach of copyright, the architect could in turn be sued for the costs resulting from the delay to the project.

It may be difficult for an architect to quantify in terms of money the potential damage to their professional reputation or standing which would be caused by a new architect continuing a project with a watered down version of their design. But practically there is no better way for a practice to protect itself than by ensuring that its work to completion of RIBA Stage 3 is subject to an appropriate front-end loaded fee, which includes a sum for the value of the copyright in design, and/or that if necessary any use of the designs beyond that stage is subject to the payment of an additional copyright licence fee.

Moral rights

Moral rights subsist in original works and are enshrined in the CDPA 1988, covering, for example, the architect's right to be identified as the author of their work and their right to object to derogatory treatment of their work.

Sometimes a client will include a provision obliging the architect to waive their moral rights. This is legitimate – moral rights may be waived, but cannot be assigned – and in most instances architects do not have particularly strong feelings on the topic and are usually happy to waive their moral rights. There is generally no financial implication one way or another with waiving moral rights. If you do want to be identified as the author of a building design, do not accept a waiver provision.

5.2.16 Payment

The level of fees

It is for the architect and the client to decide the level of the fee and the basis on which it is calculated. The fee may be expressed as a lump sum or as a percentage of the total cost of the work, or the architect may (on smaller jobs only, realistically) quote an hourly rate, although any combination of these methods may be used.

If the fee is based on a percentage of the construction budget, the architect should be alive to the possibility that the budget may be reduced if the contractor's tender comes in low – and with many contractors desperate for work, this is not as uncommon as it used to be. The architect can protect themselves from an unexpected reduction in their fee by providing for 'upwards only' adjustment; a client may query the logic of this, so another way of presenting it would be to have a minimum figure for a fee, making explicit that there is a fee level below which it becomes uneconomic for the architect to take the job.

The fee should not be inclusive of expenses and disbursements – it is difficult for an architect to assess what the value of these might be at the outset of a project. If a client insists that the fee must be inclusive of disbursements and expenses, the architect should point out that a contingency in the fee will need to be allowed which may exceed the actual costs incurred by the architect, so simply paying these amounts in addition to the fee each month may represent better value for the client.

Every client wants value for money, but no two clients assess value in the same way. The best source of practical advice on negotiating fee levels, apart from your peers, is probably the RIBA's *Good Practice Guide: Fee Management* (2012). The RIBA Fee Calculator is also a useful tool for the preparation of resource-based fee proposals, and it can be downloaded free of charge from the members' area of the RIBA's website:

• www.architecture.com

Payment provisions in 'construction contracts'

The 1996 Construction Act was introduced in an effort to ensure that fair payment practices which promote cash flow are adopted in the construction industry. As well as providing a statutory right to refer disputes to adjudication, considered in detail in Chapter 10, certain requirements in relation to the timing and withholding of payments were also imposed.

The payment provisions in any bespoke appointment should be compliant with the requirements of the 1996 Act, as amended by the Local Democracy, Economic Development and Construction Act 2009, which applies to all construction contracts entered into on or after 1 October 2011. This is good practice, although not every appointment an architect signs will automatically be subject to the Construction Acts – for example, an appointment in relation to work on a dwelling with a client who is a residential occupier will not be covered by the Construction Acts and the architect will want to expressly include contractual provisions which reflect the amended provisions of the 2009 Act. The architect should also be sure to explain fully the implications of these provisions to a consumer client; a court may otherwise be unwilling to enforce them against such a client.

The Construction Acts apply to 'construction contracts', defined as agreements for carrying out construction operations, which expressly includes an agreement to do 'architectural, design or surveying work' in relation to construction operations. The Construction Acts expressly do not apply in a number of circumstances that might otherwise be considered construction operations; as well as the residential occupier exception mentioned above, work in relation to the drilling of oil and gas, other mining operations and the nuclear industry are all excluded – these industry-specific exclusions are the result of lobbying rather than logic.

The provisions of the Construction Acts now apply to purely oral construction contracts

Under the 1996 Construction Act, the payment and adjudication provisions only applied to construction contracts which were in writing or evidenced in writing. Courts took a restrictive approach and the absence of any important written term could leave the contract liable to be declared outside the scope of the 1996 Act. The 2009 Act repeals this provision. Although it remains poor practice to agree an appointment other than in writing, many architect's appointments are at least partly reliant on provisions agreed orally; so the 2009 Act provides an important benefit, implying the protection afforded by the payment provisions of the Scheme for Construction Contracts into a wholly or partly oral appointment. It will be theoretically possible to agree orally payment provisions that are compliant with the 2009 Act without relying on the Scheme, but this should never be considered in practice.

The 2009 Construction Act is drafted to work in conjunction with the Scheme for Construction Contracts (England and Wales) amended Regulations 2011 ('the Scheme'). The Scheme contains specific obligations fleshing out the statutory principles in relation to payment and adjudication that are set out in the 2009 Act. If an appointment is a construction contract for the purposes of the Construction Acts but does not contain all of the necessary payment provisions to comply with the 2009 Act, the relevant wording from the Scheme is implied into the appointment to plug the gaps. This is different to the way the Scheme works in relation to adjudication provisions in construction contracts – if the appointment is non-compliant in any way, the entirety of the adjudication provisions in the appointment are swept away and replaced by the Scheme wording.

Instalments and withholding sums under the 2009 Act

The following issues should generally be covered in any bespoke appointment.

Instalments

For any appointment where the duration of work is to be in excess of 45 days, the Construction Acts provide a statutory right to payment in instalments. Under the 2009 Act the parties are free to agree the amounts of the payments and the intervals at which (or circumstances in which) they become due. It is good practice to agree for payment in monthly instalments to ensure a regular cash flow. There is no reason for architects to be shy about chasing up fee instalments as soon as they become overdue; this is business, and if a failure to pay is ignored once, the client may form the impression that its cash flow requirements can be prioritised over those of the architect.

Basing payment of instalments on the achievement of particular milestones is attractive to clients and has the force of logic. However, if a milestone is, for example, the completion of a particular RIBA stage, this can lead to lengthy periods when no fees are being paid to the architect, with a consequent impact on cash flow – the long contract administration Stage 5 is a good example. Combining both principles so that there is a set percentage of the fee due at completion of a stage, but monthly instalments are to be made during each stage to build up to that percentage, is a satisfactory compromise.

Architects will typically want the fee instalments to be front-end weighted, so that the biggest portions of the fee are payable in the early months. This provides a degree of protection in the event that, for example,

5

the architect is not retained to build out the project after planning permission is obtained. Clients may seek to adjust the weighting so that fee instalments for the initial stages are light, on the understanding that the architect will be involved through to the end of the project and will receive a satisfactory fee overall. If an architect agrees to this, it is sensible to include wording to oblige the client to make a payment on termination to redress the balance if, in fact, the architect is not retained beyond planning.

It is good practice to include a schedule of fee instalments in your appointment, if possible, but instalment schedules can go out of date very quickly if the schedule is too prescriptive and does not allow for updating to take account of changing circumstances, such as an expanded scope of services.

Dates for payment

Every appointment must provide an adequate mechanism for determining what payments become due, and when they become due (the 'due date') as well as a final date for the payment of any sum that has become due. An adequate mechanism may be, for example, a schedule of fee payments setting out precisely the date on which any particular payment becomes due; or wording allowing the architect to issue monthly accounts covering the services they have provided to that date. An architect should not readily accept any provision that requires them to rely on certification of payment by the client or their project manager, rather than a straight application for payment by the architect.

The process starts with the architect rendering their invoice. The parties are free in the appointment to agree the relevant period after the invoice is issued within which a sum becomes due, and the final date for payment of sums due. Under the Scheme, payment may be due on the date the invoice is rendered and the final date for payment is 17 days after that. The Act-compliant provisions in the RIBA Standard Conditions say that payment is due on the date the architect issues their account, with the final date for payment 14 days thereafter.

A typical client-drafted bespoke appointment will push the final date out to 30 days after the due date, which may in turn be several days after the invoice is rendered or 'on receipt' of the invoice. If your client is a contractor, in particular, you may be faced with an unreasonably long period before a sum becomes due in order to tie in with the contractor's own payment cycle – 35 days or longer is not unheard of. If the due date is triggered by receipt, the architect will need to check with the client that it has received an invoice and, if so, when, in order to ensure that each of the other payment-related timings can be properly calculated.

An architect should generally not accept any specific requirements as to what must be included with an invoice, especially if wording is used which requires the evidence provided with the invoice to be 'to the client's satisfaction'. A requirement to provide reasonable supporting documentation with an invoice is logical and difficult to object to.

Payment notices and pay less notices

The 2009 Construction Act is intended to simplify payment mechanisms in construction contracts, including professional appointments, by introducing a new payment notice regime. It is also intended that the new regime will be fairer for those professionals, such as architects, seeking payment from clients, and the wording in any professional appointment must reflect the new mechanism.

The basic premise has not altered following the introduction of the 2009 Act – there must be an adequate mechanism for determining what payments become due, and when, and for determining the final date for payment.

Section 110A of the 2009 Act requires an appointment to contain a provision obliging the client or their nominee to serve a payment notice not later than 5 days after the due date (usually the date the architect's invoice is issued), and the notice must specify the sum that the client or the client's nominee considers is due and the basis on which such amount is calculated. This is the 'payment notice'.

Section 110B of the 2009 Act applies where the client was obliged to give a payment notice but failed to do so. The 2009 Act entitles the architect (or any other party hoping to receive payment) to serve their own payment notice if the client fails to do so; the notice has to set out the same information as would a client's payment notice, and can be given any time after the last date when the client should have served their payment notice.

If the architect serves the payment notice in this way, the final date for payment of the sum specified in the notice is postponed by the same number of days as the number of days after the last date for the client to serve a payment notice that the architect's payment notice was given. So, if the client has not served their payment notice within the 5-day period after the due date set by the Act, and the architect serves their payment notice on the sixth day, then the final date for payment will be extended by 1 day.

5

In practice, it is far more likely that if the client does not issue a payment notice, the architect's invoice will become the payment notice. This is allowed for by section 110B(4) of the 2009 Act, which says that if the contract allows or requires an architect to submit invoices on or before the payment due date, and the architect does this, their invoice will be the payment notice, provided it sets out the sum the architect considers to be due and the basis on which that sum is calculated. The sum set out in the payment notice is described in the 2009 Act as the 'notified sum'.

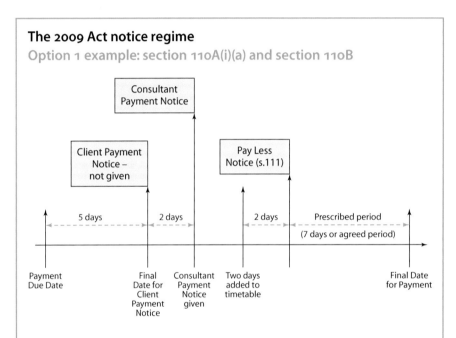

The 2009 Act notice regime

Option 1 example: section 110A(i)(a) and section 110B

The construction contract requires the payer to give an Act-compliant payment notice to the payee not later than 5 days after the payment due date.

If the payer fails to give such notice not later than 5 days after the payment due date, the payee may give a payment notice at any time thereafter. If the payee gives such a notice, the *final date* for payment of the sum specified in the notice is postponed by the same number of days after the initial 5-day period that the payee's notice was given. In the diagram, the consultant payee gave his notice 2 days after the final date on which the client could have served a payment notice; the final date for payment is pushed back by 2 days accordingly.

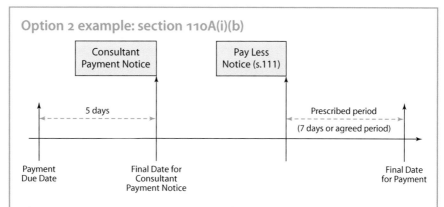

Option 2 example: section 110A(i)(b)

The construction contract requires the payee to give an Act-compliant payment notice setting out the sum the payee considers due and the basis on which that sum is calculated. If no notice is given, the clock does not start to run and the payee does not get paid.

Option 3 example: section 110B(4)

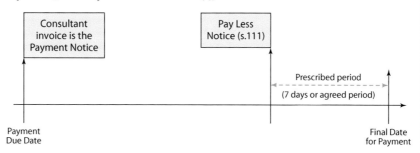

If the construction contract permits or requires the party being paid, before the date for any client payment notice, to notify the paying party of the sum that the payee considers will be due on the due date and the basis on which that sum is calculated, then the timetable will start to run from that notification.

In practice, this is how very many construction contracts will operate, including the RIBA Standard Conditions. The architect's invoice will be the payment notice, which starts the timetable running, and the sum stated in the invoice will be the notified sum.

A number of questions may arise regarding the issuing of pay less notices:

- *What if the client does not agree that it should have to pay in full the notified sum?*
  Section 111 of the 2009 Construction Act requires payment of the notified sum on or before the final date for payment, unless the client has served a 'notice of intention to pay less'. This is the same concept as under the

1996 Act, where the equivalent notice was called a 'withholding notice'. As before, it is for the parties to agree in the appointment when the pay less notice must be served. The Scheme requires service 7 days prior to the final date for payment. Most standard form and bespoke appointments provide that the pay less notice must be served not later than 5 days before the final date for payment.

The pay less notice under the 2009 Act must specify the sum that the client considers to be due on the date the notice is served and the basis on which that sum is calculated. The courts made clear, in the context of the 1996 Act requirement for 'grounds' for withholding to be given, that a notice would remain valid even if the grounds given for withholding subsequently proved not to be true or accurate; this must also be the case if the basis for the pay less notice under the 2009 Act is inaccurate.

- *What happens if the client fails to serve a pay less notice?*
  Failing to serve an effective pay less notice will leave the client liable to pay the full sum claimed without deduction. In the absence of a pay less notice, the architect will be entitled to give 7 days' notice of their intention to suspend performance of the services and, ultimately, instigate formal proceedings to recover the sum due and, depending upon the wording of the appointment, may have the right to give notice to terminate the appointment for the client's breach of their duty to pay the architect's fees.

- *Is a client ever allowed to pay less than the notified sum without giving a pay less notice?*
  Under the 1996 Construction Act mechanism, courts took a robust approach to the statutory withholding notice requirement. Arguments raised by clients to attempt to circumvent the need for serving a withholding notice tended to fail – even otherwise legally sound assertions, such as the argument that, because the 1996 Act referred to a notice as a requirement for withholding sums 'due' under a contract, a client should be able to set-off sums without serving a withholding notice. When a client exercises their right to set-off sums owed against sums claimed by the architect, their actions, legally, mean that the sums claimed by the architect in their invoice were never technically 'due' for payment. The courts have upheld the spirit of the 1996 Act by rejecting this and similar arguments, and can be expected to continue to robustly defend the 2009 Act.

There were, though, limited circumstances in which withholding notices were not required. A House of Lords case from 2007, *Melville Dundas v George Wimpey* decided that a contractual provision entitling the client to terminate a contract and withhold all future payments in the event of the insolvency of the consultant could cut across the requirements of section 111 of the 1996 Act and allow for legitimate withholding without a withholding notice. The *Melville Dundas* case was decided on the specific facts of the JCT contract between the parties. The contractor went into receivership after the final date for payment; under the contract, this gave the client a right to terminate, and withhold further payments from the contractor. But these rights had only become available to the client at a time when a withholding notice could no longer validly be served. This would make a nonsense of the clear wording of the contract.

The 2009 Act includes a provision to cater for the circumstance which occurred in the case of *Melville Dundas*, so that the client's obligation to pay the notified sum (in the absence of a section 111 notice) will not apply to contracts where the client is allowed to withhold further payment when the consultant/contractor becomes insolvent and the insolvency occurs after the time for serving the section 111 notice.

Pay when paid

'The Client's obligation to pay, and the Architect's entitlement to receive, the Fee shall be conditional upon the Client receiving from the Funder payment of a sum equivalent to the amount of the Fee requested by the Architect.'

This is a 'pay when paid' clause; the client is only obliged to pay the architect when the client has itself received payment from a third party. This issue will tend to crop up on projects where an architect is engaged as a sub-consultant, but true pay when paid wording is rarely seen in appointments intended to be governed by English law.

Section 113 of the 1996 Construction Act expressly made such provisions ineffective, and an architect should reject absolutely any such wording if proposed in a bespoke appointment. The 1996 Act allowed for pay when paid clauses to be upheld if the exclusion of the obligation on the client's part to pay was based on the *insolvency* of a third party, rather than that third party's simple refusal to pay.

Clients over time found ways around the pay when paid exclusion, for example by using wording that only obliged the client to pay if an equivalent payment to them had been certified by a third party.

The existing provisions on conditional payment conditions are tightened up considerably by the 2009 Construction Act. Section 142 of the 2009 Act extends the scope of the 'pay when paid' prohibition to cover 'pay when certified' arrangements and other ways of making payment under the appointment conditional upon an action or decision made under

5

another contract higher up the chain. Also, the 2009 Act states that an appointment does not contain an 'adequate mechanism' if it allows for the client to unilaterally say when a payment becomes due under the appointment. These are positive changes for architects and other parties dependent upon receipt of payment from clients or contractors.

However, it does not seem possible to prohibit all conditional payment practices that are arguably contrary to the spirit of the Construction Acts; for example, even under the new regime, it would be possible for a contractor client, say, to impose an extended period, perhaps months, between the due date and the final date for payment, which would have the effect of leaving the architect out of pocket until the contractor had in fact been paid.

Certain exceptions to the prohibition are retained; for example, insolvency higher up the contractual chain is still a legitimate reason for not paying an architect, if expressly provided for in the appointment.

The architect's right to suspend performance

Under the provisions of the 1996 Construction Act, if a sum is due under an appointment and is not paid in full by the final date for payment, and no effective notice to withhold payment has been given, then the architect may give to the client 7 days' notice of their intention to suspend performance, stating the ground or grounds on which it is intended performance will be suspended. The right to suspend only ceases when the client makes payment in full of the amount due.

Most bespoke appointments will expressly confer this right to suspend. Not including such a clause is poor practice, but should not affect the architect's rights. The 1996 Act, as amended by the 2009 Act, confers a statutory right and, although not expressly stated, it is thought that it would not be possible to contract out of. This right does not exist at common law.

The cost consequences of a suspension will fall to be pursued by the architect under the terms of their appointment. The time consequences are dealt with by the Act – any period during which performance under an appointment is suspended in pursuance of the statutory right to suspend for non-payment shall be disregarded in calculating the programme for completing the work under the appointment. This is more relevant to a contractor operating under an obligation to pay liquidated damages for delay, but could be relevant to an architect who has agreed strict programme obligations under their appointment.

The 2009 Act enhances the existing right, expressly allowing an architect to suspend their performance *in part* or as a whole; the possibility of a more limited suspension will, it is hoped, reduce the scope for an irretrievable breakdown in relations between the client and architect in the event that the architect exercises their right to suspend.

In addition, the amended clause provides that the defaulting client will be liable, if the architect legitimately suspends performance, to pay to the architect a reasonable amount in respect of their costs and expenses reasonably incurred as a result of exercising their right to suspend.

5.2.17 Professional indemnity insurance

'The Architect shall take out and maintain for a period expiring 12 years after Practical Completion, professional indemnity insurance cover of not less than the sum of £[ ] million in respect of each and every claim provided that such insurance is generally available in the market to consultants of the same discipline as the Architect at commercially reasonable rates and on commercially reasonable terms.'

PII cover is a requirement of the ARB Architects Code, the RIBA Professional Code of Conduct and RIBA Chartered Eligibility criteria, and it is entirely standard for a bespoke appointment to contain provisions requiring the architect to maintain such cover. The architect should be sure not to warrant that the policy they maintain will provide cover in relation to *all* of their liabilities under the appointment. There is no way of guaranteeing this.

Obligations to maintain cover with a 'reputable insurer' without 'unusual or onerous terms or exclusions' should generally be resisted; who is to say whether a particular insurer is reputable? There is no recognised way of assessing what constitutes an unusual or onerous term either. Assuming you have PII cover in place, you do not want to be forced to seek amendments to your policy or change insurer because of the terms of a particular appointment.

The terms of the obligation to maintain PII cover must properly reflect the nature and level of cover that the architect actually maintains. If your policy says that cover is on an 'each and every claim' basis, the wording of the appointment should be the same and not say, for example, that cover is maintained 'for any one claim or series of claims arising out of the same event', which may amount to something quite different. The level of cover should be no greater than the level of cover maintained; some jobs are so important that it may be worth exploring with an insurance broker the cost of increasing cover, either generally or on a project-specific basis. If the client insists on increased cover, it is reasonable that the client should contribute to the increased premium costs.

5

If the architect's PII cover contains any aggregate limits, reduced aggregate limits or exclusions, these should also be clearly expressed in the appointment in the clause requiring PII to be maintained. Aggregate insurance limits provide a level of cover (for example £1 million) in relation to the totality of claims made in a period of insurance – generally a year, because PII is generally sold on an annual basis. This is in contrast with insurance provided on an 'each and every claim' basis, which will provide the same level of cover for each claim made – clients prefer cover to be maintained on an each and every claim basis because, with only an aggregate insurance pot, the level of available cover can quickly reduce to nothing if numerous claims have been made.

It is standard for architects to have cover on an each and every claim basis, but with specific types of claim subject to an aggregate limit. These areas will usually include pollution, contamination and date recognition claims. Cover for asbestos claims is very often available only on a reduced aggregate basis, with a limit of cover of £1 million or less; many policies exclude cover for asbestos claims altogether.

A PII obligation in a bespoke appointment should usually be subject to cover being available to the architect on commercially reasonable terms and at commercially reasonable rates. Many clients prefer to express this limitation as:

'provided such insurances are available generally in the market'

or to otherwise use wording which would not allow the architect to rely on the fact that they cannot obtain such insurance because of their own claims record. This is not an unreasonable position for a client to take; one counter-argument would be that if PII is not available to a particular architect then that is a fact – putting in a contractual obligation to maintain PII is not going to change the reality. In practice it will be unusual for an architect being considered for work to have a claims record so bad that they struggle to obtain PII cover. If the point is that the architect is struggling to obtain PII cover at the client's required level, this is usually an issue that can be dealt with pragmatically by the client and the architect together. If the client considers that the architect is the most suitable for the job on every other basis, they will generally be willing to compromise, either on the level of PII or by contributing to premiums.

Evidence of insurance is usually required by clients. An architect should not accept any obligation to provide a copy of their policy, as that may allow the client to frame any claims in a way that will maximise the chance of them being covered by the policy in question; understandably, insurers take a very dim view of this. It is usual for the architect to be obliged to provide a PII broker's letter or similar evidence confirming the basic details of the insurance cover maintained (overall level, each and every claim or aggregate basis) and brokers will usually be able to produce such evidence very quickly following a reasonable request.

5.2.18   Confidentiality

'Save as may be necessary for the proper performance of their duties under this Agreement or as otherwise required by law, the Architect shall not at any time without the prior written consent of the Client disclose to any person or otherwise make use of any confidential information relating to the Client or the Project.'

Any confidentiality obligation imposed in a bespoke appointment on the architect should be reciprocal and should generally relate only to the business affairs of the other party, rather than the project in general. In practice it is usually quite difficult to establish what has been lost in the event of a breach of confidentiality in the context of a construction project, so clients are ordinarily open to reasonable amendments which limit an otherwise onerous confidentiality provision. If an appointment is being negotiated in the late stages of a project, an architect should be wary of accepting a confidentiality obligation that may capture communications the architect has innocently engaged in prior to signing the appointment, at a time when either the architect had no confidentiality obligations or thought their obligations were more relaxed. Proposing wording to ensure that the confidentiality obligation does not apply retrospectively is not unreasonable if the architect suspects that they would otherwise be entering into an appointment knowing full well that they are probably already in breach of its terms.

Any confidentiality provisions must allow exceptions for:

• taking professional advice from insurers, solicitors and accountants;
• dealing with legal proceedings;
• disclosing information already in the public domain;
• disclosing information when it is required by law to be disclosed (for example under the Freedom of Information Act 2000); and
• the purposes of the project.

A good rule of thumb is that if a communication is made for the benefit of health and safety or the structural or design integrity of the project then it should not be prohibited by the appointment.

An architect should reject any wording which would oblige them to indemnify the client in relation to any losses incurred as a result of a breach

5

of confidentiality. There is no reason why the client should not simply rely on their ability to sue for breach of contract in the usual way or seek an injunction to prevent breaches of confidentiality before they occur.

5.2.19   Assignment and sub-contracting

Assignment of the benefit of the appointment

'The Architect shall not assign or otherwise transfer any right or obligation under this Agreement.'

'The Client shall be free to assign any right or obligation under this Agreement without the consent of the Architect.'

If a contract does not contain any provisions limiting the assignment of its benefit, then the parties will usually be able to assign the benefit freely. The burden of an agreement is different; the obligations under an agreement cannot generally be transferred effectively without the agreement of both the original parties and the incoming party who is accepting the burden. For example, the architect may engage a sub-consultant to perform their services; but if they are not carried out properly, it is the architect who is still in the frame to be sued by the client.

The client will want to be able to freely assign the benefit of the appointment, and a bespoke appointment will generally confer this ability. This is again not unreasonable, but can leave the architect exposed if the benefit is transferred to a party with a history of making nuisance claims. One way for the architect to protect itself, or at least ensure they are no more exposed than any other member of the project team, is to insist on wording that would limit the client's ability to assign to only a party taking a contemporaneous assignment of the benefit of all the client's other contracts and appointments on the project; this may be expressed by saying that the assignee must be an assignee of the whole of the client's interest in the project. Some clients will be unwilling to accept such a fetter on their ability to assign, but realistically when would the client want to assign the benefit of one appointment without assigning the benefit of all their other project agreements?

Sub-contracting by the architect

'The Architect shall not assign or otherwise transfer any obligation under this Agreement. The Architect shall not sub-contract the whole or any part of the Services without the prior written consent of the Client.'

In a bespoke appointment, the client will wish to preserve their ability to pursue the architect for any default in any of their services. If there is to be any sub-consultant involvement, the client will want to retain control over such an appointment and will inevitably require the right to approve any sub-consultancy agreement and receive a collateral warranty from such a sub-consultant. This is reasonable.

No engagement of sub-consultants will generally restrict the client's ability to sue the architect for any default in the provision of their services. If, for whatever reason, the architect engages a sub-consultant to carry out work which is in fact outside the scope of the architect's own services, this will be a different matter; the architect will not ordinarily be liable for this work, unless they can be shown to have in some way assumed responsibility for it. Simply signing the sub-consultancy agreement is not usually enough in itself to amount to an assumption of responsibility.

5.2.20   Novation

The Client may at any time require the Architect to enter into a deed of novation with the Contractor substantially in the form set out in Appendix [ ] so that the Contractor takes the place of the Client under this Agreement.'

A novation is a three-way agreement made by the original employer, an incoming employer and the architect (or other service provider), under which the architect's appointment is transferred from the original employer to the new employer, so that after the novation the architect carries out their duties for the benefit of the new employer and is paid by the new employer. The terms of a typical deed of novation are discussed in more detail in section 6.3.2.

In an ideal world, an architect should simply say no in principle to novation. The risks are significant, particularly if there is an expectation that, in addition to carrying out the services for the new employer as if the new employer had always been the architect's client, the architect will also be carrying out post-novation services for the original employer.

It is, unfortunately, not realistic for an architect to take this approach. There will be circumstances in which it is commercially important for the client to novate the architect's appointment, most usually to a design and build contractor.

The important issues for the architect are that they must have confidence that their fees will continue to be paid and that their liability will not be extended by the act of being novated. The risks can be minimised if the architect knows what the terms of their novation will be, and what the terms of any ongoing agreement to provide services to the client will be, and also if they know in advance the identity of the party to whom they

5

are being novated. If there is a significant risk that the party to whom the architect will be novated does not have a sufficiently strong financial covenant to pay the architect's fees then the architect should not go through with the novation. An architect should request that the novation is subject to the client's reasonable request; if the incoming employer is unlikely to be able to pay the architect's fees then the request would arguably not be reasonable. However, many clients would be unwilling to accept this limitation.

If the architect has no option but to accept a strict obligation to enter into a deed of novation on the client's request, they could still refuse to comply with the request (in breach of contract) when it is made. This is a high-risk option and should not be considered unless the risk of carrying out services that will not be paid for exceeds the risk of being sued for breaching the obligation to enter into the novation. The only certain way to avoid this situation is to resist the inclusion of a novation obligation in the original professional appointment; if either the principle of novation or the form of novation agreement are not agreed at the time of the architect's appointment, then the architect is not legally obliged to agree to a novation.

The principles of novation are covered in further detail in Chapter 6.

5.2.21 Suspension by the client

'The Client may by written notice require the Architect to suspend the performance of all or any of the Services for a period of up to 12 months. The Architect shall resume the performance of the Services if instructed by the Client.'

It is not unreasonable for the client to be able to suspend performance if required, for example because of funding or planning issues, but the potential period of suspension can be unreasonably long. A 12-month period could in theory be followed by an instruction to resume, and then another suspension notice the next day. The architect should consider specific wording preventing follow-on suspension notices. A 12-month initial period will be excessive for most purposes in any case and a shorter period should usually be proposed.

In the event of an instruction to resume work, the appointment should allow for the architect to recover their additional costs of mobilisation. If no instruction to resume is forthcoming, the architect should be entitled to give their own notice terminating their engagement under the appointment, and they should be entitled to be paid for their services up to the date of such termination, including reimbursement of any direct loss or expense incurred during the period of suspension of services as a result of the suspension. It is generally sensible practice to issue an invoice for all sums incurred to date immediately following the issue of a notice of suspension by the client. Commercial clients will typically be unwilling to accept an obligation to pay for loss of profits in any circumstances.

5.2.22   Termination

'The Client may, in addition to any other rights and remedies which it may have, at any time at its absolute discretion by notice in writing to the Architect terminate the Architect's appointment under this Agreement.'

Trigger events

The client in a bespoke appointment will want to preserve their right to terminate the architect's appointment on notice, whether or not the architect is at fault. It is hard to argue against this as there may be many pressing commercial reasons why a client would want to bring a project, or the architect's involvement, to an end, other than the standard of the architect's own performance. An architect should insist upon this right being exercised subject to reasonable written notice, ideally a specified period of days.

In addition, it is not unreasonable for the client to have the right to terminate in the event of certain 'culpable' trigger events; these are typically set out in the appointment, even though the client may have an absolute right to terminate, because the appointment's approach to payment on termination may be different if the architect is alleged in some sense to be 'to blame'. An architect should generally argue that culpable termination is limited to material or persistent breaches of the appointment (not merely 'defaults') or the architect's insolvency.

Ideally, there should in a bespoke appointment be symmetry between the termination rights of the client and the architect, but this is generally not realistic; very few clients would be willing to accept the architect having the right to abandon their services without justification. It is reasonable that the architect should have the right to give notice of termination in the event of their services being suspended for an extended period, for example 6 months. The architect should generally have the right under the appointment to terminate in the event of the client's insolvency. It may be possible to negotiate a right for the architect to terminate in the event that the client fails to pay (and does not serve an effective pay less notice) a sum due under the appointment within, for example, 28 days of the final date for payment. This right may be subject to the architect

5

giving a further written notice to the client demanding payment. If the architect's bargaining position is particularly strong, they should try to achieve an equivalent right to terminate in the event of any material or persistent breaches of the appointment by the client, for example a failure by the client to provide information or approvals that may jeopardise the architect's ability to carry out the services effectively.

What if there is no express right for the architect to terminate?
If the architect is given no express right to terminate under the terms of a bespoke appointment, this does not mean that the architect is locked into the appointment in perpetuity, even if the client repeatedly fails to make payment or becomes insolvent. It just means that giving notice of termination comes with additional risks. If the client behaves in a way which fundamentally breaches the terms of the appointment and shows that they no longer intend to accept the obligations of the appointment – for example, by failing to make payment or by becoming insolvent – then the architect may treat this behaviour as 'repudiation' of the appointment. If the architect in such circumstances gives notice that they 'accept' the client's repudiation of the appointment, both parties will be released from further performance under the appointment. This will not prevent the architect from pursuing the client in relation to outstanding fees or for other damages resulting from the client's repudiatory breach of contract. The risk for the architect in giving notice to accept a repudiatory breach is that it could be claimed, by the client, to itself constitute a repudiation of the appointment, leaving the architect open to being sued for damages by the client.

Payment on termination

A bespoke termination clause will often provide that the architect must, within a reasonable time following the notice of termination, deliver to the client any drawings, plans, designs or other documents that the architect has produced during the course of their services. This wording is included to prevent the architect from relying on their common law right to retain such property until they have been paid in full. This right, known as the architect's lien, can be useful leverage in the event of a post-termination disagreement with the client about the level of outstanding fees. For this reason, an informed client will generally insist upon wording in the appointment to circumvent the lien. The architect may suggest a compromise to the effect that the various documents will be delivered up to the client on termination except where there is a genuine dispute over outstanding fees. Clients may still be reluctant to compromise on this principle.

It is not unreasonable for the architect to expect to be paid on termination:

'any instalments of the fee and any other sums properly due to the Architect at the date of termination together with a fair and reasonable proportion of the next instalment which would have been due but for the termination, having regard to the Services performed by the Architect up to the date of the notice of termination.'

A commercial client will generally accept this wording, subject to excluding such right to payment where termination arises as a result of the architect's material or persistent breach of the appointment or the architect's insolvency. The client will often try to include wording that puts off assessing the fees due (if any) to the architect until after completion of the architect's services by their replacement. The client will 'not be bound to make any further payment' until their additional costs resulting from the termination (and the architect's breaches, if any) have been ascertained. If the architect does not agree with the reason given for termination, they are free to utilise the appointment's dispute resolution procedures, most usually adjudication.

Finally, the client will usually seek to include wording excluding their liability upon termination, for any reason, for the architect's loss of profit, loss of contracts or other losses or expenses arising out of or in connection with the termination. If the remainder of the payment on termination arrangements are satisfactory and allow for the payment of an additional proportion of the next instalment due, this is usually reasonable. If this wording is proposed in a bespoke appointment, the client can be assumed to be alive to the issue; if it is missing, the architect may have scope to claim for recovery of lost profits in the event of termination.

5.2.23 Set-off

'Nothing contained elsewhere in this Agreement shall in any way limit or exclude the Client's rights and entitlements at common law to deduct or to set-off monies due to it or which may become due to it from or against any monies otherwise due to the Architect under this Agreement.'

'Without prejudice to and in addition to any other rights and remedies of the Client, if any sum of money shall become due and/or payable by the Architect to the Client under or in connection with this Agreement, such sum may be deducted by the Client from any sums then due or which at any time thereafter may become due to the Architect under this Agreement or may recover the same from the Architect as a debt.'

A set-off can be established by a party, if they have a viable cross-claim, as a defence to reduce or eliminate the value of claim made against them.

5

A set-off may relate to a cross-claim under the same contract as the claim being made; or it may even be based on a cross-claim under a separate contract with the claimant, if there is sufficient connection to justify the set-off. For example, in the case of *Geldof Metaalconstructie v Simon Carves Limited* concerning a claim and set-off under separate supply and installation contracts relating to the same project, the Court of Appeal took the view that it would be 'manifestly unjust' to allow the claimant to enforce payment without taking into account the cross-claim, because the two were so closely connected.

The right to set-off may be expressly provided for in an appointment, as in the wording above. There is also a common law right of set-off, but this can be excluded expressly or by implication. The client is most likely to be the party making payments under the appointment; they will be the main beneficiary of any retained common law right to set-off. The client will be reluctant to give up this advantage, as required for example by the RIBA Standard Conditions, which expressly exclude common law and equitable rights of set-off and aim to prevent any use of the set-off defence unless a sum claimed by the client has been agreed by the architect (unlikely) or awarded by a tribunal.

If a client is alive to the issues, and has a sufficiently strong bargaining position, it can be difficult to argue against the inclusion of a right to set-off. Claiming a right to set-off would not allow the client to validly withhold sums due to the architect without issuing a pay less notice; rather, the risk for the architect is that a set-off can be based on an unproven claim, so may be open to abuse by clients seeking to delay recovery of fees, or it may make pursuing a claim economically unviable bearing in mind the architect's potential legal costs in defeating the client's cross-claim. An architect may argue that wording should be included in the appointment so that set-offs must be established on the basis of a tribunal decision, but a commercial client may not accept this.

A compromise, albeit unsatisfactory from the architect's perspective, would be to allow both parties to exercise their common law ability to set-off. As discussed above, in practice this will be of less use to the architect.

5.2.24 Fitness for purpose

'The Architect warrants that the design when completed will be reasonably fit for its intended purpose.'

This principle should never be accepted. Many PII policies will not cover an obligation to ensure that the services provided are fit for the purpose that the client requires. This is because an architect may be in breach of a fitness for purpose obligation even if they have exercised reasonable skill and care in carrying out their services. A building is either fit for its purpose or it is not; the fact that an architect may have performed faultlessly to get there is beside the point. This is usually not a justifiable risk for an architect to take.

5.2.25 Liquidated damages

'In connection with any failure by the Architect to complete the Services in accordance with the Programme and/or any applicable milestone, the Architect shall pay to the Client £[   ] for each day or part thereof of any such delay.'

It is unusual for a client to seek such wording even in a bespoke appointment, but it does still happen. This should not be accepted by an architect. Claims based on a penalty or liquidated damages are often not covered by PII policies.

In reality, any delay is likely to be the result of a combination of factors that may have nothing to do with the architect's own performance. It is generally unrealistic for a client to expect an architect to guarantee that a particular programme will be achieved and to pay damages for delay in the event that the architect does not meet the programme requirements. A reasonable compromise is for the architect to accept an obligation to exercise reasonable skill, care and diligence in accordance with the normal standards of their profession to meet any milestones or programme dates.

5.2.26 Limitations on liability

Depending upon the relative strength of the parties' bargaining positions, the architect should seek limitations on liability in the areas set out below in this section. A limitation in time is reasonably standard even in a bespoke appointment; other limitations are generally not. The client will generally be reluctant to accept limitations on liability, but they may be agreed in exchange for compromise by the architect in other areas.

5

Limitation in time

Unless otherwise provided, the statutory limitation periods (discussed in detail in Chapter 2) will apply. It is sensible for the architect to seek to include wording to clarify that, subject to any shorter period provided by statute, no actions or proceedings may be brought under 'or in connection with' the appointment after the expiry of 12 years (6 years if the appointment is a simple contract rather than a deed) from the date the architect performed their last service under the appointment; or, if earlier, the date of practical completion under the building contract.

The use of the words 'in connection with' should apply the same limitation period to actions in tort, including negligence. This can be further clarified by expressly applying the stated limitation period to:

'actions in contract, tort, for breach of statutory duty'

or otherwise, and this is the position adopted in the RIBA standard forms of appointment.

The client may not be willing to accept the imposition of a limitation period on actions in negligence which would prevent the use of the 'latent defects' limitation period provided by statute. In addition, the client may argue that the limitation period should only start to run after the certification of making good defects under the building contract, generally a year after practical completion. Architects should resist this effective extension to the limitation period. The architect can argue reasonably that they will have completed their most important design services possibly years before that point.

Net contribution

Net contribution is discussed in detail in section 4.1.7 in the context of the RIBA Standard Conditions clause 7.3. Consultants have had particularly good grounds for requesting the incorporation of a net contribution clause since the 2002 House of Lords case *Co-operative Retail v Taylor Young*, which seemed to suggest that it would be impossible for an architect, following a claim from the client, to recover a contribution under the 1978 Contribution Act against a contractor if the contractor happened to be jointly insured with the client. The principle appeared to be that, if the client's loss was covered by the joint names policy, the contractor would never be liable to the client for the same loss as was the architect. In fact, the contractor had no liability to pay compensation for a jointly insured loss at all; the client's remedy against the contractor was to insist that they proceeded with due diligence to carry out the remedial works, and the client would be obliged to authorise the release to the contractor of the insurance money paid out. The architect would have no contribution claim against the contractor in these circumstances.

In fact, the House of Lords in the *Tyco v Rolls-Royce* case clarified that there is no principle of English law that would prevent one jointly insured party from suing another for damages arising out of a jointly insured risk, but for consultants, including architects, there is still a distinct risk of being left unable to claim a contribution from the contractor in these circumstances.

Commercial clients remain generally reluctant, but an architect can justify the inclusion of net contribution wording in principle if they have only a limited role in the project, and the prospect of being liable for the whole of the client's loss where other parties are jointly responsible would be disproportionate and unfair. If the architect has concerns over the financial strength of the contractor, and their potential insolvency risk, this may also be a reason to argue for inclusion of a net contribution clause. In reality it may be difficult to convince a commercial client to accept the inclusion of net contribution wording in an appointment because of the inevitable increased risk of the client being unable to recover 100% of their losses in the event of a default.

An overall cap on liability

An overall cap on liability limits the architect's liability to the client under the appointment to a specified sum. The arguments for an overall cap are similar to those for net contribution, although more clients seem willing to accept an overall cap on liability in principle, on the pragmatic grounds that they are unlikely in practice to be able to recover more from an architect than the level of the architect's PII cover.

The potentially misleading sense of security that an architect can derive from obtaining an overall cap on liability is dealt with in section 4.1.7 in relation to the RIBA Standard Conditions clause 7.2.1. The only truly safe overall cap would be set at the sum actually recovered by the architect from their insurers and would apply to claims in relation to the project overall, requiring equivalent wording in the appointment and any collateral warranties:

'The liability of the Architect under this Agreement or otherwise in connection with this Project whether in contract, tort, for breach of statutory duty or for any other claim shall not exceed the amount, if any, recovered by the Architect under its professional indemnity insurance.'

The architect may sweeten the pill somewhat by providing that the limitation shall not apply to the extent the architect fails to maintain PII cover or fails to report a claim in accordance with the requirements of their policy. Even so, commercial clients will very rarely accept such restrictive limits; they would argue that there are in practice no equivalent artificial limits on the potential level of their losses.

Limitation on the types of loss that may be recovered

Ideally, in the event of a claim, the architect would want to be able to rely on a term in the appointment limiting in a reasonable way the losses that may be recovered by the client – for example, excluding liability for 'indirect or consequential' losses, limiting recovery to the 'reasonable costs of repair, renewal or reinstatement' of the defective building or even seeking to exclude the architect's financial liability altogether and instead include an obligation to re-perform the relevant services at no cost. Informed clients will generally be unwilling to accept such limitations in an appointment, and will argue that there are no such limitations on the types of loss that they may actually suffer.

5.2.27 Disputes

A bespoke appointment, even one with a 'consumer' client, should generally provide a right to refer disputes to adjudication, to be conducted in accordance with the Scheme. It is good practice to provide for mediation as an option, but this should not (and cannot, in construction contracts to which the Construction Acts apply) be allowed to prevent or hinder the parties' ability to refer disputes to adjudication at any time. The fallback position should be the agreement of the parties to submit to the jurisdiction of the English courts.

5.2.28 Confirmation letters

'The Architect hereby confirms that the Works undertaken by the Contractor pursuant to the contract for the construction of the Project have been completed in accordance with the Employer's Requirements … and in the opinion of the Architect a Statement of Practical Completion can be issued by the Employer.'

It is becoming increasingly common, particularly on major projects, for the client to request that each consultant on the project sends them a letter stating that they are satisfied that the works conform with the specifications and recommending that the practical completion certificate be issued. There is often no obligation to provide such a letter under the consultants' appointments, and the request is often made just weeks or days before practical completion is planned to take place.

The intention behind obtaining such confirmation letters is to impose a layer of additional responsibility on the various consultants; to oblige them to some degree to assume responsibility for checking the completeness and quality of the work of the contractor.

An architect faced with such a last-minute request should generally refuse. There may be strong commercial pressure to sign, but there is nothing to be gained by assuming additional liability which the architect's appointment does not require. If the commercial pressure to provide some form of confirmation is overwhelming, an architect may consider limiting their confirmation only to aspects of the contractor's work that are clearly related to the architect's services, and further limiting the confirmation by reference to the architect's subjective knowledge and the exercise of reasonable skill and care; for example:

'We hereby confirm that to the best of our knowledge the architectural aspects of the Works undertaken by the Contractor pursuant to the contract for the construction of the Project have been completed in accordance with the architectural aspects of the Employer's Requirements. We make this confirmation in accordance with the terms of the Appointment and exercising the reasonable skill and care of the ordinary skilled architect.'

However, even this watered-down wording does not address the fundamental concern with providing an 11th-hour confirmation letter. The imposition right at the end of the project of such an obligation means that the architect has missed the opportunity to monitor and review the work, in sufficient detail to give the confirmation, as the project progressed.

5

Chapter 6

Collateral warranties, third party rights and novation

This chapter:

- examines why collateral warranties are requested;

- reviews the typical clauses included within a collateral warranty;

- provides negotiation tips and suggested alternative wording;

- explains the advantages and disadvantages of agreeing schedules of third party rights and deeds of novation.

6.1   Overview of collateral warranties

6.1.1   The network of collateral warranties on a typical project

Construction projects often require a network of collateral warranties to be put in place. Figure 5 shows a typical example.

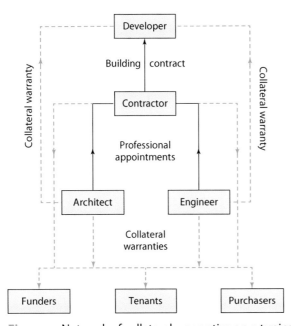

Figure 5   Network of collateral warranties on a typical project

6.1.2   Why do interested third parties 'need' collateral warranties?

Because of the doctrine of privity of contract, only those persons who are parties to a contract can sue for breaches of the contractual obligations. An architect may be sued by the client for breach of the architect's appointment; the freehold landowner, or a third party who takes an interest in the completed building, such as a tenant, funder or purchaser, cannot sue the architect for breach of their appointment with the client. If the building is defective, these third parties will want to recover the diminution in value of their interest – a purely economic loss. But the law now severely restricts the ability of claimants to recover pure economic losses in negligence, so interested third parties typically insist that the client provides a contractual route for recovery of such losses from the contractor, the design team and the sub-contractors.

6.1.3   What is a collateral warranty?

It is generally not good practice to refer to a collateral warranty by the shorthand term 'warranty'. This book aims to do so only when there is no scope for confusion between a 'collateral warranty' – a short collateral contract – and a 'warranty', which is a name for a specific material obligation that may feature in any contract. A collateral warranty generally contains a number of warranties.

Freehold landowners of the site, future tenants, purchasers and funders now regularly receive the benefit of collateral warranties – individual contracts between the beneficiary (the party receiving the benefit of the collateral warranty) and the relevant member of the project team.

Like any contract, a collateral warranty has to be properly executed by the parties. This will usually mean execution as a deed. Any collateral warranty should always be executed in the same way, either under hand or as a deed, as the underlying appointment. An architect should never agree to greater liability under the collateral warranty than in their appointment, in scope (what they have to do or the standard they must achieve), quantum (the sums they may be liable for) or duration (the length of the limitation period on actions under the contract); equally, the beneficiary is unlikely to be willing to accept the lesser protection of a collateral warranty executed under hand if it knows that the client has the comfort of an appointment executed as a deed.

Usually, if a project is sufficiently complex or high-value for the architect to be asked to provide collateral warranties, the architect will have been appointed by deed.

These individual collateral contracts, generally short in format, are separate from the underlying professional appointment or building contract that the party giving the collateral warranty (the 'warrantor') has entered into with the client. But, although separate, the collateral warranty typically refers back to the obligations in (and hence is 'collateral' to) the relevant underlying agreement.

If collateral warranties are required from an architect, they are being expected to extend the scope of their liability to third parties who would otherwise in all likelihood not be able to sue them. The architect should consider, on a project by project basis, whether it is appropriate for them to be giving collateral warranties at all.

If a project is small in scale and low in value, the architect's fee is equally small and its services limited, and if other members of the team are not being required to provide collateral warranties, then the architect should argue that a request for collateral warranties is disproportionate. The architect's professional indemnity insurers will also have a view about whether its insured should be accepting this type of additional liability on a project. If the client wants collateral warranties and the architect wants the job, they should price the risk accordingly. This may involve a significant increase on a fee for a very small project, which in itself may discourage unnecessary requests for collateral warranties.

6.1.4 How does an architect become obliged to give a collateral warranty? Who is likely to want one?

To make the arrangement work, there must be a clause in the architect's appointment explicitly obliging them to provide collateral warranties to particular parties or in specified circumstances. This is known as a collateral warranty 'enabling clause'. The architect and their lawyer should consider whether a particular collateral warranty obligation is too extensive in terms of the number required or the nature of the potential beneficiaries.

A client on a large-scale commercial project will understandably want to be able to obtain collateral warranties in favour of future purchasers and tenants, to increase the marketability of their development. A purchaser generally has no ability to sue the seller for defects in a development; a tenant with a full repairing covenant in their lease (the market norm) will be obliged to carry out, at their own expense, repairs on the property they have rented.

Any third party funder of a project will require collateral warranties in order to protect their investment. On completion, the funder has to be sure that the development achieves a sufficient market value to provide adequate security for the loan it has provided to the developer. A funder will in fact usually require a provision in any collateral warranty it receives allowing it to 'step in' to the shoes of the client and take over the appointment of the architect, any other important designers and the building contractor, in order to complete the development if, for whatever reason, the client falls out of the picture.

6.1.5 Forms of collateral warranty wording

There are two main standard forms of collateral warranty that an architect may be asked to enter into. One form is drafted by the Construction Industry Council and is known as CIC/ConsWa, published in 2003/2005, with versions in favour of a funder, purchaser or tenant, or client post-novation. The other main standard form is drafted by the British Property Federation and known as BPF/CoWa, again with one version for a funder and one for purchasers/tenants. These collateral warranty forms are generally insurable and provide significant limitations on liability to protect the architect's position; if you have to sign a collateral warranty, these are the safest options.

Many clients are happy to use these forms, but equally many prefer to use their own bespoke forms, and on important or high-value commercial projects it is more likely than not that bespoke forms of collateral warranty will be proposed.

In any case where collateral warranties are required, you should check with your professional indemnity insurer to make sure that they are satisfied your policy covers both the collateral warranty wording proposed and the overall number of collateral warranties that may be requested. Insurers will want to have the chance to approve the collateral warranty terms.

All types of collateral warranty, bespoke or standard form, will typically cover the same territory; but bespoke forms, drafted by solicitors acting for clients, tend not to include the level of protection for the consultant that would be present in an industry standard form.

There is one important rule of thumb. If a specific obligation is included in a professional appointment, for example a list identifying prohibited materials, the equivalent provision in the collateral warranty must be the same or no more onerous. The architect will perform their services in accordance with the obligations in their professional appointment so, if a collateral warranty imposes a stricter obligation, there is a possibility that the architect will be in breach of the collateral warranty obligation.

The architect's 'warranty' itself

This is the core provision of the collateral warranty. The architect will be expected to warrant that, in respect of their professional services under the appointment, they have complied with the terms of the appointment and have exercised and will continue to exercise reasonable skill, care and diligence. As discussed in the context of professional appointments above (section 5.2.6), the standard of care for an architect will, in the absence of any other wording, usually be that of the ordinary skilled architect. If a client seeks to impose a higher standard, this should generally be resisted.

Many PII policies contain an exclusion of cover for any contractual performance warranties that would not have existed but for the wording of the contract itself; that is to say, any performance warranty in excess of the warranty of reasonable skill and care implied by law. Although it is unlikely that an insurer would take this point in respect of the enhanced skill, care and diligence wording that clients often seek, it is possible if the PII policy is based on the ordinary professional standard; particularly if the insurance market is 'hard', and if there are other aspects of the architect's behaviour which, in addition, the insurer may view as meriting a denial of cover.

Enquiries by the client do not affect the architect's liability

A provision will usually be included to the effect that the architect's obligations and liabilities shall not be released or diminished by any enquiry or inspection carried out by or on behalf of the beneficiary. This is fair. The architect is not prevented from seeking a contribution from any such independent surveyor that the beneficiary may have appointed, if the beneficiary sues the architect for a loss they have incurred and if that surveyor is liable to the beneficiary for the same loss, for the purposes of the 1978 Contribution Act.

The architect's acknowledgement of payment

Some bespoke forms of collateral warranty require the architect to acknowledge that, at the date of the collateral warranty, the professional appointment remains in full force and effect and the client has paid all sums properly due to the architect under the appointment. The intention seems to be to prevent the architect from raising any set-offs in relation to claims by the collateral warranty beneficiary. It is difficult to see how an architect can be expected to agree such a provision when signing the professional appointment – and it must be agreed then, because the draft form of collateral warranty must be attached as an appendix to the appointment – because at the time the collateral warranty is requested the architect may be in dispute with the client over fees, so any such provision should be deleted.

The risk of agreeing that the beneficiary is 'deemed' to rely upon the architect's performance

In a bespoke collateral warranty the client may include wording such that the architect acknowledges that the beneficiary has relied and will rely on the satisfactory performance by the architect of their obligations under the appointment. This should not usually be accepted. Some beneficiaries will be entirely reliant on the contractor and the professional team. But a beneficiary who has considerable experience in the construction industry, for example a repeat-player anchor tenant, an established developer or even a fellow construction professional, may arguably not have relied particularly on the architect's collateral warranty, but may have relied on its own experience or in-house or retained professional advice. Ordinarily, when seeking to establish a claim against the architect, the beneficiary would have to prove that it had relied on the architect's performance.

The obligation to avoid specification of prohibited materials

As mentioned in section 5.2.10, in the context of professional appointments, an architect should generally resist prohibited materials obligations based on the outdated 'list' format. The vast majority of products that might reasonably be prohibited are adequately dealt with in the relevant British Standards, European Standards or the 2011 BCO guidelines and a material that complies with these documents can be expected to perform satisfactorily.

Maintenance of PII by the architect

As with the equivalent provision in the architect's professional appointment, the obligation to maintain PII should properly reflect the level of insurance actually being maintained. It is standard for the obligation to be subject to such insurance being available at commercially reasonable rates and on commercially reasonable terms. Ideally, the test for what is commercially reasonable should be linked to the architect's subjective position, rather than the general availability of PII in the market.

How many times should the beneficiary be allowed to assign the benefit?

It is the market norm for the benefit of a collateral warranty to be assignable by the beneficiary once, and for their assignee to have the ability to make one further assignment – two assignments in total – without the consent of the warrantor being required. Thereafter assignment should either not be permitted at all (which should be the architect's preferred position) or permitted only subject to the architect's written consent, such consent not to be unreasonably delayed or withheld.

Clients will generally accept the principle of a maximum limit of two assignments, but may try to include wording to the effect that assignments of the benefit to companies in the same group as the beneficiary, or to parties providing finance to the beneficiary, will not count as one of the two permitted assignments. This should not usually be accepted. The effect of an assignment of the benefit of a contract is generally the same, whoever the assignee is; the architect has no control over the assignment and finds they are in a contractual relationship with an unknown third party. These are serious risk factors and it is not unreasonable for the architect to expect certain limitations on their potential exposure. But each such clause should be considered in the context of the circumstances of the project – how much of a risk does free assignment to such parties really represent? The architect can gain some comfort if they include wording to the effect that any assignment of the benefit must be an assignment of the whole of the beneficiary's interest – the risk is easier to manage if all of the obligations are owed to one party; in addition, wording can be included so that assignment is only possible at the same time and to the same party as the beneficiary assigns the whole of its interest in the project.

Such restrictions may be viewed by the client as having a negative impact on the marketability of the project, and may not be acceptable. This issue is not merely a theoretical risk for the architect, though; there is a real risk of assignment to a party with the specific intention of facilitating a claim for an existing breach. For example, the case of *Larkstore v Technotrade* involved the assignment by one party of the benefit of a geotechnical survey to a subsequent purchaser of the site, *after* an actionable breach of contract under the surveyor's report had arisen, and several years after the transfer of site ownership. The court found nothing wrong with the assignment of the right to sue the surveyor for breach of contract; but if the surveyor had included wording in their appointment to the effect that the benefit of the report was only assignable at the same time as the benefit of the rest of the client's interest, they would, on the facts of the case, have escaped liability to the subsequent purchaser of the site.

The obligation to grant a copyright licence

Generally, the same considerations apply here as apply to the copyright licence wording included in the underlying appointment. Ideally, the provision of a copyright licence should be linked to continuing payment of the architect's fees, as is the case in the RIBA standard forms of appointment. Clients in a strong bargaining position will be unwilling to accept this, because, they would say, a fee dispute between the client and the architect should not affect the tenants, purchasers or funders. This is not unreasonable, but an architect with a stronger bargaining position could argue at least for the inclusion of wording which would allow for the copyright licence to be suspended in the event of a fee dispute which has proceeded to adjudication or litigation. This would counteract any arguments about spurious claims being used to hold the client to ransom; an architect would not adjudicate or litigate unless they thought they had a good case.

Provisions allowing the beneficiary to 'step in' to the underlying appointment

In a collateral warranty to a funder, or to a party who has agreed to purchase the whole of a project prior to completion, or in a collateral warranty back to the client after a novation, it is usual to provide step in rights.

Taking the position of the funder as an example, their return on their investment is dependent upon satisfactory completion of the project before it can be sold or let. The funder will not want to risk an important member of the project team, such as the architect, being able to leave the project prior to completion if, in the view of the funder, it is more likely that the project could be completed on time and on budget with the original architect. For this reason, the funder will typically require step in rights in any collateral warranty they receive from an architect, which would allow the funder to 'step in' to the architect's appointment in the position of the architect's client by giving notice in certain specified circumstances.

The right to step in may be reactive or proactive and a sensible funder will want both. If, for example, the original client has stopped paying the architect's fees and the architect has given notice to terminate their appointment, the funder's step in right under their collateral warranty from the architect will allow the funder to give notice to the architect saying that the funder requires the architect to carry on, with the funder being responsible for all payment of fees on stepping in (including those outstanding at the date the architect gave notice to terminate). This is a reactive step in. The funder may want to proactively step in when, for example, the funder/client relationship has broken down and the funder wants to build the project out, having removed the client, to protect their investment.

Step in operates to restrict the architect's ability to terminate their own appointment for breach of the client's obligation to make fee payments, but this is usually acceptable in principle as long as the incoming party commits to paying all outstanding fees and all fees going forward after the date of step in:

'It is a condition of any notice of intention to step in given by the Beneficiary under this clause that the Beneficiary or its nominee accepts all the obligations of the Client under the Appointment, including liability for payment and including payment of any sums outstanding at the date of such notice.'

If the collateral warranty beneficiary can appoint a nominee (not every funder will have the capacity, ability or inclination to take over running a project as client directly) to step in, the exercise of this right must be subject to the beneficiary agreeing to act as guarantor for the nominee's payment obligations.

The step in clause should make clear that there is a limited period during which the collateral warranty beneficiary may serve their step in notice. In the context of a reactive step in, it is usual for the beneficiary to receive 21 days' prior written notice of the architect's intention to terminate their appointment, and the beneficiary must serve notice of their intention to step in within that period.

There will be projects where more than one party is entitled to issue a step in notice under their collateral warranties. Any issues of 'priority' of step in should be taken out of the hands of the architect and should be dealt with in the background funding and development agreements. The architect should be entitled to treat any first step in notice they receive as valid and binding.

Governing law, notices and third parties

It is important for a collateral warranty to include provisions setting out the agreed position in respect of certain basic formalities. There should be a clause setting out the law governing the contract – this should always be the same as applies to the underlying appointment – and there should be a provision giving details of the names, addresses and procedure for giving written notices under the collateral warranty.

There should also be a clause setting out the position under the collateral warranty with respect to the application of the Contracts (Rights of Third Parties) Act 1999. There is generally no reason why the architect, as the warrantor, would want this Act to apply. The Act allows third parties in certain circumstances to take the benefit of a contract, but a collateral warranty is for the most part all one way; there is no real benefit for the architect, only obligations. The standard way to 'exclude' the effect of the Act is to include wording such that:

'No term of this Deed may be enforced solely by virtue of Section 1 of the Contracts (Rights of Third Parties) Act 1999.'

What limitations on liability should be included?

In a collateral warranty, clients are generally more receptive to the inclusion of limitations on liability, although there may be some resistance in relation to funder collateral warranties. This is because of the powerful position of the funder on many large projects; and also because it is more likely that the funder will be in place early in the project (not necessarily the case with tenants and purchasers) and will be able to exert through their solicitors direct influence on the form of funder collateral warranty.

In addition to a limitation on actions in time, a net contribution clause and an overall cap on liability, it is very important that the architect includes wording that ties their liability under the collateral warranty to their exposure under the underlying professional appointment:

'The Architect shall have no greater liability to the Beneficiary under this Deed in scope, quantum or duration than it would have to the Beneficiary if the Beneficiary had been named as joint client with the Client under the Appointment and shall be entitled in any action or proceedings for loss suffered by the Beneficiary to rely on any limitation of liability in the Appointment and to raise equivalent rights in defence of liability as it would have under the Appointment.'

This is generally acceptable to clients, although a client may seek to restrict the 'scope, quantum or liability' drafting, arguing that it is too wide. A commercial client will also usually try to prevent the architect from exercising any right of set-off against the collateral warranty beneficiaries; the argument put forward will be that the beneficiaries are not in a position to influence a payment dispute between the client and the architect. If a client is not alive to the point, however, the ability to raise set-off arguments against collateral warranty beneficiaries can be a potentially useful way to encourage the client to compromise on a fee payment issue.

'Liability' is not the same concept as 'duty'; an architect may owe the same duties to the client and to the beneficiary of the collateral warranty, but in the event of a claim may have greater liability to the beneficiary. It is important that the wording 'no greater liability' is insisted upon.

6.2   Overview of third party rights

6.2.1   The principle of third party rights

The Contracts (Rights of Third Parties) Act 1999 ('the TPR Act'), which came into force in May 2000, made a profound change to the law on privity of contract (discussed in section 2.2.1). Section 1 of the TPR Act provides that a person who is not a party to a contract (described in the Act as a 'third party') will be entitled in their own right to enforce a term of the contract if the contract expressly provides that they may, or if the term in question purports to confer a benefit on them.

To achieve this, the TPR enabling clause in the appointment must expressly identify the potential beneficiary by name, or otherwise the potential beneficiary must be identifiable as a member of a particular class or as answering a particular description; for example, 'any tenant of the whole or any part of the completed development'.

Once a beneficiary has been identified, for example once a tenant has signed a lease, the client should give notice to the architect that the architect's TPR obligation will extend to this particular beneficiary. It is safest for the client (and the beneficiary), although not strictly required by the TPR Act, for an acknowledgement of service of the notice of TPRs to be sent to the architect, and for this to be signed and returned by the architect, confirming their specific agreement to the grant of TPRs to the particular beneficiary. If the architect genuinely disputes that the beneficiary is in fact within the scope of the class of parties in favour of whom TPRs may be required, now is the time to raise the issue. If the architect is correct, the client may wish to offer an addition to the fee in exchange for accepting the additional risk; but if the proposed beneficiary is outside the scope of the TPR obligation, there is nothing the client can do legally to force the architect to agree to extend the scope of their obligation.

Conversely, if the proposed beneficiary is within the scope of the TPR obligation, because they are expressly identified individually or as part of a group, there is nothing the architect can do legally at that stage to deny the grant of TPRs.

6.2.2 Collateral warranties or third party rights?

Many bespoke appointments provide options for the client to request either collateral warranties or TPRs. This flexibility may be required because different third parties have different preferences. Some developer clients favour TPRs; other potential beneficiaries, banks in particular, still prefer collateral warranties. Does it make a difference to the architect?

Some insurers are wary of their insureds granting TPRs, and prefer the relative familiarity of collateral warranties. When asked to sign an appointment with a provision for the grant of TPRs, check that your insurer is comfortable with the principle and that there is no specific exclusion in your PII policy.

Even if covered by your insurance, there are particular commercial disadvantages of agreeing in the appointment to confer TPRs. If the beneficiaries are not identified individually, but as a class, how can the architect judge the potential risk of the beneficiary making a claim against them?

Also, once a TPR obligation has been agreed in the appointment, there is no going back if, at the time the client gives a TPR notice, the architect considers they would rather not be bound. There may be valid reasons why the architect would wish not to give TPRs in favour of a particular beneficiary; for example, the architect may know the beneficiary to have a history of making unwarranted claims, which could be a drain on the architect's time and resources.

In theory, the same could be said of an obligation to provide collateral warranties – there is no going back once the obligation is agreed in the appointment – but in practice this is not strictly true.

Unless and until the architect puts pen to paper (assuming they have not agreed a 'power of attorney' provision in their appointment), the proposed collateral warranty beneficiary has no contractual rights against the architect and the client cannot force the architect to sign.

It is unlikely that a court would grant an order forcing an architect to sign a collateral warranty if, in breach of contract, they refused to do so. More likely, a court would seek to assess the worth of the missing collateral warranty in damages. That may be a particularly unsatisfactory result for the client, and the proposed beneficiary.

In practice this type of dispute may arise in particular where the client and architect have fallen out over fees. An architect, with little other commercial leverage, may deliberately choose to breach their contractual obligation, and refuse to sign a collateral warranty, in the hope that the client will as a result agree to compromise on the fee dispute. This is not good practice, but it can be a commercial reality and is an advantage that an architect subject to a TPR obligation does not have. Some professional appointments seek to undermine the architect's ability to 'hold the client to ransom' in this way by setting out a defined level of compensation for failure to provide a collateral warranty. However, the level of compensation must be commensurate; a clause that obliges the architect to provide collateral warranties as a condition precedent to any payment of fees is unlikely to be upheld by a court, as it would constitute an unenforceable 'penalty', as discussed in the case of *Gilbert-Ash v Modern Engineering*.

6.2.3   The form of a third party rights schedule

In a bespoke set of appointment documents, if a schedule of TPRs is attached as an appendix, it will tend to closely follow the form of a collateral warranty. The comments set out above in relation to the form of a collateral warranty generally apply to the form of any proposed schedule of TPRs.

6.3   Novation

6.3.1   The risks of novation

The most common context for a novation is a project where the contractor is wholly or largely responsible for both the design and the construction. The client will typically have engaged consultants early, to develop a design for the project on the basis of which the design and build contractor will have been able to produce a more accurate tender price for the works than if the design had not been sufficiently developed.

The client will favour novation of the design consultants whom they had initially engaged, partly (as they would see it) to ensure a degree of continuity in the design effort, but also because it is often preferable to have a single point of responsibility, rather than be faced with the prospect of suing multiple parties if anything goes wrong. The design and build contractor, for their part, will be reluctant to accept their role as the single point of responsibility to the client without the protection (and ability to control) that is provided by being the direct employer of the consultants who have actually produced the design.

The usual solution is for the contractor, when they sign up to the project, to take over the appointments of the key designers from the client. This process commonly takes place at or around RIBA Stage 4, after planning permission has been granted, at the time the building contract is executed. Novation requires that the rights and obligations of the original parties are transferred, with the client dropping out of the picture and the contractor taking over their contractual right to sue, as well as their obligation to pay the consultants' fees, as if they had been a party to those contracts from the outset.

An architect should not generally enter into a deed of novation with a building contractor whose own contract remains outstanding, simply because the potentially uncertain terms of the contractor's future involvement in the project could negatively affect the architect.

Novation can work well, but there are three key areas of risk:

- the architect must be confident in the financial strength of the incoming employer;
- the terms of the novation must be very clear; and
- the architect should be very wary of accepting an ongoing role performing services for the original client after the novation.

There are, in theory, two types of novation:

- a basic switch of employer from the client to the contractor; and
- a novation 'ab initio', whereby the new employer is deemed to have been the architect's client from the outset.

The formal position of the RIBA and the Construction Industry Council is that consultants should, where possible, avoid ab initio novation agreements.

A client who wishes to novate will generally want to achieve an ab initio novation, and if novation is provided for in a bespoke appointment, this will be the intention. Some commentators have expressed difficulty with the legal fiction involved in novation ab initio and have expressed concerns with the expectation that the architect, who, for example, at one stage would have been advising the client about tenderers for the building contract, would logically be assumed to have been acting for the contractor when the architect was giving this advice – which obviously does not make sense. In truth, no type of novation is easier to justify logically than another; any novation presents the architect with practical difficulties.

Viability of the incoming employer

It will hopefully be a rare occurrence that the client on a project should ever want to transfer the appointment of a consultant to a party who will not be able to pay the consultant's fees. But it may occur if the original client knows that its money is running out and wishes to avoid claims for fees from the design team; in such circumstances, there may be no intention to complete the project, and a novation may be proposed, to a new client, to extricate the original client from their contractual ties to the consultant. An architect faced with an obligation to novate in these circumstances has a stark choice – go through with the novation, or breach the contract and take their chances against the original client. Including wording to provide that the obligation to accept novation is subject to a standard of reasonableness would go some way to protecting the architect's position.

Clarity of novation terms

It is possible for consent to novation to be inferred by the conduct of the parties. If an architect does not take care to protect themselves by insisting upon very clear novation terms, a purported novation can be used by unscrupulous clients to muddy the waters with regard to the client's payment obligations. Unless the documentation used to record the novation is very clear, the novated party can be left in an unenviable position – working for two masters, or, worse still, working without a clear contract with either master. Any proposal that the architect should enter into an 'informal' novation arrangement without a written deed should be rejected.

The *Camillin Denny v Adelaide Jones* case is an example of what can go wrong. The architect brought proceedings to enforce an adjudicator's decision that had been made against their client; but the client claimed that there had been a novation under which it was replaced as the architect's employer by another company. If this was correct, the adjudicator's decision would not have been enforceable against the original client. On the facts, the court found in favour of the architect; but the architect would no doubt have preferred to avoid incurring increased legal costs having to fight the client's spurious novation argument.

As an architect you can protect yourself by approaching a purported novation with caution. Take legal advice, and do not be afraid to ask common sense questions:

- Why is the novation being suggested, and why now?
- Am I obliged under my appointment to accept novation?
- Is there an agreed form of novation deed?
- Is there proof that the proposed new employer formally exists as a legal entity?
- Is there any evidence of the proposed new employer's financial standing?
- Will the new employer be able to pay my current outstanding fees as well as my fees going forward?
- Are the other design consultants being novated at the same time?

The importance of a formal professional appointment and, if the principle of novation is accepted, a formal deed of novation executed by all parties cannot be overemphasised.

Post-novation services for the original employer

It is by no means uncommon for the original client to expect the architect, after novation to the design and build contractor, to continue performing services for them, for example monitoring the construction phase and reporting on progress. This is not in itself unreasonable; the client's interest in the project after novation will remain unchanged, and it makes sense for the architect, with their existing knowledge of the project and existing lines of communication with the client, to continue to advise the client on certain matters. But it is not good practice either.

If an architect does agree to accept this arrangement (it can sometimes be very hard to argue against if the client has a strong bargaining position at the time the appointment is negotiated), they must be aware that conflicts of interest are likely to arise; the wording of the novation should expressly deal with this possibility.

6

A client who wants the architect to perform services for them post-novation may try to bring this about in a number of ways. Most commercial clients will want a collateral warranty from the architect on novation (known as the collateral 'warranty back') to cover the work previously carried out by the architect for the client; legally the original client becomes just another third party after novation and gives up their right to sue for breach of the professional appointment. Some clients will attempt in addition to include in the collateral warranty wording that imposes positive ongoing obligations to provide further services. A client may instead try to include an obligation to provide further services in the novation deed itself; or may have sought to cater for the eventuality by including a schedule of post-novation client services in the professional appointment. Perhaps most sensibly, a client may propose a supplemental services agreement, entirely separate from the novation and any collateral warranty back. It is possible, on the basis of judicial comment in the case of *Blyth and Blyth v Carillion*, that combining the novation with ongoing obligations to the original client may call into question the effectiveness of the novation as a whole.

The deed of novation should, in circumstances where the parties know that the architect will be performing some ongoing services for the original client, make clear that this work will be carried out separately from the post-novation work for the contractor. If possible, the architect should have different individuals working for the two employers and the novation should express the obligation to keep the work separate. If there is any question of the architect carrying out services that go beyond reporting on progress or passing on reports, for example an obligation to provide support to the client in the event of disputes (which may include disputes with the contractor) then the novation should provide a confidentiality obligation to prevent individuals within the architect firm working for one party disclosing information to those working for the other. Sometimes it will simply not be possible for the architect to effectively provide a service or guarantee the separation of personnel required in a credible way. If it cannot be done, the architect should not enter into an obligation to do it, whatever the commercial pressure.

One way of relieving the pressure on an architect, where the client requires extensive post-novation services, is to confront the issue explicitly in the novation with a clause that contemplates the possibility of post-novation services for the original client under a supplemental agreement, and which goes on to consider the existence and resolution of conflicts of interest. The architect should be given the right to notify at the same time both the client and the contractor in the event of a conflict, and the novation deed should provide for a period within which the parties endeavour to agree how the conflict should be addressed. However, such a clause can only work if there is a default position that applies if the parties cannot agree how to resolve the conflict; if the novation is to be effective and survive, the clause must allow for the ongoing services for the contractor to take precedence. The clause must provide that, if the parties cannot reach agreement within the given timescale, the particular service which has caused the conflict or, if necessary, the whole supplemental agreement with the original client, shall no longer be of any effect.

Do the circumstances give rise to a built-in conflict of interest?

Was the architect aware from the outset that their appointment was likely to be novated to a contractor? If not, there is a greater risk that the architect's prior performance will contain elements that are incompatible with their future role as the contractor's architect. If this is the case, and if there is no obligation to novate, then the architect should be very wary of agreeing to do so, no matter how great the commercial pressure to agree. Would the architect have carried out their services differently if the contractor had been their client from the outset, or if the architect had known from the outset that, through a deed of novation, the contractor was going to be deemed to have been their client? If the answer is yes, and if it is too late to go back and make appropriate adjustments, then the architect should again proceed only with extreme caution.

6.3.2 Typical terms of a novation deed

A deed of novation should generally be as short and uncomplicated as possible. Any references to the nature of the architect's ongoing services (if any) for the client should be removed and the detail of those services should be set out in a separate agreement between the client and the architect. If additional client services are being provided under a separate agreement, it may be appropriate to include 'ethical wall' and conflicts resolution wording in the deed of novation.

Under the terms of the novation, both the architect and the original client should:

'release and discharge the other from any and all obligations and liabilities owed under the Appointment.'

This release and discharge should be entirely mutual in the novation deed, notwithstanding any supplemental agreement or collateral warranty back given by the architect.

As discussed above, a client will typically want to provide that the mutual undertakings of the main contractor and the architect:

'to perform and agree to be bound by the terms of the Appointment in every way'

should take effect as if the contractor and the architect had been the parties to the professional appointment from the date of its execution.

Following the case of *Blyth and Blyth v Carillion* it has become usual for clients to include wording in a deed of novation to the effect that:

'The Architect agrees that in defence of any claim brought by the Contractor, they shall not contend that the Contractor is precluded from recovering any loss resulting from their breach of the Appointment solely on the ground that the Client for whom such duties or obligations were originally performed has suffered no loss, or a different loss.'

Blyth and Blyth is a case still considered by many to have been oddly decided, in which the court held that following a novation, the contractor was unable to recover their losses against the novated consultant because, at the time the consultant performed the action that ultimately caused the contractor's loss, the consultant had been acting for the original client; and the original client had not suffered any loss. The court decided that the contractor's right to recover losses in respect of the pre-novation services, through the novation, was limited to the measure of losses appropriate to the original client.

To avoid the possibility of confusion, best practice is to list in the deed of novation those pre-novation services performed by the architect that cannot sensibly be regarded as having been performed for the contractor, and to expressly exclude them from the scope of the novation.

The architect should not 'warrant' to the contractor 'that it shall be liable' for *'any'* losses suffered by the contractor; any language similar to this, which suggests an indemnity, should be deleted.

The deed of novation should provide, subject to the *Blyth and Blyth* wording above (which means that wording takes precedence):

'The Architect shall have no greater obligation or duty to the Contractor under this Deed than it would have had if the Contractor had been named as joint client with the Client under the Appointment and the Architect shall be entitled to rely on any limitation or exclusion in the Appointment and to raise the equivalent rights in defence of liability as it would have against the Client under the Appointment.'

Finally, in addition, it is helpful for the architect to include wording which waters down the legal fiction that the architect should be judged as if it had always been acting solely for the benefit of the contractor. This is an important qualification to make, particularly in the context of the architect's work in producing the employer's requirements:

'Provided always that the Contractor acknowledges that the Architect, in performing its obligations under the Appointment prior to the date of this Deed, was acting solely on behalf of and in accordance with the instructions of the Client.'

Apart from these provisions, and clauses stating which national law applies and (assuming English law) excluding the effect of the Contracts (Rights of Third Parties) Act 1999, there is arguably nothing else that a deed of novation should include, and any additional provisions should only be agreed with caution.

Chapter 7

The architect's role within a construction project

This chapter:

- provides hints and tips for managing risks when pitching for work;

- describes the different role specifications that an architect may agree;

- provides an overview of the services expected to be provided by an architect during each RIBA stage.

7.1 The relationship between the architect and the client

7.1.1 The importance of the architect to the client

This is very often the key relationship on the project. Although for larger projects the situation may be more complex, and will vary depending upon the procurement method and whether other consultants, such as a project manager, are involved, the architect's role may be nothing short of advising the client at every stage from the first idea to the finished building, from vision to reality.

7.1.2 What should the architect look for in a client?

The decision-making process an architect goes through when deciding whether or not to take on a client is covered in Stage 0 in the *RIBA Job Book*.

Every commercial relationship involves an element of risk, but developing an effective strategy for this stage will help you avoid taking on clients and projects that present serious foreseeable risks. One good approach is to create a 'scorecard' setting out a list of relevant questions that would need to be answered prior to involvement in any project. The answer to each question is given a rating, for example 1 to 5, with 1 representing a low risk and 5 a high risk – the importance of each answer will be specific to your business – and the final score will give an overall picture of whether the potential risk associated with the job or client is outweighed by the potential reward.

This kind of tick-box approach works best when combined with common sense analysis of the results based on experience; over-reliance on a tick-box approach creates problems when the decision-makers stop thinking.

Many well-known and highly successful practices use scorecards, covering broadly strategic/practice management issues – the fit of a project with the firm's business plan, the likelihood of obtaining repeat business – as well as issues that may have a direct impact on the potential scope of the firm's legal liability. The weighting given to each answer will vary from practice to practice, as will the threshold that needs to be reached before a project becomes attractive; some architects are more risk averse than others. An example of a 'legal' scorecard is given below.

Project risk assessment scorecard: legal risks

1. *Client risk*

☐ Has the client legal entity been clearly identified and verified?
☐ Have we worked successfully for this client before, directly or indirectly?
☐ Is the client financially stable?
☐ Does the client have a history of withholding fees/making claims?
☐ Does the client have a clear idea of what it wants to achieve, set out in a written brief?
☐ Is the client's vision achievable/reasonable in light of time/budget expectations?
☐ Is the client knowledgeable about the design and construction process?

2. *Project risk*

☐ Do we have any information about the likely contractor or other consultants?
☐ Have we worked with them successfully before?
☐ Are the required services clear?
☐ Do we have the experience and expertise to provide the required services?
☐ Are we able to resource the required services within the likely fee?
☐ Do we have the resources to comply with the client's project timescale?
☐ Do current staff have capacity to handle the project workload and remain effective?

3. *Contract risk*

☐ Is the selection process reasonable?
☐ Are contract negotiations and contract terms likely to be reasonable?
☐ Will sub-consultancy agreements be required?
☐ Will we be obliged to provide collateral warranties or third party rights?
☐ Will local collaboration be required?
☐ Is the contract based on English law?
☐ Will we be able to form a project team to the necessary standard?
☐ Is novation a possibility?

7

7.1.3   What does the client want from an architect?

The RIBA produces a number of guides and brochures, available free of charge, that aim to inform and manage the expectations of clients who may be considering consulting an architect. These range from *'Working with an architect for your home'* for domestic clients through to *'Commissioning architecture'*, aimed at business and institutional clients. Another detailed RIBA note called *'It's useful to know …'* provides detailed guidance to help clients understand the architect's role in a building project. *A Client's Guide to Engaging an Architect* (November 2009 edition) is available from the RIBA Bookshop and is perhaps the most thorough source of information for clients about the role of the architect, the process of design and construction and the regulatory framework. Guides such as those produced by the RIBA, the marketing literature of individual practices and the preconceptions of clients themselves combine to shape a client's expectations.

The RIBA material emphasises not merely 'the value of an architect' but encourages potential clients to view the engagement of an architect as a necessity. Clients are informed that all architects are trained to define the client's objectives and develop designs that imaginatively interpret the client's vision. Architects are trained to secure the approvals necessary to ensure that a project can go ahead, and to manage the construction phase, by helping the client to select the right procurement route, select a suitable contractor, obtain competitive prices, oversee co-ordination of design and integration of any sub-contractor designed elements and monitor progress, quality and safety on site.

The guide *'Commissioning architecture'* encourages sophisticated commercial clients to understand the value of consulting an architect in terms of time, money, utility and beauty:

> Consulting an architect at the earliest planning stages opens the door to cost savings, both in the construction and operation of the building, through innovative design solutions. Using an architect to manage your project and co-ordinate the work of consultants and contractors can save you time and money in the long run.

Client expectations are high, and demands follow expectations.

It is important from the client's perspective that they are properly protected in the event of a problem with the project. In terms of the potentially overlapping roles of their team of professional consultants, the client will want to be certain that the respective roles and responsibilities are well defined so that no individual task falls between the cracks. This can only be achieved if the schedules of services in each professional appointment have been thought through and drafted accurately, so that every service that needs to be performed in order to make the project work will be completed by one of the consultants.

7.2 The architect's services

7.2.1 Defining the architect's services

The schedule of services is the part of an architect's appointment that sets out 'what' they will be doing; the terms and conditions of appointment set out the standard that the architect must achieve when performing the services.

The architect is obliged by the ARB Architects Code and the RIBA Professional Code of Conduct to have agreed a written appointment, setting out both the terms and conditions of appointment and their services, prior to providing any services.

It is in the interests of both the client and the architect that the client knows and understands what services the architect will be providing. If the architect's schedule of services has not been drafted by the client, it must be fully explained to the client; failure by the client to properly understand the architect's role and responsibilities during the design, planning and construction process is the root cause of many disputes and complaints against architects.

The *RIBA Job Book* is essential reading; an architect must be able to understand and explain their services and the actions they must take in practice during each defined RIBA stage. The *Job Book*, now updated to bring it into line with the RIBA Plan of Work 2013, is a valuable tool even on projects where the architect has agreed an amended or bespoke schedule of services. The RIBA stages are long established and firmly based in a logical order, and this logical ordering has been carried through into the RIBA Plan of Work 2013. Often a client's bespoke schedule of services will be more prescriptive about the individual tasks that the architect must carry out, but it will be rare for a client to propose a schedule of services that bears no relation at all to the RIBA stages. An architect will not be required to perform every service contemplated by the RIBA stages on every project, and there may be additional client requirements on individual projects, but the RIBA Plan of Work 2013 and stage descriptions in the various task bars set out in general terms the potential extent of an architect's role.

The RIBA Standard Conditions of Appointment 2010 (2012 revision) Schedules booklet also contains a number of fundamental role specifications which may be agreed with a client for a particular project. An architect may be appointed to carry out one or a number of the separate defined roles; although when appointed as lead designer their services will include not only the lead designer role specification, but also the architect role specification. When an architect is appointed to perform a specified role as set out in the Schedules booklet, they are generally responsible for the performance of the stated activities that form part of that role specification *throughout* – over the course of all the RIBA stages for which the architect is appointed.

As part of the RIBA Plan of Work 2013 it was necessary to redefine the roles contained in the various RIBA appointment documents, including the RIBA Standard Conditions of Appointment 2010 (2012 revision). The redefined roles now comprise:

• Client
• Client Adviser
• Project Lead
• Lead Designer
• Architect
• Building Services Engineer
• Civil and Structural Engineer
• Cost Consultant
• Construction Lead
• Contract Administrator
• Health and Safety Adviser.

The most important of the role specifications are described below – those of project lead, lead designer, architect and contract administrator.

The project lead and lead designer role specifications

The project lead services are always required, whether or not other consultants are appointed. Dale Sinclair's books, *Assembling a Collaborative Project Team* (2013, RIBA Publishing) and *Leading the Team: An architect's guide to design management* (2011, RIBA Publishing), are recommended reading in relation to project team formation and design co-ordination. As emphasised in these books, the project lead (lead consultant in the old pre-2013 terminology) and lead designer roles, and the duties undertaken by them, are central to the design process and so to the delivery of a successful project. On the vast majority of projects, the architect will be appointed to undertake both roles.

What skills are required to carry out these duties? *Leading the Team* covers this area and comments as follows:

The lead consultant role is more management-orientated and does not necessarily have to be undertaken by a designer. The lead designer's role requires design skills and, more importantly, any practice undertaking this role would need to have the relevant professional qualifications and professional indemnity insurance.

The practical measures that should be taken by a project lead and lead designer in order for them to be considered to have exercised reasonable skill and care in the performance of their duties are also considered in detail in *Leading the Team*.

The architect's (as designer) role specification

The duties to be carried out as part of this role specification apply equally if the architect is appointed as lead designer. The architect's duty extends beyond using reasonable skill and care to ensuring that the content of their designs is accurate and adequate in terms of functionality, impact and buildability; the architect must also use reasonable skill and care to provide designs that can be built safely, and maintained safely and cost effectively. The architect's duty in this role also encompasses self management – for each RIBA stage the architect must establish a programme for the performance of their own services, and the architect must have due regard to the cost of implementing their design.

The contract administrator's role specification

The RIBA role specification begins with the architect inviting tenders and then working with the client to appraise the tender returns. The contract administrator's role specification also includes:

- preparing the building contract and arranging for signatures;
- the actual administration of the terms and mechanics of the building contract; and
- liaising with other consultants to gather information sufficient to enable the contract to be properly administered.

The role of the architect as contract administrator is considered in detail in the next chapter of this book.

7.2.2   The RIBA Plan of Work 2013

The RIBA Plan of Work 2013, which can be customised to meet project- or practice-specific requirements, is available at www.ribaplanofwork.com. It organises the process of briefing, designing, constructing, maintaining, operating and using building projects into a number of key stages and task bars (Figure 6). Architects should bear in mind that the RIBA stages and task bars are indicative rather than prescriptive; the precise content,

www.ribaplanofwork.com

The RIBA Plan of Work 2013 organises the process of briefing, designing, constructing, maintaining, operating and using building projects into a number of key stages. The content of stages may vary or overlap to suit specific project requirements. The RIBA Plan of Work 2013 should be used solely as guidance for the preparation of detailed professional services contracts and building contracts.

Tasks ▼ / Stages ▲	0 Strategic Definition	1 Preparation and Brief	2 Concept Design	3 Developed Design	4 Technical Design	5 Construction	6 Handover and Close Out	7 In Use
Core Objectives	Identify client's **Business Case** and **Strategic Brief** and other core project requirements.	Develop Project Objectives, including **Quality Objectives** and **Project Outcomes**, **Sustainability Aspirations**, **Project Budget**, other parameters or constraints and develop **Initial Project Brief**. Undertake **Feasibility Studies** and review of **Site Information**.	Prepare **Concept Design**, including outline proposals for structural design, building services systems, outline specifications and preliminary **Cost Information** along with relevant **Project Strategies** in accordance with **Design Programme**. Agree alterations to brief and issue **Final Project Brief**.	Prepare **Developed Design**, including coordinated and updated proposals for structural design, building services systems, outline specifications, **Cost Information** and **Project Strategies** in accordance with **Design Programme**.	Prepare **Technical Design** in accordance with **Design Responsibility Matrix** and **Project Strategies** to include all architectural, structural and building services information, specialist subcontractor design and specifications, in accordance with **Design Programme**.	Offsite manufacturing and onsite **Construction** in accordance with **Construction Programme** and resolution of **Design Queries** from site as they arise.	Handover of building and conclusion of **Building Contract**.	Undertake **In Use** services in accordance with **Schedule of Services**.
Procurement *Variable task bar	Initial considerations for assembling the project team.	Prepare **Project Roles Table** and **Contractual Tree** and continue assembling the project team.	*(The procurement strategy does not fundamentally alter the progression of the design or the level of detail prepared at a given stage. However, **Information Exchanges** will vary depending on the selected procurement route and **Building Contract**. A bespoke **RIBA Plan of Work 2013** will set out the specific tendering and procurement activities that will occur at each stage in relation to the chosen procurement route.)*			Administration of **Building Contract**, including regular site inspections and review of progress.	Conclude administration of **Building Contract**.	
Programme *Variable task bar	Establish **Project Programme**.	Review **Project Programme**.	Review **Project Programme**.	*(The procurement route may dictate the **Project Programme** and may result in certain stages overlapping or being undertaken concurrently. A bespoke **RIBA Plan of Work 2013** will clarify the stage overlaps. The **Project Programme** will set out the specific stage dates and detailed programme durations.)*				
(Town) Planning *Variable task bar	Pre-application discussions.	Pre-application discussions.	*(Planning applications are typically made using the Stage 3 output. A bespoke **RIBA Plan of Work 2013** will identify when the planning application is to be made.)*					
Suggested Key Support Tasks	Review **Feedback** from previous projects.	Prepare **Handover Strategy** and **Risk Assessments**. Agree **Schedule of Services**, **Design Responsibility Matrix** and **Information Exchanges** and prepare **Project Execution Plan** including **Technology** and **Communication Strategies** and consideration of **Common Standards** to be used.	Prepare **Sustainability, Maintenance and Operational Strategy** and review **Handover Strategy** and **Risk Assessments**. Undertake third party consultations as required and any **Research and Development** aspects. Review and update **Project Execution Plan**. Consider **Construction Strategy**, including offsite fabrication, and develop **Health and Safety Strategy**.	Review and update **Sustainability, Maintenance and Handover Strategies** and **Risk Assessments**. Undertake third party consultations as required and conclude **Research and Development** aspects. Review and update **Project Execution Plan**, including **Change Control Procedures**. Review and update **Construction and Health and Safety Strategies**.	Review and update **Sustainability, Maintenance and Operational and Handover Strategies** and **Risk Assessments**. Prepare and submit **Building Regulations** submission and any other third party submissions requiring consent. Review and update **Project Execution Plan**. Review **Construction Strategy**, including sequencing, and update **Health and Safety Strategy**.	Review and update **Sustainability Strategy** and implement **Handover Strategy**, including agreement of information required for commissioning, training, handover, asset management, future monitoring and maintenance and ongoing compilation of **'As-constructed' Information**. Update **Construction and Health and Safety Strategies**.	Carry out activities listed in **Handover Strategy** including **Feedback** for use during the future life of the building or on future projects. Updating of **Project Information** as required.	Conclude activities listed in **Handover Strategy** including **Post-occupancy Evaluation**, review of **Project Performance, Project Outcomes and Research and Development** aspects. Updating of **Project Information**, as required, in response to ongoing client **Feedback** until the end of the building's life.
Sustainability Checkpoints	Sustainability Checkpoint — 0	Sustainability Checkpoint — 1	Sustainability Checkpoint — 2	Sustainability Checkpoint — 3	Sustainability Checkpoint — 4	Sustainability Checkpoint — 5	Sustainability Checkpoint — 6	Sustainability Checkpoint — 7
Information Exchanges (at stage completion)	**Strategic Brief**.	**Initial Project Brief**.	**Concept Design** including outline structural and building services design, associated **Project Strategies**, preliminary **Cost Information** and **Final Project Brief**.	**Developed Design**, including the coordinated architectural, structural and building services design and updated **Cost Information**.	Completed **Technical Design** of the project.	**'As-constructed' Information**.	Updated **'As-constructed' Information**.	**'As-constructed' Information** updated in response to ongoing client **Feedback** and maintenance or operational developments.
UK Government Information Exchanges	Not required.	Required.	Required.	Required.	Not required.	Not required.	Required.	As required.

© RIBA

*Variable task bar – in creating a bespoke project or practice specific RIBA Plan of Work 2013 via www.ribaplanofwork.com a specific bar is selected from a number of options.

Figure 6 RIBA Plan of Work 2013 stages

sequence and any overlapping of stages and tasks will be governed by the procurement route adopted for the project. The *RIBA Job Book* contains detailed discussion and visual representation of the potential stage sequences by procurement method.

The major advantages of the Plan of Work 2013 are greater flexibility and adaptability. Where the RIBA Outline Plan of Work 2007 aligned only to one procurement route (traditional) and made assumptions about the timing of planning applications, the RIBA Plan of Work 2013 is suitable for all forms of procurement and can be tailored to project, practice and client requirements. Project-specific or practice-specific versions can be generated electronically from the basic RIBA Plan of Work 2013 template.

The RIBA Plan of Work 2013 sets out eight stages and eight task bars. Stages 0–7 are now aligned with the Construction Industry Council's schedule of services and the Government's 'Digital Plan of Work', allowing greater integration of architects within the wider construction industry.

The stages are fixed, but certain of the task bars contain content which can be varied, used or not used as appropriate to the needs of the project. The task bars relating to Procurement, Programme and Planning are variable; the Sustainability Checkpoints and UK Government Information Exchanges task bars may be 'switched' on or off altogether.

7.3 Strategic Definition, Preparation and Brief: RIBA Stages 0 and 1

7.3.1 Defining the client's requirements through development of the brief

Stage 0 emphasises the necessity for strategic brief and definition of a project prior to creation of a initial project brief. It is intended that the strategic appraisal will address issues as fundamental as whether a new building is required at all or whether a refurbishment, extension or a rationalised space plan would be more appropriate.

During Stages 0 and 1 the architect must take reasonable steps to establish whether the project envisaged by the client is feasible and buildable. Everything starts with the client's initial statement of requirements, describing the building required by the client and the actions necessary to achieve it. This may begin as a detailed document produced by the client or, with less experienced clients, it will typically be a document produced by the architect following discussions with the client of their needs, objectives and business case. On the basis of this initial statement/ brief it is the architect's duty to complete feasibility studies and present options to the client to allow them to decide whether it is realistic and desirable to proceed.

The initial brief should be as comprehensive as possible. Any development of the initial brief should be recorded in writing. Fee and timescale will be based on an assessment of the initial project brief; be sure to record in writing any necessary adjustments as the initial project brief develops, along with the client's agreement to any increase in your fee estimate or overall timetable.

Establishing *feasibility* and a *usable brief* will involve an investigation by the architect of the site itself, having obtained from the client all the information reasonably necessary for the architect to ensure that the initial project brief is as accurate as possible, including such information as site ownership and boundaries, proposed use of the building (including individual areas within the building), desired lifespan and time for delivery. It is the architect's responsibility to check who precisely the client is and whether the party providing the information does so with the client's authority. The architect should also be mindful to check the information they are given by the client against their own observations of the site:

- Do the dimensions of the site or its topography call into question the feasibility of the project?
- Is the client's budget realistic?
- Is ground investigation of the site required and, if so, who should the client engage to carry out the survey?

It is good practice to develop a comprehensive checklist questionnaire to establish your client's needs and objectives, business case and possible constraints on the development, and to meet with the client as often as is necessary to discuss their responses until you are sure that the initial project brief fully expresses the client's wishes and no important detail has been left out.

The architect may during these stages be expected to advise the client on the need for the appointment of other specialist consultants, such as a quantity surveyor or project manager, with whom the architect might be expected to work to produce an initial cost plan and overall programme.

7.3.2   Advising the client on procurement

During Stage 1, the architect is likely to be required to advise in relation to the need for a building contractor and the most appropriate form of 'procurement route' (traditional contracting or design and build, for example) and form of building contract.

To allow for compatibility with all forms of procurement, the RIBA Plan of Work 2013 has a generic Procurement task bar. Users generating a bespoke RIBA Plan of Work can select the type of procurement from a pull-down list. The practice- or project-specific Plan of Work subsequently generated will contain a task bar that includes the specific procurement and tendering activities at each stage for the chosen procurement route.

On many projects, the procurement route is likely to be considered and agreed during Stage 1. In such circumstances a tailored project-specific Plan of Work can be generated at the end of Stage 1 to reflect the chosen procurement route.

Whilst it is recommended that a project-specific Plan of Work is created at the end of Stage 1, the pull-down options in the electronic version allow a degree of flexibility. If the procurement strategy, or for that matter the planning strategy or project programme, have not been settled by the end of Stage 1, a holding bar can be placed in the project-specific RIBA Plan of Work 2013 and a new plan generated when the outstanding items have been finalised.

Procurement advice is not always the architect's responsibility. The architect's appointment should make clear whether they have a role to play in this area; often this will be the responsibility of a project manager or quantity surveyor, or the client may require input from all three. Entire books have been dedicated to the task of selecting the best procurement route for a project – RIBA Publishing's *Which Contract?* is particularly helpful – but the relevant factors to take into account are largely common sense. The aim is to identify the client's optimum balance between:

- cost control;
- timing of completion;
- quality of construction;
- risk sharing; and
- client control over design.

7.4   Concept Design and Developed Design: RIBA Stages 2 and 3

The architect has a wide-ranging role during these stages. They will be reviewing the procurement route and advising the client in relation to, among other things, project costs and statutory requirements, while also developing and reviewing their design and co-ordinating it with the designs of the other consultants.

7.4.1 Reviewing the procurement route

The procurement options can and should be refined after Stage 1 to take account of the development of the brief and any other relevant new information. By the time the tender documents are issued (Stage 4 – although depending upon the procurement route the tender or first stage tender may take place earlier than this stage) they will need to be specific about not only the procurement route but also the precise form of building contract to be used. The architect's duties, in addition to advising the client on the form of building contract, include giving advice on the need for any amendments to the contract terms to suit the particular needs of the project or the client, advising on the choices to be made when certain optional clauses are available within a contract (dispute resolution methods for example, or whether to sign a contract under hand or as a deed) and, very importantly, advising on the need for the client to take further specialised legal advice.

The architect's duty to exercise reasonable skill and care demands that the various choices are presented and explained to the client and that the client is enabled to make an informed decision in each case. It is important that the client understands both the advantages and disadvantages of the available options. Advice to the client is an ongoing process. If, once the client has made their decision, it subsequently becomes apparent that a change in circumstances means that the selected route is no longer the most suitable, it is the architect's duty not only to be alive to the issue but to bring it to the client's attention and advise again on the best course of action.

There are numerous forms of construction procurement and an even greater number of standard form building contracts. The most popular options are, broadly defined, 'traditional' contracting, design and build, and 'management', whether management contracting or construction management. These options are considered in more detail below in the context of RIBA Stage 4.

7.4.2 Providing and revising cost estimates

During these stages, the architect may be expected to provide information for cost planning and to take responsibility for the provision of initial cost estimates and the revision of these estimates during the course of the project. These services may be provided by the architect in lieu of a quantity surveyor, or the architect may assist a client-appointed quantity surveyor in this role. If the client wishes the architect alone to assume this role, it may be appropriate for the architect to engage their own quantity surveyor; this happens rarely in practice, but in those circumstances where it does, the client is entitled to assume that the architect will be responsible for providing cost information using the requisite degree of reasonable skill and care set out in the architect's appointment. The client will bring an action against the architect in the event of negligence; it will be for the architect to bring an equivalent claim against their sub-consultant if necessary.

Will the architect have satisfied their obligation to exercise reasonable skill and care simply by engaging a suitably qualified quantity surveyor as a sub-consultant? Can they use this as a full defence against the client's claim for negligence? The answer is, maybe. The court in the case of *Co-operative Group Limited v John Allen Associates Limited* (at paragraph 180) said that an architect can discharge their duty to use reasonable skill and care by relying on the advice of a specialist provided that the architect acts *reasonably* in doing so:

- Was assistance sought from an appropriate specialist?
- Was it reasonable to seek assistance from another professional at all?
- Was there information which should have led the architect to give a warning?
- Does the client have an alternative remedy in respect of the specialist's advice?
- Should the architect have advised the client to seek advice elsewhere?
- Should the architect have sought professional advice before engaging the specialist?

7.4.3   Ensuring compliance with statutory requirements

During these stages, the architect has to consider their design and the project overall in the context of a number of statutory requirements, and must advise the client accordingly. The architect will need to:

- consider their role under the applicable health and safety legislation;
- make applications for planning permission, listed building consent and conservation area consents as appropriate; and
- advise the client in relation to any party wall notices that may be necessary.

One further important statutory requirement, Building Regulations approval, is usually sought later, during Stage 4 (section 7.5.1).

The architect's role under health and safety legislation

The architect has a duty during these stages, and throughout the project, to:

- advise the client of their duties under the Construction (Design and Management) Regulations 2015 ('CDM Regulations') and other health and safety legislation;
- comply with their own duties as a designer under the CDM Regulations, as well as their duties under other health and safety legislation; and
- if the architect is not acting in this capacity itself, assist the principal designer by providing information to them and co-operating with them and advising the client to require other members of the project team to do the same.

The CDM Regulations apply to all projects, with limited exceptions, where there is more than one contractor. Any building project that will involve more than twenty people on site at any time and will last longer than 30 days, or will involve more than 500 person days of construction work, must be notified to the Health and Safety Executive. The CDM Regulations impose statutory duties on designers and contractors, and also on clients – whether or not the work in question is for the client's own residence.

The CDM Regulations require the client to take reasonable steps to ensure that any contractor or consultant appointed on a project (including the architect) is competent to carry out their role. The client is also obliged on each project to appoint a consultant health and safety compliance specialist, the 'principal designer'. This may be the architect, if they have the appropriate skills and experience, but otherwise the architect will have a duty to be aware of the principal designer's role and to co-operate with and provide information to them as reasonably necessary.

Even if the architect is not the principal designer, the duties of a designer under the CDM Regulations are extensive. The designer should not commence work, other than initial design work, on a notifiable project unless a principal designer has been appointed. In practice this means that an architect should not progress work beyond Stage 1 in the absence of a principal designer. A designer has to ensure that they are competent for the job and also that that the client is aware of their duties in relation to the CDM Regulations before beginning work on the project. When preparing the design, the designer must as far as is reasonably practicable avoid creating risks to the health and safety of those who will be carrying out the construction work, and also of those who will use, maintain, clean and repair or eventually demolish the completed building. The designer has an ongoing duty to review their design risk assessments during the course of construction of the project, whether instructed to do so or not.

Whilst it remains relatively rare for designers to face health and safety charges, it is by no means unheard of. In 2010 the Health and Safety

Executive ('HSE') decided to prosecute both the contractor and the designer, Oxford Architects Partnership, in relation to the death of a technician who fell over a low parapet while repairing an air conditioning system on a recently completed building.

The architect pleaded guilty to failing to take safety into account in the building's design, and not ensuring that the project's planning supervisor (principal designer in the current terminology) considered design safety. It was found by Bristol Crown Court that the technician had to climb a ladder located less than a metre in front of a low wall at the edge of a flat roof to get to the cooling unit; the access ladder was too close to the edge, the parapet was too low and the ladder was 'very wobbly'.

The HSE subsequently commented that the architects had created the risk by changing the design of the build; originally the air conditioning unit was going to be placed elsewhere. Neither the contractor nor the architect had reviewed the project risk assessment after the building design changes, because they were rushing to complete the project. The HSE prosecution under the CDM Regulations led to the architect being fined £120,000 and ordered to pay £60,000 in prosecution costs.

Applying for planning permission

The architect's services will always include an obligation to apply for any necessary statutory consents and approvals, one of which will usually be planning permission. An architect must be able to advise the client as to what (if any) permission is required, who to approach and how best to go about obtaining it, having first reviewed any relevant local authority guidance as well as the statutory requirements, in particular the Town and Country Planning Act 1990. The client should also be advised of the likely time and costs associated with making the application for planning permission.

It is very important the client understands that no architect can warrant, undertake or guarantee that they will obtain planning permission, or Building Regulations approval for that matter.

An architect must reject an obligation to 'obtain' such approvals, as the ultimate decisions are made by third party local authorities, outside the architect's reasonable control.

Planning control is essentially concerned with ensuring that the right projects are built in the right places, and ensuring the harmonisation of new buildings and building alterations with their surroundings. Planners are concerned with the environmental impact generally of developments, their usability and the impact of the development on third parties. Some brief official guidance covering planning and building regulations approval is provided on Directgov's Planning Portal website:

• www.planningportal.gov.uk

Certain types of small-scale alterations and extensions to buildings come within the definition of 'permitted development', for which planning permission is not required, but for the most part any substantial project will require planning permission.

Applications are made by way of a development plan to the local planning authority; again, the Planning Portal website has a powerful search engine, which will tell you the name of the appropriate local planning authority based on the postcode or site location information you provide. The Planning Portal also provides information about whether the local authority accepts planning applications through the website, along with links to guidance produced by the relevant local authority and contact addresses and phone numbers. There is no shortage of freely available information that the architect can use to refine their development plan in accordance with the relevant local authority's stated requirements, to maximise the chances of making a successful application.

As well as the full application for planning permission, based on a fully realised development plan, it is possible to apply for 'outline permission', a confirmation that the local authority looks favourably on the development in principle, subject to acceptance of the detailed development plan at a subsequent date. An application for outline permission can save a good deal of time and expense if the architect reasonably considers that, for example, the proposed project would be unusual for the particular location being considered.

The architect must be very sure of the accuracy of their drawings when submitting the planning application; the architect will potentially be liable to the client for the losses incurred if permission is not granted because of a failure by the architect to exercise reasonable skill and care in any aspect of making the application. The architect should consider the implications of any deviations from the permission granted in the final built project. It is not sensible to change a design at all once full planning permission has been granted; some local authorities will require the application to be re-submitted in its entirety and any significant variation will require a further planning application.

One final aspect of the architect's duty, particularly in the context of a design and build project, is to ensure that the conditions (if any) on the basis of which planning permission was granted are properly communicated to the party – be it the client or the contractor – who has assumed the risk of satisfying those conditions.

Planning applications are typically made at the end of Stage 3, using the output from that stage. However, the RIBA's member consultation during the development of the RIBA Plan of Work 2013 identified a common trend among clients to request that planning applications be submitted earlier in the process, for example using an enhanced concept design at the end of Stage 2.

Dealing with party wall issues

The Party Wall etc. Act 1996 came into force on 1 July 1997 and applies to the whole of England and Wales, apart from the four Inns of Court in London. For a more detailed review of the law and practice relating to party walls, specifically aimed at architects, see *Party Walls: A Practical Guide* by Nicol Stuart Morrow (RIBA Publishing, 2010).

The 1996 Act defines party walls, party fence walls and party structures, and sets out both the rights and obligations of property owners involved in building work affecting such walls and structures at the boundary of their properties. The work covered by the 1996 Act may be the construction of a new party wall or structure on a boundary, the alteration or repair of existing party walls or structures, or the excavation of land within a specific distance and angle, prescribed by the 1996 Act, of a party wall or structure. The Act sets out the procedures for notification of neighbouring owners, which must be followed if a building owner wishes to carry out any such work, as well as the mechanism for the appointment of party wall surveyors, if necessary to resolve a dispute about the proposed work. An architect owes a duty of care to their client to be aware of the requirements of the 1996 Act and to advise their client accordingly. It is also the architect's duty to ask the right questions of their client, and make reasonable enquiries if the client is unable to provide the necessary information, about the nature and extent of neighbouring interests in the first place, as well as to bear in mind the management of those interests when producing their design.

A building owner proposing to carry out work covered by the 1996 Act must give their neighbour written notice; depending upon the type of work proposed, the notice must be given either 1 or 2 months before the work is due to start. The neighbouring owner then has 14 days to indicate their agreement or objection to the works taking place; silence is taken as an objection. If the works are not agreed, a dispute is said to exist; party wall surveyors must then be appointed by each owner to agree a party wall award. It is possible for both parties to agree a single, impartial surveyor to make the award.

A suitably experienced architect – there is no required formal qualification – may act as their client's party wall surveyor. A party wall surveyor performs a statutory function and their role is to impartially facilitate the resolution of disputes under the 1996 Act, not to fight their client's corner. This can be a difficult balance for the architect to strike, and for the client to understand. In the event that an architect is required to act as party wall surveyor, it is very important that the architect explains fully the different nature of their role in performing that function; the client is not generally permitted any input in the resolution of the dispute once the mandatory appointment of party wall surveyors has taken place. The architect should also be sure to conclude a separate written appointment covering the party wall surveyor role. If there is any doubt about whether the architect will be able to maintain impartiality, or whether the client will allow them to, then the architect should suggest that the client engages an alternative architect or surveyor to take on this role.

7.4.4   The designer's duty to the client

An architect's basic obligation, in the absence of any higher contractual obligation, is to produce and develop their design using the reasonable skill and care of the ordinary competent architect. The architect should never accept an absolute obligation in relation to their design; some clients may expect the architect to guarantee a particular outcome by warranting that their design will be fit for the stated purpose. An architect simply cannot give such a guarantee, and their PII policy will not cover claims made on such a basis.

The architect's choices in terms of the specification of materials and workmanship must be such as would be supported by a responsible body of their peers. The design itself must be 'buildable' – ordinarily this will mean that the design can be constructed by a building contractor with the skills and experience that might reasonably be expected of them. In some circumstances the architect may be entitled to assume that the building contractor will possess a special higher degree of skill and experience, for example on a high-value, high-profile or architecturally unique project. Generally, however, if the architect has made unrealistic assumptions about the standard of workmanship required to build out the design, they will be found to have performed negligently.

The architect must also exercise reasonable skill and care in verifying the assumptions on which their design is based, or in ensuring that the client knows additional information is required to verify the assumptions on which the architect has based their design. As an illustration, if an architect is not to be considered negligent, they must have based the site levels in their drawings on sufficient knowledge of the relevant site surveys. A designer also has a duty to warn other designers if their design cannot be fully relied upon without further verification of the design assumptions.

As mentioned above in the context of specialist advice on cost estimates, if the architect engages or otherwise relies upon the advice of a specialist in producing an element of their design, this may amount to a discharge of the architect's duty to use reasonable skill and care in producing their design, but only if in all the circumstances it was reasonable for the architect to have relied on the advice of the specialist in question.

The designer's duty is not confined to producing a design that appears reasonable and buildable on paper. It is a continuing duty during construction that may be triggered by events on site. If the architect is engaged by the client to perform inspection duties during the construction phase, the architect must use reasonable skill and care to react to 'trigger events' by reviewing their own design as necessary; they must check that it will work in practice, and must correct any errors that become apparent, issuing instructions to the contractor for remedial work if required. The architect must react to trigger events and act immediately, not wait to see if a problem resolves itself; an architect can be negligent by omission (a failure to act) in the same way that an architect's acts may be negligent.

A trigger event is any circumstance during the building phase which would alert a reasonably competent architect to the potential need for review of the design, and may include queries received from the contractor as well as circumstances on site that the architect has directly observed. It is unlikely that the ongoing duty to review the design exists in the absence of a trigger; it is also unlikely (although technically possible) that the duty to review persists after practical completion of the works.

There is a more detailed commentary about the architect's duties of inspection below, in the context of RIBA Stage 5 (see section 7.6), and comprehensive information is available in the RIBA's *Good Practice Guide: Inspecting Works* (2009).

7.5   Technical Design: RIBA Stage 4

7.5.1   Seeking building control approval

It is the architect's duty to advise the client which Building Regulations the project will have to comply with, whether Building Regulations approval will be required and, if so, to use reasonable skill and care to give the notices necessary to obtain it. As with planning permission, an architect must not accept an obligation to obtain Building Regulations approval – that is not within the architect's reasonable control.

Building Regulations aim to secure the standards of health and safety for those who will use or be otherwise affected by buildings, and to set the basic standards to be achieved in the design and construction of buildings to promote energy conservation and the welfare and convenience of disabled people. The statutory framework for building control in England and Wales is created by the Building Act 1984 and the Building Regulations made under the Act. The Building Regulations focus on the safety, durability and sustainability of design, building methods and materials used. Building Regulations approval is likely to be required for a broader range of work than planning permission, including even some small-scale internal alterations, such as loft conversions.

Directgov's Planning Portal website is again useful, providing:

- basic guidance on building control requirements;
- a search engine for identifying the correct local authority for your project; and
- links to the relevant local authority's own building control guidance.

Two types of building control service are available:

- the building control service provided by the relevant local authority; and
- an approved private building inspector engaged by the client.

An architect must be competent – through their own experience and knowledge of the available options and their advantages and disadvantages in particular circumstances – to advise the client in relation to which service would be most appropriate, and also which procedure would be most appropriate:

- the building notice procedure: a simple notice to the local authority of the developer's intention to carry out works, which the local authority does not 'accept' or 'reject'; or
- the full plans procedure: requiring the deposit of full plans for the development with the local authority or approved inspector; if using the services of a local authority, the plans must be accepted or rejected within a period of 5 weeks, which may be extended to 2 months by agreement.

The architect should also be able to advise on the timings and associated costs of the different procedures.

Following the official guidance is not enough in itself to satisfy the architect's professional duty of care; if in any doubt about the nature, extent or content of the advice to be given to the client, take your own legal advice.

One word of caution; the architect may produce design documentation that is approved by the building control service, but the architect must still comply with the requirements of the Building Regulations themselves and not rely solely on this approval. There is an important potential advantage in using the services of a private building inspector rather than the local authority service; a private inspector is more readily accountable, must carry PII and will be liable to a claim for negligence in the event they approve drawings which are not in compliance with the Building Regulations.

An architect may also be required by a client to carry out a Fire Safety Risk Assessment – in relation to non-domestic premises – for the purposes of the Regulatory Reform (Fire Safety) Order 2005. The 2005 Order replaced most of the previous fire safety legislation, and obliges anyone who has 'some level of control' in relation to non-domestic premises to take reasonable steps to reduce the risk from fire and ensure safe means of escape in the event of a fire.

In relation to projects carried out in England only, on a single site, whose estimated cost is in excess of £300,000 plus VAT, a site waste management plan must be prepared in compliance with the Site Waste Management Plans Regulations 2008 before construction work begins. The 2008 Regulations are concerned with the management of waste generated by construction projects, the minimisation of such waste and the efficient and appropriate removal of any such waste through re-use, recycling or other disposal. An architect may well be expected to advise the client in relation to their obligations to appoint a principal contractor to prepare a site waste management plan – or that the client should take on the task of preparing the plan – and to advise in relation to the potential criminal penalties for failure to comply with the Regulations.

7.5.2 Tenders

Identifying the procurement route

By Stage 4 (or potentially much earlier) in order to obtain meaningful tenders, the procurement route and proposed form of building contract must have been defined. The most popular options are discussed below in broad terms. It should be borne in mind that there are many shades of difference between 'pure' traditional contracting, for example, and 'pure' design and build; and that the roles and responsibilities of the architect

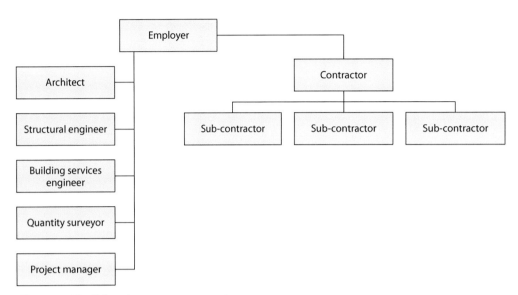

Figure 7 Traditional procurement route

may vary considerably even on two projects procured on the same fundamental basis.

Essential features of traditional contracting

This probably remains the default option for many less-experienced clients on low-value projects. An architect is appointed by the client to carry out and substantially complete the design in sufficient detail to enable tenders to be obtained; the contractor tenders on the basis of that substantially completed design for the job of building it out. The client signs the building contract with the contractor, and professional appointments with the architect and any other consultants. The client is protected by these direct contractual relationships and may sue any of these parties for breach of contract if they are responsible for a design or construction defect. If the contractor engages sub-contractors to carry out specialist elements of work, these sub-contractors are likely to be required to sign collateral warranties to establish a direct contractual relationship with the client.

If the production information is issued in sufficient detail to enable meaningful tenders to be obtained, and the 'bills of quantities' (setting out the quantities of each element required to complete the works) are also sufficiently detailed and accurate, traditional contracting offers the client the closest thing to price certainty. It is possible to opt for traditional contracting without specifying quantities; the measurement risk is with the contractor in such a scenario, and as a result the client may receive fewer bids for the work.

The potential for a degree of price certainty will be to some extent lost if the design is not sufficiently detailed at tender stage, and if there is insufficiently detailed design or quantities information at tender stage then it is an option (although rarely used in traditional contracting) for the architect to consider advising the client to engage in a 'two-stage' tender. In this process, initial tenders are received on the basis of the available information and, once a preferred contractor is identified, the second stage of the process involves firming up the price for the works as the design becomes more detailed. Two-stage tendering is a possibility whenever a client is keen to get a project up and running quickly, and where the development of a design will benefit from the contractor's early input on the method of construction.

In addition to cost certainty, traditional contracting also emphasises quality of detailing, if not necessarily construction – where there is no contractor design input whatsoever, the design team designs, the contractor builds, and both are subject to the direct control of the client. The lines of contractual responsibility are generally clear-cut in the purest form of traditional contracting, and this way of procuring construction is intuitive, even for an inexperienced client.

There are two potentially important disadvantages to traditional procurement. Because of the need for production information to be issued in sufficient detail to form the basis of meaningful tenders, work on site may begin later than would be the case with other procurement routes – for example, design and build or a management contract. If reducing the overall programme for the project is an important issue for the client, the architect should consider steering them towards a procurement route in which design development and work on site may proceed in parallel, although in practice traditional procurement can match the timescales produced by other procurement routes if operated efficiently.

The second important disadvantage for the client is the lack of a single point of responsibility; in any dispute about defects in a building, there are always likely to be arguments about whether the defect was caused by faulty design or faulty construction work. The client's legal fees will increase considerably if it is necessary to bring actions against both builder and designers in order to recover damages.

Essential features of design and build procurement
The main advantage for the client of design and build procurement, in its purest form, is the simplicity of a single point of responsibility. The contractor is responsible for the whole of the design and construction of the finished project. The client has a contractual relationship with

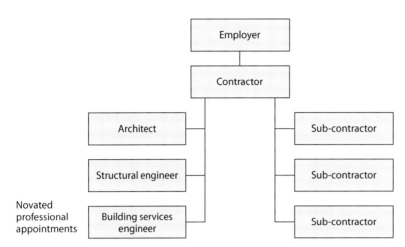

Figure 8 Design and build procurement route

the contractor through the building contract and will want to receive collateral warranties from any design professionals and specialist sub-contractors engaged by the contractor. Design and build construction can be relatively quick because the building work can potentially begin before the design is finalised. There is a degree of cost certainty too – the contractor is generally expected to commit to a fixed lump sum even though the design is still to be fully developed. As a result, the client should expect the contractor to build a premium into their price to take account of the risk of making the price commitment based on incomplete information.

The perceived main disadvantages of design and build are the potential for:

- lack of quality in detailing;
- lack of incentive for innovation; and
- loss of control over the detailed elements of the specification.

The client effectively hands over control, and it is down to the contractor to bring all the elements of design and construction together. This is the price the client pays for passing on the bulk of the project risk.

In reality, the design work is likely to be carried out by the same parties under both a traditional procurement route or design and build. There are contractor-designed elements (performance-specified work) in very many traditional projects, often undertaken by specialist sub-contractors; and in many design and build projects the majority of the design work will be carried out by specialist sub-contractors along with the architect and other consultants originally engaged by the client but subsequently 'novated' to the contractor. The key issue for an architect in this position after novation is to be satisfied that they have explained fully enough to the contractor what additional detailing the contractor may need to address in their own design.

Two-stage design and build procurement, where specialist sub-contractor design can often be completed before the building contract itself is agreed, offers potential advantages for the architect, as early contractor involvement means early sharing of the design responsibility.

Essential features of management contracts
Management contracting and construction management are two broadly similar concepts which offer particular advantages to a sophisticated and experienced client. Both are reliant on the skills of one key appointee, the management contractor or the construction manager; their skills in managing the timescale for the deliverables and placing contracts with specialist contractors for the completion of elements ('packages') of the work can allow the client to enjoy time and quality benefits, with the added advantage of flexibility to modify and develop the design deep into the construction phase.

This all comes at a price, of course. There is an inherent uncertainty as to the final cost of the project with either management route and the

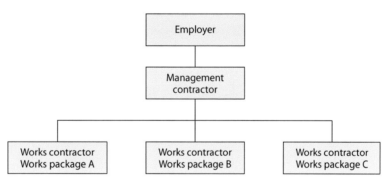

Figure 9 Management contract procurement route

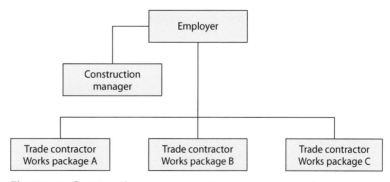

Figure 10 Construction management procurement route

risk is almost entirely with the client. The manager's job is to manage; responsibility for actual performance failings will lie with the individual contractor or consultant. The scope for overlapping liabilities is great and can make it difficult for the client to identify where final responsibility lies in the event of a problem.

What are the architect's fundamental duties during the tender process?

At Stage 4 it is the architect's duty to prepare production information in sufficient detail to enable a tender or tenders to be obtained. The design must have reached a stage of development – including all architectural, structural and mechanical services information and specifications – to enable tenders to be sought. The level of detail produced by each designer will depend on whether the construction on site will be built in accordance with the information produced by the design team or based on information developed by a specialist sub-contractor. The technical work of the core members of the design team should be completed during Stage 4. It is important that any fabrication design, which can only be completed after the contractor is appointed, is clearly identified in the tender documents.

It is also part of the contract administrator's role specification – and consequently the architect's duty if they are appointed to perform this role – to invite and appraise a tender or tenders. The architect's duty in this context is generally understood to be the preparation and/or collation of the tender documentation in sufficient detail for a tender or tenders to be obtained.

In reality it is not uncommon for a quantity surveyor to actually issue the tenders, even if the architect is appointed as contract administrator, but it is certainly best practice for this to be part of the contract administrator's function.

The tender documents must encompass far more than a statement of the client's vision of what they want built, in a specification and contract drawings. The architect (or quantity surveyor) has to consider the desired end product in the context of:

- the client's budget;
- the overall programme;
- which other parties (contractors, consultants) will need to be engaged;
- what those other parties' roles and responsibilities will be; and
- which building contract and procurement route should be used.

The architect is also required to consider and advise the client on the extent of the architect's own responsibilities.

The architect also has a role in assisting the client to appraise the tenders received, most likely in a formal report to the client. The assessment of tenders and selection of the building contractor is best seen as a collaborative process, but many clients will ultimately be looking to the architect for a recommendation. The exercise of reasonable skill and care in this context requires that the architect's advice must be logically supportable. Assertions within a tender relating to the contractor's skill, capacity, experience, reputation or insurance cover should be checked by the architect; information that is not verifiable should not be presented to the client as fact. The architect's report should cover:

- a review of the tenders received by cost;
- a review of the tender sums against the pre-tender estimate and project budget;
- a review of tenderers' proposed contract periods;
- an assessment of the tenderers' ability to comply with project requirements;
- a note on non-compliance with the tender requirements and other errors and omissions; and
- conclusions and recommendations.

For the purposes of contract law, a contractor's tender is usually an 'offer' to carry out the work for the price stated by the contractor. It is the architect's responsibility to make sure the client understands the rules for acceptance. The contractor's tender can generally be withdrawn any time before it is accepted; the architect must also make sure that the client understands any rejection of the tender or partial rejection ('you can have the job if you do it for 20% less') will mean that the tender cannot subsequently be accepted, though the contractor may accept the client's counter-offer to take the job on at a different price or on the terms of the original tender. The architect must also bring to the client's attention any time limit for acceptance that the contractor has put in their tender.

What if no tenders come in on or below the client's budget? That is not necessarily evidence that the architect has negligently over-designed or over-specified in the tender documents – the general climate for tenders may just be high because there is so much work about – but disappointing tenders can damage the architect/client relationship and lead to claims, whether justified or not. An architect should always keep well informed about the likely level of tenders in order to manage the client's expectations, and must ensure there is a clear paper trail showing how the architect has used reasonable skill and care in linking decisions about design or specification back to the client's own requirements.

7.6 Construction and the architect's duty to inspect: RIBA Stage 5

The architect's services may include a duty to visit the construction works as they are being carried out on site in two capacities:

- as designer; and
- as contract administrator.

The architect will be looking to use their visits to:

- assess progress and quality;
- meet the other professionals and contractors on site as necessary;
- give – or gather information to give – any required comments or approvals; for example, in relation to design information provided by contractors or specialists; and
- gather the information to perform their contract administration duty – to enable them to issue certificates, architect's instructions and notices.

An architect should never agree a service requiring 'supervision' of the works. For around the past 30 years the RIBA standard forms have referred to a service of periodic 'inspection', which the case of *Consarc Design Limited v Hutch Investments Limited* confirmed is a less onerous duty than 'supervision'. Supervision, unlike inspection, may potentially involve the architect in giving directions as to how the work should be carried out; an architect has no authority, ordinarily, to direct a contractor or sub-contractor in this way.

The duty to inspect is onerous enough. Going about the task without method, or rigidly sticking to a pre-conceived site visit programme, are not going to be enough to amount to reasonable skill and care. The architect's inspection regime must be tailored to the project in question, not based on personal habit, and must be appropriate to the precise work being carried out on site at any particular time during the course of a project. The frequency of site visits will vary according to the stage reached in the works. Each visit should have a definite purpose based on the current state of play. Before going on to site the architect should have a clear idea of what they are looking for rather than waiting for something to jump out at them. That said, it is a good idea to combine method with an element of unpredictability, to limit the potential for an unscrupulous contractor to carry out sloppy work they know can be covered up before the next targeted inspection of that element. Vary the times or dates of inspections, and always indulge in a non-specific poke around outside your main areas of inspection during a visit.

A court's assessment of an architect's performance in carrying out their inspection role will not be results-based. An architect undertakes to exercise reasonable skill and care; they do not guarantee a particular result. It is a given that some defective work, even potentially serious defective work, may not be identified even by an architect exercising reasonable skill and care.

The discharge of the architect's duty is all about the adequacy of their approach.

The architect must therefore take particular care:

- in gathering information before a visit;
- in judging when and how often to visit and what to look at on a particular visit;
- in identifying what level of detail is appropriate for inspecting a particular element of work in the context of its completeness;
- in assessing what actions are necessary when the architect gets back to their office.

The test an architect must satisfy is: would a responsible body of architects have discharged their inspection duty in the same way? The architect should make sure they keep a thorough contemporaneous log of their site inspections, ideally chronologically in a bound notebook, in case the architect's actions ever need to be considered by a court or other tribunal.

It is worth noting that ordinarily the architect's duty to inspect the works and identify defects is owed to the client alone; the contractor cannot claim against the architect for failing to identify the contractor's own defects. This will not be the case, though, in the context of a design and build project where the architect's appointment has been novated to the contractor and the architect has agreed a contractual inspection duty.

7.7 Handover and Close Out, and In Use: RIBA Stages 6 and 7

During the post-completion phase the architect advises the client in relation to the resolution of defects and makes final inspections as appropriate. In practice it is not uncommon on design and build projects for Stages 6 and 7 services to be limited or not required.

It is important that the architect ensures the client is aware that through this inspection role, the architect is not in any way assuming responsibility for the work of others. During Stage 6, the architect will also have a role in settling, or providing information to others such as the quantity surveyor to enable them to settle, the final account.

A phrase used increasingly in bespoke appointments is the need to ensure a 'soft landing' – in practical terms, for example, providing copies of the O&M manuals months (rather than days) in advance of project handover so that the client can be properly familiarised with the new building. The Building Services Research and Information Association has published a soft landings framework document to give structure to the obligations and procedures required to bring about a soft landing in practice:

• www.bsria.co.uk/services/design/soft-landings/

RIBA Stage 7 is dedicated to post-occupancy services. The architect may be required to advise in relation to the operation and maintenance (O&M) of the completed building. It is good practice and common sense for the architect at Stage 7 to debrief with the client; to evaluate with the client how the building is performing post-occupation (known as post-occupancy evaluation) and to seek feedback from the client on how the architect and the other members of the project team performed during the course of the project.

This is an important way in which the architect can seek to manage their legal risk. Debriefing post-occupation can give early warning of the factual presence of defects, but it can also give early warning of a client's dissatisfaction and potential to bring a claim under the appointment. The debrief is an opportunity for the architect to manage the client's expectations, to prevent actual or perceived problems turning into claims. Client feedback can also provide invaluable business development information for the architect. Data from the 2010–2011 RIBA Business Benchmarking Survey showed that 55% of architects' work is repeat business from existing clients.

The architect may also be required to provide services in relation to the resolution of disputes with the contractor or other members of the professional team; such services should always be considered an 'additional service', subject to an additional fee, because of the inherent unpredictability of the time and costs associated with providing such assistance.

Chapter 8

The role of the architect in relation to the building contract

This chapter:

- provides an overview of the architect's role as contract administrator;

- describes the standard of performance the architect must achieve as contract administrator;

- explains the potential for liability of the contract administrator to the client and the contractor;

- discusses the specific powers and duties of the contract administrator.

8.1 Managing relationships with the client and the contractor

In most projects, the architect is one of the first parties approached for advice by the client. The architect is often appointed early, and helps to shape the client's thinking in terms of the overall form of the project, and in particular which procurement route to choose. The architect will have a role in producing the information on which the tenders of bidding contractors are based; and the architect will have a role in assisting the client (best described in the context of a building contract as the 'employer') to assess the tenders and select the best contractor for the job. In a design and build project, the architect will lead and co-ordinate the production of the employer's requirements. So, even before the building contract is placed, the architect is providing services and making decisions that may impact upon the contractor.

Once the building contract is in place, the architect's contract administration role is defined by the terms of the building contract. Their professional appointment may refer simply to an obligation to administer:

'the building contract up to and including practical completion [RIBA Stage 5]'

and:

'administration of the building contract after practical completion [RIBA Stage 6]'

but the detail of what their key powers and duties are is all in the building contract itself.

The terms of any two building contracts are likely to differ. This chapter seeks to highlight the generic challenges to the architect of managing their relationship with both the employer and the contractor, before and after the building contract is in place; and to shed light on the typical duties of a contract administrator and the way in which those duties should be approached in practice, by reviewing the role with specific examples taken from the JCT SBC/Q Standard Building Contract with Quantities 2011 (SBC).

8.1.1 The architect's position under a design and build contract

SBC is a 'traditional' building contract; the contractor is engaged to build out the design fully completed by the architect (this is not always the case – there is an option for a contractor's designed portion of the design work), and the architect acts as an independent contract administrator. Contrast this with the position under a design and build contract, such as JCT's DB

2011. The contractor is responsible for completing the works and for the design comprised within the contractor's proposals. There is no independent certifier; the employer's agent issues and receives all applications, consents, instructions and statements on the employer's behalf.

Does the architect have a role under a design and build contract?

It is not common for an architect to act as the employer's agent in design and build procurement. If an architect is so appointed, they must be given full authority by the employer to act as their agent for all purposes under the building contract. This role should of course be set out in the schedule of services to the architect's appointment. The role of employer's agent is very different from that of contract administrator; architects who are more used to traditional procurement should be cautious if approached to carry out this role on a design and build project.

8.2 The architect as contract administrator ('CA')

8.2.1 The CA's role

For the purposes of this chapter, 'CA' is used as an abbreviation for contract administrator, and refers specifically to the *architect* as contract administrator.

To a layman, it must be surprising that the architect's role can be so wide-ranging. The design work, and the architect's part in shaping the specification for a project, are relatively easy to understand. The role of the architect as CA is that much harder to grasp. Their position is ambiguous. At times the CA is expected to be the employer's agent, for the purpose of securing the efficient completion of the contract works, such as when they instruct variations to the work; at other times, in their decision-making capacity, they must be entirely independent, such as when assessing extensions of time or loss and expense claims. In applying the terms of the contract, when they are called upon to exercise their professional skill and judgement in holding the balance between the employer and the contractor, the architect's duty is to act independently, honestly, fairly and impartially.

The CA's role under any contract, bespoke or standard form, is hugely important. It is also, surveys show, one of the leading sources of claims against architects. The RIBA Insurance Agency recently analysed its claims data for the period 2005–2011 and contract administration/project management was the second most common source of claims against architects, representing 33% of claims (the leading source was negligent design, representing 56% of claims, and third was planning, representing 12%).

The duty to act fairly does not confer on an architect the immunity from being sued that an arbitrator or adjudicator can expect. Some examples of typical claims which may be made against an architect in this area include:

- negligence in respect of the extent of an extension of time award and loss and expense to be allowed to the contractor;
- over-certification of the value of works that were in fact defective or incomplete;
- failure to advise that default notices should be issued when a contractor is failing to make due progress with the contract works;
- wrongly issuing a certificate of practical completion where there remain substantial incomplete or defective works, resulting in the incorrect authorisation of payment of retention money to the contractor and prejudicing the employer's rights to require further substantial works from the contractor;
- wrongly issuing a notice terminating a building contract; and
- wrongly allowing substantial contract works to proceed before the building contract has been signed.

8.2.2   Can the contractor claim against the architect?

Before the building contract is in place, the architect is unambiguously acting for the employer; in law the architect is the 'agent' of the employer when, for example, producing the tender documentation. In contrast (as will be seen) with the prevailing view of the position relating to the architect's conduct as CA, there is clearly no reason in law why the architect should not be liable to the contractor for their actions and statements during the pre-contract phase. For example, the architect may be vulnerable to a claim from the contractor if any negligent misstatements made by the architect to the contractor during the tender process induced the contractor to tender in circumstances when they would otherwise not have done so.

What if the architect, in performing a function under the building contract such as certifying payment or assessing an extension of time, negligently (or deliberately) fails to exercise their independent professional judgement and strike a fair and impartial balance between the interests of the parties? Is the architect only concerned to avoid opening the way for a claim by the contractor against the employer? Or is it possible, even in the absence of a contractual relationship, for the contractor to claim directly against the architect?

The 1974 case of *Sutcliffe v Thackrah* made clear that architect CAs are not protected from negligence actions – in contrast to the position of a judge, arbitrator or adjudicator – and so opened the way for claims from the employer. In the *Sutcliffe* case, the CA was liable to the employer for the adverse effects of negligent over-certification in interim certificates.

In the 1990 case of *Pacific Associates v Baxter* the Court of Appeal appeared to make equally clear that a CA, whether architect, engineer or any other consultant, could not be sued by the contractor for negligence in the certification process. In the *Pacific Associates* case, the Court was mindful that the contractor had an alternative remedy under the building contract and could have challenged the certificate in question by arbitrating against the employer. The JCT suite of contracts, in common with other standard form building contracts, similarly provides a mechanism through which the contractor may dispute contentious decisions of the CA. As a result the architect will, in most cases under most building contracts, not be vulnerable to a direct claim in negligence from the contractor in relation their contract administration duties.

This position is not entirely clear cut, though, and architect CAs should be wary of the continuing possibility of a direct contractor claim. Until the *Pacific Associates* case it was widely assumed that a CA could in fact be vulnerable to a negligence claim from the contractor, and there may still be circumstances where a court will be willing to find that the architect had a duty of care to the contractor. For example, there may be circumstances where the contractor has no other avenue for recovery against the employer under the building contract, and where an assumption of responsibility by the architect and reliance by the contractor can be clearly established.

It is worth bearing in mind that these comments relate to the architect's liability in negligence. If, for example, the architect deliberately colludes with the employer to under-certify, there is no doubt that the contractor would be in a position to bring a claim – according to the case of *Lubenham Fidelities v South Pembrokeshire DC* – against the employer, in contract, and the architect, in tort (not the tort of negligence, but the separate tort of inducing breach of contract). The evidential threshold for proving fraud or collusion is high, but successful claims are by no means unheard of.

8.2.3 What does it mean in practice to act independently, honestly, fairly and impartially?

When the architect holds the balance between the employer and the contractor and is required to make a decision under the contract which affects them both, how do they discharge their duty to be independent and fair?

Being independent does not require you to make decisions in a vacuum. You can discuss with your client what you consider to be your options in a particular scenario, and how you are minded to act to discharge your duties. You can listen to their opinions as to how you should act. You can listen to the contractor's views too. You may seek (and pay for) your own legal advice on how to respond to a particular situation. You can share this legal advice with your client, the employer, and the contractor if you wish. But the architect will have failed to discharge their duties if they come so much under the influence of one party to the detriment of the other that the architect can no longer be said to be acting independently.

In the real world, it may often be the case that a client struggles with the concept of an architect, whose fees they are obliged to pay, acting in a way that they perceive to be unfavourable to them. The architect must manage their client's expectations. There may be times when the employer client seeks to encourage the architect, subtly or not, to make a particular decision in a particular way; the architect may feel compelled to make their decision in that way even though, if the client had not exerted pressure, the architect would have done something different. The pressure may take the form of an overt threat to withhold fees or instigate a claim for negligence; or may involve an appeal to the architect's desire for the project to be successfully completed and for all parties to maintain good working relationships. The latter is, if anything, harder for most architects to deal with. It seems that a strong sense of wanting to do the right thing by all parties goes with the territory of being a professional architect. This can lead practitioners into dangerous territory. If an architect departs from their legal and contractual obligations out of a misguided sense of needing to keep everybody happy, the party most likely to suffer the consequences is the architect. It may seem counter-intuitive, but the only acceptable course is for the architect to be very firm about sticking to the letter of their duties – not trying to interpret how to act in the right 'spirit'.

If you consider that one or other party has overstepped the mark in trying to influence you, you should send a warning letter or e-mail reminding that party of your obligation to remain fair and independent in your decision-making capacity. If the employer, your client, is making it impossible for you to discharge your duties effectively, tell them. Explain the options. If you are effectively prevented from performing your role, you have to resign. If you act correctly to the letter of your professional appointment and your duties under the building contract, you cannot be criticised; if you choose to act differently, you will be vulnerable to a claim in contract or tort, as well as to accusations of professional misconduct.

8.3   Specific powers and duties of a contract administrator

8.3.1   Assessing extensions of time

The employer's first job after the execution of the building contract is to give possession of the site to the contractor, if this has not been given already. The CA's first job after the execution of the building contract is to arrange for the contract and other documents, schedules and information to be released to the contractor. Included among this information is the programme setting out the projected date for completion of the construction works. Without possession of the site and a managed flow of information, the contractor will not be able to properly carry out the works. Failure to provide either would amount to a serious breach of contract on the part of the employer.

What if it becomes reasonably apparent to the contractor that the progress of work is being delayed, whether or not they are likely as a result to miss the contractual completion date? SBC, in common with other standard form building contracts, allows the contractor to claim an extension of time for completion by giving notice under clause 2.27.1 to the CA. In order to claim an extension of time, the cause of delay must be a 'relevant event' as defined in SBC. These relevant events include acts of prevention by the employer and those acting on its behalf, along with a number of other events beyond the reasonable control of the contractor or the employer. For a more detailed review of the law and practice relating to extensions of time, see the RIBA's *Good Practice Guide: Extensions of Time* (2008).

It is vital for the employer to recognise that any act of prevention on their part can be deemed to be a relevant event under the building contract, allowing the contractor to claim an extension of time. This is because of the 'prevention principle' of English law; if the employer has prevented the contractor from performing a particular obligation under the contract, such as the obligation to complete the works by the date for completion, the employer cannot insist upon the performance of that obligation by the contractor. As a result, the contractual time for completion of the works would fall away, leaving time 'at large'. This is a favourite phrase used by contractors, which simply means that the contractor in this scenario would have to complete the works within a reasonable time. This would be bad enough for the employer, but the news gets worse. As well as the contractual completion date, most employers will include in their building contracts a requirement that the contractor must pay liquidated and ascertained damages (LADs) to them in the event of a delay in completion; but the law will not allow the employer to benefit from its own wrong by claiming LADs when the contractor is delayed because of an act of prevention by the employer.

The contractor is obliged to give notice of delay whether or not they are being delayed by a relevant event (so they must give notice even when they know they will not be entitled to an extension of time); the notice must be given 'forthwith' to the CA, setting out the cause or causes of delay. Following receipt of the contractor's notice, the CA must assess whether the delay has been caused by a relevant event, and whether the delay is going to cause the contractor to miss the planned completion date. The CA is required to make their decision as soon as reasonably practicable, and in any event within 12 weeks of receipt of the required particulars of delay, fixing a new completion date if necessary and notifying the contractor in writing.

How should the CA go about assessing the extension of time claim?

The quality of the CA's assessment will depend largely upon the quality of the information available to them; the main source of information will be the contractor's delay notice, but site meeting minutes, discussions with other professionals involved in the project and the architect's own observations from site visits may all assist. As with most aspects of the architect's work, the question of whether the architect as CA has discharged their duty to assess the extension of time claim using reasonable skill and care is not results-based. It is a question of whether the architect's method was appropriate for the claim in question, based on the information available; in some circumstances an impressionistic assessment will suffice, but in others a calculated, scientific approach will be required.

What if the contractor's progress has been delayed by two causes acting at the same time, one being the contractor's fault and the other a relevant event? The Scottish case of *City Inn Limited v Shepherd Construction Limited* provided guidance. The Inner House of the Court of Session (the Scottish equivalent of the civil Court of Appeal) decided that where two causes are operative, only one of which is a relevant event, and neither can be described as the dominant cause, it will be open to the CA, approaching the issue in a fair and reasonable way, to apportion the delay in completion between the competing causes. How the CA applies this principle is open to question. The *City Inn* judgment may be indicative of a desire to move away from the mechanical application of critical path analysis, which should be welcomed. Assessing an extension of time remains a question of fact; the CA may consider any factual evidence acceptable to them and has a wide discretion, to be exercised reasonably, to decide what information is important.

8.3.2 The CA's role in relation to liquidated and ascertained damages

It is usual for the employer to wish to include a provision in any building contract entitling them to levy LADs in the event of completion of the works being delayed by the contractor. Fixing the correct level of LADs is crucial; the figure, usually expressed as an amount per week of delay, must be a genuine pre-estimate of the employer's likely losses assessed at the date the contract was made. If the figure cannot be logically supported and appears excessive there is a possibility that a court will strike the LADs provision out of the contract as an unenforceable penalty. In the absence of an LADs provision, the employer will be able to claim for their actual delay damages, if they can prove that the contractor was responsible for the delay and that the delay caused their losses.

A sensible LADs provision is to the benefit of both the employer and the contractor. The employer need not take action to prove their losses in the event of a delay, saving both parties legal costs, and the contractor knows what their maximum weekly exposure will be. Sometimes the genuine pre-estimate proves to be an underestimate, which suits the contractor; sometimes the calculation will work in favour of the employer.

In order for the employer to levy liquidated damages under SBC, the CA must have properly discharged their duties in considering all extension of time claims, and must also have issued a non-completion certificate under clause 2.31, stating that the contractor has failed to complete the works by the contract completion date. The non-completion certificate is a pre-condition to the employer's ability to levy LADs; the employer must also give the contractor a notice, any time before the date of the final certificate, stating that they may require payment of LADs. It is the architect's duty to advise the client in relation to the service of such notices and they will in all likelihood be asked by the client to draft the employer's notice, and the demand for LADs, as well as the certificate of non-completion the architect must give in their capacity as CA.

The employer is able to claim LADs up until the date of practical completion under the building contract. It makes no difference whether the employer has taken possession of the works. For example, in the case of *Hall v Van Der Heiden* the employer moved back into their house while the (hugely delayed) refurbishment work was still going on. The employer levied LADs when the contractor failed to complete on time; the contractor argued that the LADs figure had become a penalty because once the employer moved back into their house they were no longer incurring any costs as a result of the contractor's delay. The court refused to accept this argument; if the LADs figure was a genuine pre-estimate of likely losses at the date the contract was made, it cannot subsequently cease to be valid.

8.3.3 The CA's power to give instructions and require variations

Clause 3.10 of SBC gives the CA sole power to issue instructions to the contractor. The employer has no power to give effective instructions directly to the contractor, although in practice, particularly on small domestic projects, the employer often finds it impossible to resist directly instructing the contractor. If the contractor acts on a direct instruction (they are not obliged to), a court may subsequently decide that the employer and contractor had decided to amend the building contract. The practical effect is that no directly instructed work should be valued in an architect's certificate unless it has been included in an architect's instruction. The architect is placed in a difficult position; project costs can quickly unravel if additional work is being instructed without the architect's knowledge.

If the architect as CA finds their position undermined in this way they should warn the employer to desist; if the employer ignores the architect's advice, the architect's ultimate sanction is to treat this behaviour as a repudiation of their appointment – the employer is preventing the architect from properly carrying out their services – and walk away from the project.

All architect's instructions must be in writing, but no particular form is prescribed by SBC. The RIBA produces architect's instruction templates, sold in pads of 100, which, if used by the CA, may eliminate any scope for confusion about the status of a particular communication. The contractor must, with some specified exceptions, comply with every valid architect's instruction.

Some instructions give guidance, such as advising the contractor in relation to discrepancies between contract documents, but many instructions will require the contractor to vary the works. Variations may be instructed because of unexpected difficulties encountered on site, but may equally result from a unilateral change in the design desired by the employer. Any variation may result in the adjustment of the contract sum; a variation is also a relevant event and so may allow the contractor to claim an extension of time. The CA may be responsible for determining the consequent adjustment to the contract sum, either alone or assisting the quantity surveyor, or facilitating the agreement between the employer and the contractor of the value to be attached to the variation. The CA will certainly be required to assess any extension of time claimed as a result of the variation.

The employer's power, through the CA, to vary the works is not limitless. For example, it is not generally possible to omit work in order to give it to another contractor, or to instruct additional work that bears no relation to the scope of work originally envisaged.

8.3.4 Certifying practical completion and making good

Clause 2.30 of SBC requires the CA to forthwith issue an appropriate certificate when, in their opinion, the works have reached the stage of practical completion. Practical completion is an extremely important stage in the project:

- one half of the retention fund is typically returned to the contractor;
- the defects rectification period begins; and
- the contractor's liability for LADs ends.

In the run-up to practical completion, more than at any other time in the life of a project, the CA is likely to come under considerable pressure from both the employer and the contractor as they seek to influence the CA's decision. It is extremely important that the CA's decision about the state of completion of the works is based on established principles and truly represents the reasonably held opinion of the CA. Although 'practical completion' is nowhere defined, the CA should bear in mind the following.

- The contractor must have complied with their obligation to provide as-built drawings and information requested for the health and safety file.
- All the construction work that has to be done has been completed.
- The CA does, however, have discretion to certify practical completion where there are very minor items of work left incomplete.
- The works can be practically complete if there are latent (undiscovered) defects.
- The works cannot be practically complete if there are patent (known) defects.

This guidance, from decided cases and the accumulated experience of seasoned commentators, should not be seen as an unattainable counsel of perfection. Exercising caution and acting in accordance with best practice will reduce the scope for claims arising from the issue of the practical completion certificate.

It is almost usual to see CAs issuing a certificate of practical completion accompanied by an extensive list of snagging items, which may include incomplete or defective work. The employer may well be desperate to take possession of the building, but once practical completion is certified, the employer loses a significant amount of leverage, and they may struggle to ever encourage the contractor to finally tie up all the loose ends. Even if the employer applied pressure on the CA to certify practical completion, it is the CA who is in breach of their duty of care if they certified practical completion before they reasonably believed it had been achieved.

The default defects rectification period under SBC is 6 months, but employers will typically expect a period of 1 year. The defects rectification period is a contractual window during which the contractor has a right to return to site to remedy identified defects; the contractor would otherwise have no such right and would simply be liable to a claim in damages – a defect is suggestive of a breach of contract on the part of the contractor.

The rectification period is intended to allow for the rectification of defects that are not apparent at the date of practical completion; that is why it is bad practice to certify practical completion subject to a schedule of patent defects, however minor. The CA may issue instructions to the contractor, requiring the making good of any defect, shrinkage or other fault, at any time up until 14 days after the expiry of the rectification period; alternatively, or in addition, the CA may list all outstanding defects appearing during the rectification period in a schedule of defects, that schedule to be delivered to the contractor no later than 14 days after expiry of the rectification period. In either case it is the contractor's duty to make good, within a reasonable time, the defects, shrinkages or other faults specified. Alternatively, the CA may instruct that the employer accepts the defective work, in which case an appropriate deduction is made from the contract sum; this may be a viable option in the context of very minor defects, but the CA must advise the employer to proceed with caution if considering this option as the full extent of the problem may not be apparent.

The architect may need to advise the employer on a course of action if the contractor is showing no signs of being willing to comply with an instruction to rectify defects. This may happen if the contractor decides that the cost of making good exceeds the sum of retention money that is likely to be released when making good is certified; the contractor may have an idea that the employer intends to dispute the sum to be returned, or may consider that particular defects cannot be brought into line with the contract documents and as a consequence making good will never be certified. Faced with this scenario, the CA may issue a notice requiring compliance with their instructions, allowing the employer (if the contractor has not complied within 7 days) to bring in another contractor to do the work and deduct the resulting costs from the contract sum.

When in the opinion of the CA the contractor has made good all the defects notified to them, the CA must issue the certificate of making good. The final certificate cannot be issued without the CA first having issued the certificate of making good, if there were any defects at all.

8.3.5 Assessing the value of the works carried out

The building contract must, in order to comply with the Construction Act (1996 or 2009 varieties), set out an adequate mechanism for deciding what amount of payment is due to the contractor and when. SBC sets out a payment cycle of due dates at one month intervals up to practical completion and, unless otherwise agreed, intervals of two months thereafter:

- the contractor may make an application for payment;
- this application may be accepted, or more likely the quantity surveyor will be instructed by the CA to calculate the gross valuation of the work carried out by the contractor to date;
- the CA issues interim certificates for payment accordingly, not later than 5 days after each due date for payment; and
- the CA will ultimately issue the final certificate.

The architect's duty to inspect the works is important for their duty as CA to issue certificates for payment. The quantity surveyor generally measures and values the works as they progress; their valuations should exclude the value of incomplete or defective work. But it has recently been reconfirmed, in the case of *Dhamija v Sunningdale Joineries*, that the quantity surveyor owes no duty whatsoever to their client, the employer, in relation to issues of quality. The quantity surveyor need only be concerned with getting their sums right; they are entirely reliant on others, in particular the architect, to advise them of the presence of defective or incomplete work that should not be valued. The employer in the *Dhamija* case had asserted that the quantity surveyor had a positive duty to bring defects to the attention of the architect, and that the quantity surveyor was also under a duty only to value work that was properly executed. The court rejected these suggested duties of care as having no basis in law. The architect cannot rely on the quantity surveyor to point out areas of defective work.

8.3.6 Advising on retention

It is generally accepted that the employer should be entitled to deduct a percentage from each interim payment due to the contractor (the rate is

8

now 3% under clause 4.20 of SBC) to create a fund which the employer may use to remedy any defects which emerge. SBC creates the right for the employer to deduct the retention money, but it is the duty of the CA to advise the employer of the need to comply with the contractual rules on the treatment of the retention money and to operate the retention mechanism properly during the payment process and also when certifying practical completion and making good – half of the retention fund is released to the contractor on the occurrence of each event.

At the date of each interim certificate the CA must prepare, or instruct the quantity surveyor to prepare, a statement to be issued to the employer and the contractor specifying the amount of retention deducted in arriving at the interim certificate value. SBC requires the employer to hold the retention fund in trust for the contractor, to protect the retention money against the employer's potential insolvency. If the contractor requests that it be done, the employer must arrange for the retention fund to be held in a designated bank account separate from the employer's normal trading account. It is the architect's duty to advise the employer on the steps to be taken, most likely by advising the employer to take specialist advice from their solicitors or accountants.

How prescriptive the contractor can be in insisting where the employer opens the account is open to question, but the architect should advise the employer to proceed with caution; the courts have demonstrated a willingness to grant mandatory injunctions to force the employer's hand if a suitable separate account has not been set up. The architect may also be asked to advise the employer in relation to compliance with the bank's account opening procedures; a bank will want to see evidence of the existence of the trust which the account is being set up to satisfy. The trust is established by the building contract itself; a full certified copy should suffice, and the particular trust provisions will need to be brought to the bank's attention.

If the architect is asked to advise in relation to the operation of the trust account by the employer, they should in most cases suggest that the employer consults a specialist accountant. Some key principles were established in the *Bodill & Sons v Harmail Singh Mattu* case, including the need to ensure that the account name is sufficiently clear to enable it to be described as a designated trust account, and the contractor must be given 3 working days' notice prior to the removal of any sums from the trust account.

What if the employer has a claim against the contractor for a sum equivalent to or greater than the retention fund? Certainly it appears that a court in such circumstances will not require the fund to be set up in a separate trust account.

The employer is also entitled to set-off sums they claim against sums that would otherwise be taken as retention under an interim certificate; such sums will never find their way into the retention trust account.

Finally, the architect should caution the employer against including retention provisions in the building contract which may result in the employer having sole control over when and whether retention money is released. In the Scottish case of *AMW v Zoom* the court had to consider a scheme being constructed in three blocks, with retention for all blocks only being released on practical completion of the final block. The court heard that the first two blocks had been successfully completed before the employer decided not to proceed with the third. As work on the third block would never start, it would never reach practical completion and as a result the retention for all three blocks would never be released. The court decided that this was not an adequate payment mechanism for the purposes of the Construction Acts.

8.3.7   Certification for payment

The CA's duty is to issue interim certificates for payment at monthly intervals, after the work carried out to that date has been valued. The issue of the CA's certificate is a condition precedent to the contractor's entitlement to payment. The contractor may refer a dispute to adjudication if the CA's certificate is late or is not issued at all. The employer then pays the contractor on the basis of the certificate, less any amounts to be deducted or withheld; if the employer considers they have grounds for withholding sums, the architect must advise on timing for the service of the appropriate pay less notice and the information it must contain.

The final date for payment of each interim certificate under SBC is 14 days from the date it was issued. The architect should advise the employer of the potential consequences of a failure to make payment in accordance with the certificate if no pay less notice is served; the contractor will have a right to claim interest on the sum not paid (clause 4.12.6) and will be entitled to give notice of their intention to suspend the works (clause 4.14) if payment in full is not forthcoming.

The CA will in due course be obliged to issue the final certificate (SBC clause 4.15.1) following the issue of the certificate of making good defects (if there are any defects), within the time periods provided for in the contract. The process for calculating the final adjusted contract sum to be included in the final certificate begins with the contractor; they must provide 'all documents necessary' to enable the CA, with the quantity surveyor, to make the calculation. In theory, though, if the contract has been operated correctly throughout, the CA and quantity surveyor should already have all the information from the contractor required to finally adjust the contract sum. If the contractor does not provide any further information at the end of the project within the timescale set out in the contract, the quantity surveyor should be instructed to make the calculation on the basis of the information already held and the CA should issue the final certificate accordingly within the period required. The final date for payment of the final certificate is 28 days from the date it is issued.

The issue of the final certificate is a serious responsibility for the CA; they must be certain that they have properly and fully discharged their duties as CA prior to issuing the certificate, and must ensure that the final certificate itself is unambiguous and complies with the requirements of the contract as to form, substance and content. Take legal advice as necessary before issuing. The final certificate is so important because it has a conclusive effect in relation to a number of issues under the contract. It is conclusive that:

- where matters (including the quality of materials or goods or standards of workmanship) have been expressly stated to be for the CA's approval, they have been approved;
- proper adjustment has been made to the contract sum;
- all and only such extensions of time, if any, as are due under clause 2.28 have been given; and
- reimbursement of all direct loss and/or expense has been made in final settlement of any claims the contractor may have had.

Either the employer or the contractor may challenge the final certificate in whole or in part by issuing proceedings within 28 days of its issue; to the extent it is challenged in such proceedings, the certificate ceases to be conclusive.

8.3.8 The CA's role in relation to termination

Termination of the contractor's employment by the employer

It is usual for a building contract to provide both the employer and the contractor with a right to terminate the contractor's employment in certain circumstances. It is the employment that is terminated; the contract is not terminated, and the parties continue to be bound by it and liable under it after termination.

SBC allows the employer to terminate following the occurrence, prior to practical completion of the works, of particular breaches of contract by the contractor, set out in clause 8.4. In the event of such a default:

- the CA may give notice to the contractor specifying the default;
- if the contractor continues the specified default for 14 days following receipt of the notice then the employer may, on or within 21 days from the expiry of that initial 14-day period, give a further notice terminating the contractor's employment;
- if the employer does not give this notice, the contractor's employment will continue, but if the contractor repeats the specified default then the employer may without warning give notice terminating the contractor's employment, within a reasonable time of the repeated default.

The CA's role and advice in relation to the procedures

The notice procedures must be followed strictly; the CA's warning notice must clearly express the default forming the potential grounds for termination. The CA must be wary of taking part in a termination by the employer that may be construed as unreasonable or vexatious.

It is important for the CA to know and understand the notice mechanism, and the particular contractor defaults which may allow for an initial notice to be given, as well as the rights and obligations of the parties after such a termination.

For example, the employer has extensive rights which they may exercise to facilitate the completion of the works by another contractor; or the employer may instead choose not to complete the works. In these circumstances the architect will be required to advise the employer in relation to the mechanism to be followed for identifying any outstanding payment due to the contractor.

Termination by the contractor, or by either party

The CA will be expected to advise the employer in relation to the contractor's rights to terminate under the contract for any one of a number of employer defaults specified in clause 8.9. In such circumstances, the contractor may follow the same notice procedure as is available to the employer in the event of a contractor default, the one difference being that the employer cannot do anything without the CA's initial default notice. The contractor may give the initial 14-day notice, then a termination notice after a further 21 days if the default continues. The contractor may also terminate for employer insolvency.

Either party may terminate, prior to practical completion of the works, if a serious 'force majeure' event – i.e. beyond the control of the parties – occurs. The architect must use reasonable skill and care to advise the employer in relation to their rights and obligations in such circumstances, as well as advising in relation to and operating the accounting mechanics to be followed in the event of such a termination, or in the event of termination by the contractor.

The CA's role and advice in applying the principles to the facts

As well as operating the termination mechanisms precisely as required by the contract, the CA must exercise their judgement in borderline cases, particularly in relation to SBC clause 8.4.1.2, which allows for a default notice to be given if the contractor fails to proceed regularly and diligently with the works. A CA may be sued for negligence by the employer for failing to issue a default notice; but default or termination notices may also be challenged by the contractor in adjudication or litigation. If a notice is found to have been issued negligently, it is the CA who will be in the frame for a subsequent claim by the employer.

As CA, the architect may already have given the default notice, but they will typically also be required to advise (along with the employer's solicitors) on the correct course of action to be taken subsequently:

- Is the specified default continuing or has it been remedied?
- Is issuing a termination notice an option?
- Is termination the right option?

Repudiation: termination rights other than those provided for in the contract

The architect should advise the employer in relation to the possibility of repudiation under the contract. If a breach of contract by one party is so serious that it indicates an intention to no longer be bound by the contract, then the other party may treat this as 'repudiation'; they can accept the repudiation, terminate the contract, and sue for damages incurred as a result of the breach. Repudiation is a common law right, available even if the contract does not provide a right to terminate for the specific breach of contract in question.

Chapter 9

Professional indemnity insurance

This chapter:

- explains why an architect needs professional indemnity insurance;

- describes the extent of the cover such insurance provides;

- gives an overview of the provisions of a typical professional indemnity insurance policy;

- discusses the risk management strategies an architect can adopt to reduce the possibility of claims.

9.1 The need for professional indemnity insurance

9.1.1 What does PII do?

Professional indemnity insurance (PII) is an essential safety net. There are many ways in which an architect can manage the risks inherent in practising architecture (discussed more fully in section 9.3): carrying out proper due diligence in respect of new clients, keeping up to date with current practice by attending training courses, negotiating appointment terms to include limitations on liability, and so on. PII is best seen as part of a spectrum of measures that an architect can take to reduce the risk of claims occurring in relation to their work and to cope with claims if and when they do arise. PII is the vital final element that will provide protection for the architect when all the other risk management procedures have failed to prevent a claim arising.

As a general point, PII provides cover only in respect of the architect's liability to other parties, such as the client; it is not equivalent to a fully comprehensive motor insurance policy, for example, which may directly benefit the insured party by providing a fund with which to purchase a replacement car in the event of theft. PII indemnifies the architect, protecting them in relation to the financial consequences of claims by others. PII policies are typically renewable annually, and operate on a 'claims made' basis; this means that the policy responds to claims made, or notified to the insurer as possible claims, during the currency of the policy only. The negligent act which is the root cause of the claim may have occurred in a previous period of insurance or even when the architect had a different insurer or different cover.

This should not be a problem for an architect who maintains cover with the same scope and at the same limit of indemnity year on year, or who has a growing practice and is increasing the scope and level of their cover. But if for whatever reason an architect has reduced the scope or level of their cover, this could leave the architect exposed.

The activities and liabilities covered, the people covered and the level of cover will all depend upon the wording of the specific PII policy. The amount you will have to pay (the 'premium') to secure cover will also depend on your specific circumstances; the insurer will take into account a number of factors, including:

- the level of cover you are seeking;
- the size of your practice;
- the nature of your clients and the work you carry out for them; and
- your previous claims record.

As well as circumstances specific to the insured party, the level of premium charged will also be dependent upon the state of the insurance market as a whole. If the market is 'hard', an architect may find it difficult to obtain cover at a reasonable premium. Conversely, in a 'soft' insurance market, premiums will be reduced, and the scope of cover potentially extended, as insurers try to keep hold of their existing portfolio of business. The insurance market is inherently cyclical, but the cycle is unpredictable.

The RIBA endorses the RIBA Insurance Agency (a division of a well-known UK insurance broker) as its official insurance broking partner; their website is a useful starting point for an architect looking to obtain PII for the first time:

- www.architectspi.com

9.1.2   Professional standards and client expectations

Both the ARB and the RIBA have strict rules relating to the maintenance of PII cover. Put simply, PII is a compulsory requirement for practising architects.

The RIBA Code of Professional Conduct, Guidance Note 5, states:

> Members practising architecture are exposed to the risk of being sued for negligence or breaches of contract. Some form of insurance should therefore be held which will generally cover liabilities arising from such claims. Holding appropriate insurance cover is a requirement of an RIBA Chartered Practice.

The RIBA guidance also refers to the ARB requirements.

Standard 8 of the ARB Architects Code provides that:

> You [the architect] are expected to have adequate and appropriate insurance cover for you, your practice and your employees. You should ensure that your insurance is adequate to meet a claim, whenever it is made. You are expected to maintain a minimum level of cover, including run-off cover, in accordance with the Board's guidance.

Current ARB guidance is that:

> the minimum level of indemnity provided by PII should be £250,000

for each and every claim, however small the turnover of a practice may be. The question of what is 'adequate and appropriate' cover will in each case depend upon the size of the practice and the nature of its work.

Even if the ARB and the RIBA Codes were not so prescriptive, it would still be vital for an architect to maintain PII cover. Almost every client will

9

expect an architect to have appropriate insurance, as part of the enhanced service that a client should receive from a regulated professional.

Sophisticated clients will also be aware of the potential insolvency protection benefits conferred by virtue of an architect maintaining PII cover. If an insured party becomes insolvent, a claimant may seek to recover its losses from the insurer under the Third Parties (Rights against Insurers) Act 1930, which will eventually be updated by the Third Parties (Rights against Insurers) Act 2010. The 2010 Act has received Royal Assent but is not likely to come into force before 2013 at the earliest. Ordinarily, if an insured party becomes insolvent before a claim is paid out, the insurance money will become an asset of the insured's insolvent estate and the third party claimant would only receive a fraction of the money. Under the 1930 Act, the insured's rights against the insurer can be transferred to the third party claimant, allowing the claimant to obtain the benefit of the indemnity in full.

9.1.3   Obtaining cover

The role of the insurance broker is central. The broker is the link between the architect and the insurer who agrees to carry the risk in return for the premium. The broker seeks to find the best fit between insurer and insured. A broker is an expert who can assist you with finding the right policy and level of cover for your business, at the right premium. They should help you to assess the nature and value of the work you undertake, as well as where you want your practice to be in the future; enhanced PII cover can help you find a place in the next league up. A good broker sees their relationship with the insured as a long-term prospect. Good brokers tend to be very loyal; they will fight your corner with the insurer at renewal time to secure the best premium for you.

Insurance brokers typically get paid on a commission basis, the commission being calculated as a percentage of the premium. Sometimes, a broker will instead be paid a flat fee; or a combination of commission plus fee. Perhaps controversially, the broker may also receive a fee or commission from the insurer; a broker should generally be under an obligation to disclose upon request the source of their earnings.

Utmost good faith

The key document underlying any policy of insurance is the proposal form, an application for insurance cover to be completed by the architect, which in its most basic form will usually require at least the following information:

- full name and address of the party or parties to be covered by the policy;
- annual turnover and profits of the insured; and
- confirmation in respect of any claims or potential claims made against the insured for a specified period, often the 5 years preceding the date of the proposal form.

Insurers need to be able to accurately assess a risk in order to decide whether to take it on at all and, if so, what premium to charge. The proposal form has to be completed fully and accurately – there is nothing to be gained by withholding relevant information or presenting information in a potentially misleading way in order to convey a more favourable picture of your business. Insurance contracts are contracts of 'utmost good faith'. Both the insurer and most importantly the insured are under a duty to disclose in a clear and accurate way every material fact relating to the proposed insurance. If the insured architect breaches this duty, they may have given the insurer cause to deny cover in the event of a claim.

What is a material fact?

Your broker should give advice on what is and is not material for the purposes of the proposal form.

- Material issues will include anything that may be likely to influence a prudent insurer's judgement (an objective test, independent of the views of the particular insurer and insured) when making their decisions about whether to provide cover and what level of premium to set. When in doubt, err on the side of caution and disclose.
- The test is not simply what is known by the insured, but what that party ought reasonably to be expected to have known about. This implies a duty to make reasonable enquiries as to whether there is any additional information that should be disclosed.

There are no hard and fast guidelines as to what precisely may be considered material. An insured is partly reliant on their broker, and partly on common sense. Existing or likely claims made against an architect will be material. Patterns of behaviour which have not yet led to a claim but which may make the architect a more risky insurance prospect may also be material; for example, a practice of failing to adequately review professional appointment terms.

A proposal form will typically remind the party seeking cover that:

'Failure to disclose could prejudice your rights to indemnity in the event of a claim or cause insurers to void your policy.'

9

and will end with a declaration section:

'I declare that after enquiry and to the best of my knowledge, the statements made and particulars given in this proposal are true and I have not misstated or suppressed any material fact. I undertake to inform the Insurer of any material alteration to these facts occurring before completion of the Contract of Insurance and during the policy period.'

The party seeking cover will have to sign this declaration.

The onus of proving non-disclosure is with the insurer, but the effect of the insured party signing the declaration on the proposal form is that the insured is taken to have *warranted* the accuracy of the information supplied and the truth of the answers given. This warranty will be interpreted strictly; the insurer will have the right to void the policy if any inaccuracy or non-disclosure at all can be shown.

Who should be covered by the policy?

The professional codes of practice make clear that any architect who undertakes professional work should ensure that their work is covered by insurance, whether the work is carried out (according to the ARB's 'PII Guidance' leaflet, available online):

> through a partnership or company or as a sole trader, as an employee or in a private capacity.

An architect, even an employed architect, has a duty to ensure that insurance is in place to cover their work. The policy will make clear who is covered; coverage needs to be drawn sufficiently widely and should include the legal entity of the practice (LLP or company, for example), partners, directors, members, consultants and employees, as well as former partners and former practice entities that have become part of the current practice. Sub-consultants, and joint ventures entered into by the insured architect, are not usually covered.

Professional work includes all work an architect may carry out, in whatever context: paid or unpaid, formally appointed or giving free advice as a favour. If someone is relying on your professional expertise, you may be liable to claims in the event that anything goes wrong.

The need for PII cover does not end when you retire, because claims may be made in relation to work you have carried out for many years after the date you completed that work. If you were an employed architect most recently prior to your retirement, or a partner in a larger firm, and your firm continues in business after your departure, you should continue to be covered by the firm's PII policy – but you should take care to check that this is in fact the case. If you were in business on your own account, or your old firm ceases to trade after your retirement, you will need to make your own PII arrangements. One other point – the Partnership Act 1890, which governs practices set up in the traditional way as partnerships, provides that a retired partner could remain liable, to any person who has not had notice of their retirement, for acts or omissions of the partnership occurring even after their retirement. An advertisement in the *London Gazette* (the official newspaper of record for the UK; first published in 1665 and now available online, it is the place to find official information as diverse as legal notices relating to current company appointments and military despatches from the Battle of Waterloo) is adequate notice to persons who have not had previous dealings with the partnership, but those who have had prior dealings with the firm must be directly notified that a partner has retired.

• www.london-gazette.co.uk

The ARB recommends a minimum of 6 years' 'run-off' cover to provide insurance protection for an architect immediately following retirement. This is a minimum recommendation; a 6-year extension may in fact be inadequate, given that the long-stop date for claims for latent defects is 15 years. In addition, actions in respect of negligence or breach of duty causing personal injury or death are not, in certain circumstances, subject to any specific long-stop limitation period.

The decision you make about the extent of run-off cover required will be informed by the nature of the work you were carrying out prior to retirement. Risks associated with large-scale, complex, high-value projects require more than the minimum recommended cover.

9

Can a claimant bring an action for damages resulting from negligence or breach of contract against the architect's estate after their death?
Unfortunately, yes; the Law Reform (Miscellaneous Provisions) Act 1934, section 1(1), states:

> on the death of any person … all causes of action [in contract or tort or otherwise] subsisting against or vested in him shall survive against … his estate.

Damages can even be recovered if the estate has been distributed to the beneficiaries named in the architect's will, and in an extreme case the ultimate sanction of the claimant would be to compel the executors to seek refunds from the beneficiaries. You should consider maintaining PII cover to protect your estate in the event of your death at least for the 6/12 year contractual liability period; this may provide a degree of financial comfort in otherwise profoundly upsetting circumstances.

The risk of such an action against the estate of an architect who was formerly employed by a practice constituted as a company or an LLP is much reduced, as individual directors, employees or members (of an LLP) generally enjoy immunity from personal liability for the organisation's debts and obligations to third parties.

9.2 Specific provisions of a typical PII policy

There is no such thing as a standard insurance policy wording – the precise words and emphasis used differ from insurer to insurer and policy to policy – but certain phrases and usages do tend to crop up repeatedly. PII policies also all tend to cover the same issues.

9.2.1 The schedule

This element of the policy, also known as the slip, contains the core details of the policy:

- policy number;
- name and address of the insured;
- policy period (almost always a calendar year);
- limit of indemnity;
- excess;
- territorial limits;
- premium;
- name of the insurer, or names if there is more than one; and
- percentage of the risk the insurer covers (their 'participation').

9.2.2 The insured

The definition of the insured party should generally cover the firm itself, if it is a separate legal entity such as a company or LLP, as well as any:

- predecessor business entities;
- subsidiary or related group companies; and
- partner, director, member, consultant or employee who has been engaged in the professional business of the firm.

9.2.3 Limit of indemnity

The limit of indemnity is the stated maximum amount that the insurer will pay in respect of damages payable by the architect to a claimant. A good PII policy will state that legal defence costs and expenses will be in addition to the limit of indemnity, otherwise legal costs will eat into the headline indemnity figure.

The limit of indemnity may be expressed in two main ways:

- **Each and every claim cover:** The headline indemnity limit, say £5 million, may apply to 'each and every claim'; this generally has a clear meaning in practice (unless the policy contains a more restrictive definition of 'claim', a point which should be clarified with your broker) – the full limit of indemnity applies to each claim received during the period of insurance. In our example, the architect may potentially recover £5 million in respect of every single claim.

  This cover may be expressed in a subtly different way as applying to 'any one claim or series of claims arising out of any one event'; this overtly applies an aggregate limit if the 'claims' arise out of the same 'event'. The practical effects of the latter can lead to serious arguments in the event of multiple claims being made.

- **Aggregate cover:** PII cover may also be purchased with an explicit aggregate indemnity limit. The practical effect of this is that, taking our £5 million indemnity limit as an example again, a single pot of £5 million will be available to service all claims received during the period of insurance. If the first claim in the year results in the insurer paying out £4 million, the available indemnity limit for subsequent claims in that period of insurance will be £1 million only.

Most architects maintain, and most clients expect, PII cover on an each and every claim basis

However, within the headline limit it is common for there to be other discrete limits applying to specific types of loss. Usually, claims relating to pollution, contamination and date recognition will be subject to an aggregate limit equivalent to the overall limit of indemnity, even if the limit of indemnity under the policy generally applies on an each and every claim basis. Cover for asbestos claims, if it is provided at all, will very often be at a reduced aggregate limit; for example £1 million in the aggregate, when the headline limit of indemnity is £5 million each and every claim.

9.2.4 Excess

This figure, otherwise known as the 'deductible', may be familiar from typical motor insurance policies. It is the sum that the insured must pay in relation to each claim, and below which the policy does not respond. Because most claims will be small, covered in whole or in large part by the excess on each policy, the insurer is able to keep the premiums they charge to manageable levels. Generally, if an architect arranges with the insurer a low excess, they can expect to pay for that through a higher premium than would otherwise apply. An excess is also an incentive for the insured to avoid as far as possible poor practice that leads to claims.

9

Some clients will, in the insurance clause of a professional appointment, attempt to restrict the possible level of excess under the architect's PII policy by requiring that the excess shall not be unreasonable or onerous (although it is unclear what these would mean in practice) or by specifying an upper limit. The architect should not accept such restrictions; generally any attempt on the client's part to be prescriptive about the detailed content of the architect's PII policy should be resisted.

9.2.5 The insuring clause

'The Insurer shall indemnify the Insured for legal liability from any claim first made against the Insured and notified during the period of the Policy, up to the limit of indemnity stated in the Policy, in consequence of breach of professional duty of care by the Insured arising from the performance of the Insured's Professional Business or by any other person or company acting on behalf of the Insured.'

The insuring clause in the PII policy is the basis of your PII cover. Such clauses tend to be rich with meaning, and if you have any doubt about what is and is not covered by the policy, ask your broker to explain. Over time many of the stock phrases that appear in insuring clauses have taken on defined meanings and a broker should be able to explain the practical effect of any of the words used.

The insurer provides an indemnity to the insured architect. The money paid out by the insurer will compensate the insured for their actual economic losses. Even if the headline amount of cover under the policy is higher, the insured will only be able to recover the level of loss that can be proved to have been suffered. PII is intended to place the insured in the position they would have been in had the claim not been made.

The indemnity is given in relation to the insured's legal liabilities. In theory, to become a legal liability for the purposes of a PII policy the insured must first have been found liable to pay damages by a court or other competent forum; in practice, an insurer will typically take over conduct of the insured's defence against the claim.

Some policies go on to list specifically what is meant by a legal liability, others rely on the understood meaning of the phrase. Essentially, what is covered is every liability that can create an obligation on the part of the insured to pay *damages* – not, for example, any fines that might result from a criminal process. Legal liabilities resulting from negligence or breach of contract would include liability for:

- property damage;
- personal injury;

- consequential and economic losses; and
- costs of redesign and repair.

Because 'legal liability' is very widely drawn, PII policies will invariably include qualifications setting out what *is not* covered, in the form of 'exclusions', discussed in the following section.

Under the insuring clause set out above, the legal liabilities must result from a claim first made and notified during the period of the policy. It is irrelevant when the damage occurs; all that matters is when the claim is made against the insured and notified to the insurer.

To activate the policy:

- the claim must relate to a breach of professional duty; and
- the breach must have occurred during the course of the insured's professional business.

These requirements narrow the focus of the insurance cover to professional negligence, as opposed to negligence in any other area linked to the architect's working life. If the architect negligently crashes into someone else's car, causing damage, this damage will not be covered by a PII policy because it was not incurred as a result of a failure by the architect to discharge their professional duty of care. 'Professional business' may be defined by the PII policy to further limit the scope of the cover, for example by describing the architect's professional business as:

'advice given or services performed which the insured is reasonably qualified to provide by virtue of qualification or experience.'

In this way the insurer seeks to ensure that their insured only engages in business activities that are within the reasonable scope of the insured's professional competence.

9.2.6 Exclusions: points to look out for

Exclusions may come in many forms, dealing with:

- types of loss;
- types of claim;
- areas of work;
- contractual arrangements (liabilities of an architect as part of a single-project joint venture are often excluded); or
- geographical coverage (the United States and Canada are particular favourites for exclusion, but an insurer may be wary of providing coverage for any overseas projects).

Warranties and penalties

The most important standard exclusion clause relates to the type of legal liability that will trigger policy coverage. Historically, PII coverage was intended to protect the insured against the risk of damages for negligence. Nowadays, the scope of coverage is better understood as protection against civil liability as a whole, including contractual liability, but with limits; proof of negligence is still a basic requirement for a claim under most PII policies.

Many insurers, while providing a relatively broad civil liability cover, do nevertheless seek to exclude coverage for contractual liability to the extent that such contractual liability goes beyond that which would have been imposed on the architect anyway, at common law, in the absence of the contract. The exclusion clause may read:

'The policy will not indemnify the Insured in respect of a claim under any performance warranty or guarantee unless the liability of the Insured would have existed in the absence of such warranty, guarantee or similar provision.'

Strictly understood, this clause would exclude liability for certain claims under collateral warranties; for example, in relation to purely economic losses, for which the law of negligence now provides no actionable duty of care. To avoid this outcome, many policies go on to specifically include cover for liabilities arising under collateral warranties.

The sample wording above seeks to make sure that all claims are based on proof of negligence, in order to exclude cover for claims based on a more onerous duty of care – such as a claim based on the breach of an indemnity or a fitness for purpose clause. Any such claim would in all likelihood not be covered by a standard PII policy. Taking the example of a fitness for purpose obligation, an architect's design might not be fit for purpose even though it has been produced using reasonable skill and care; there is no need for the claimant to prove negligence if they can show that a design is not fit for purpose.

The sample wording can be read even more restrictively. In the absence of a contractual duty of care, the common law duty imposed on any professional, including an architect, is to carry out their work exercising the reasonable skill and care to be expected of an ordinary skilled professional – nothing more. So in theory, any enhanced standard of care contained in a professional appointment or collateral warranty may call into question the architect's PII coverage because the PII policy is likely to be based on the common law standard. PII policy wording may expressly provide that the insured must not agree to any duty more onerous than the exercise of reasonable skill and care; or this may be implied, as in the sample wording above, by referring to liability that would have existed in the absence of the contractual provision.

An architect should always seek to limit their duty of care to the standard of the ordinary skilled professional; although, as discussed above in the context of duty of care clauses generally, it would be rare for an insurer to take this point in isolation as a basis for denying cover. The enhanced duty of care is discussed further in section 5.2.6.

Asbestos, pollution, contamination and date recognition

It is quite usual for pollution, contamination and, less often, date recognition (a nod to the concern that took hold in the build-up to the year 2000, when many predicted a deluge of claims relating to a potential failure by computer systems to respond properly to the changeover from '99' to '00' – it never came!) claims to be subject to an annual aggregate limit even if the PII policy overall provides cover on an each and every claim basis. Claims relating to asbestos are likely to be subject to a further reduced annual aggregate limit, or in some policies excluded altogether.

These exclusions and limitations reflect the exceptionally unpredictable nature of the risks involved; the discovery during a project of an asbestos issue could result in a claim which has a quantum and a longevity out of all proportion to the architect's fee for involvement in the project. It is important that the wording of any professional appointment or collateral warranty insurance obligation properly reflects not just the headline PII figure, but also any internal limitations or major exclusions within the policy.

Client reactions

It is generally not realistic for a client to object to a proposed amendment that is required to bring the appointment into line with the PII cover actually maintained by the architect. There is no advantage for the client in insisting upon imposing an obligation which is not covered by the architect's insurance, and this argument is often enough to convince a client. Some clients will require written proof from the insurer or broker that the architect's interpretation is correct and that the existing wording would jeopardise the architect's cover. Other clients will refuse to compromise.

It will sometimes be possible to agree a one-off amendment to the policy (an 'endorsement') to deal with the client's concern, but this will

9

not always be possible or may only be available subject to an increased premium, which could make the change unrealistic for the architect.

If the architect has checked with their broker that a particular provision in an appointment or collateral warranty does create a PII policy coverage issue, and the client is still unwilling to compromise and no amendment to the policy is possible, the architect is left with a commercial decision to make. It is never sensible to agree a contractual obligation that is known or suspected to be outside the scope of your insurance. But you should weigh up the importance of the job and the client against the likelihood of the uninsured obligation leading to a claim and the potential size of any such claim. Overall, is the risk one that can be borne by your business without the benefit of PII cover?

9.2.7   Notification requirements

Every PII policy will contain a clause setting out how and when the insured must inform the insurer in the event of a claim, or potential claim, with wording such as:

'The Insured shall, as a condition precedent to their right to be indemnified under this policy, give notice to underwriters as soon as possible during the period of insurance of any claim or of the receipt of notice of any intention to make a claim and shall, regardless of any previous notice, give notice in writing immediately on receipt of any claim form, particulars of claim, arbitration notice, adjudication referral or any other formal document commencing legal proceedings of any kind.

The Insured shall give during the period of insurance full details in writing as soon as possible of any circumstance or event which is likely to give rise to a claim of which the Insured shall first become aware during the period of insurance.'

In the wording above, the giving of notice by the insured is expressly stated to be a condition precedent to cover; so any failure by the insured to comply strictly with the obligation to give notice as soon as possible will give the insurer reason to refuse to indemnify the insured. The notice has to be given at the right time and with the correct content. Dust off the policy itself – what does it require you to do? Speak to your broker to ensure your approach is correct.

The notification clause wording raises further questions for the architect:

• How soon is 'as soon as possible'?
• What is a 'circumstance or event which is likely to give rise to a claim'?

- Is there any disadvantage in simply notifying every incident or communication that may remotely lead to a claim?
- Can the insurer reject a notification if it is too tenuous?

Every case depends on its particular circumstances, especially in relation to timing of the notification. In 2008, in the case of *Aspen v Pectel* the High Court had to consider PII policy wording that required the insured to give 'immediate written notice with full particulars of any occurrence which may give rise to an indemnity'. The insured had not notified insurers of a fire on one of the insured's projects in 2004. Nearly 3 years later the insured received a copy of a solicitor's letter from the client alleging liability on their part; notification was then sent to the insurer, but the insurer denied coverage on the basis that notification had not been given in line with the policy requirements. The Court agreed, and held that the fire itself was an occurrence which may have given rise to a claim and therefore notice to the insurer should have been given immediately afterwards. In the 2009 case of *Laker v Templeton*, the Court of Appeal took a more lenient approach when it had to decide whether an insurer was entitled to deny cover because the insured's notification followed not the event itself, but the instigation of a formal dispute resolution procedure against the insured. The difference may have been the policy wording; the policy being considered by the Court of Appeal required notice to be given immediately of circumstances which were '*likely*' to give rise to a claim. It is a fine distinction, but the formulation 'circumstances which *may* give rise to a claim' seems to require more notifications than the phrase 'circumstances which are *likely* to give rise to a claim'.

In practice it is best to err on the side of caution and provide as much information as you can to the broker and insurer as soon as possible. Take advice from your broker in borderline cases – they have a duty to advise you whether action is required, and it is what they are there for – but if there is any doubt it is best to notify. An excessive number of notifications may have an impact on the premium your insurer decides to charge when it comes to renewal time; but failure to promptly notify a claim has the potential to be far more expensive, if the insurer declines cover as a result. An insurer can reject a notification; but an insured party should in such circumstances be persistent and repeat the notification. If the event does develop into a full blown claim, the insured's persistence will have been justified, and if it does not there is generally no harm done by the insured's cautious actions.

If notification is necessary:

- make sure that the form and content are in line with your policy requirements;

9

- make sure that the correct party is notified, as set out in the policy;
- put the notification in writing; if you have given an initial notification by telephone in an emergency, follow this up with notice in writing;
- even if day-to-day contact about your PII policy is with your broker, you should also inform the insurer directly;
- if it is unclear whether you should give notice to your local office or to the insurer's head office, copy your notice to both.

What to put in the notice

In addition to any basic content requirements set out in the terms of your PII policy:

- make clear that the notice being given is a formal notice under your policy;
- include as much detail as possible about the circumstances of the claim;
- stick to the facts, and never try to put a particular (for example, unduly positive) spin on the situation – this could lead to problems later on if the notice, on reflection, could be considered misleading;
- remember that if the notice is too narrowly drawn, it may not effectively cover all the aspects of the claim that you wish to notify; it can be difficult to achieve the right balance, but the notification must be detailed but also sufficiently widely drawn as to cover all elements of the claim;
- if new elements of the claim emerge after the initial notification, these should be subject to a separate notice if it is clear that they have not already been covered.

It is in the interest of the architect that the PII policy wording incorporates an 'innocent non-disclosure' clause. This may offer some protection against refusal of cover in circumstances where there is an innocent late notification without any intention to mislead or defraud and which does not prejudice the insurer's position. The PII policy wordings arranged through the RIBA Insurance Agency, for example, incorporate an innocent non-disclosure clause, and also offer the added benefit of allowing a RIBA member insured with the RIBA Insurance Agency to refer any dispute with the Agency to the President of the RIBA, in addition to the possibility of arbitration in the event of a dispute. As a minimum requirement, the architect should ensure that any PII policy they take out incorporates an arbitration clause to deal with disputes.

9.2.8   **Practical ways to comply with the policy notification requirements**

Every firm should have a designated individual (with a deputy to cover holiday and illness absences) who is available to facilitate the notification process and deal with other issues relating to the firm's PII cover and risk management more generally. In most practices, acting as 'insurance manager' will not be a full time role and can be combined with other duties. The important point is that other people within the practice are aware of the role, know what the insurance manager does and have the ability and the confidence to contact them when an issue arises. The insurance manager should be the focus for queries about potential claims; theirs should be the first number that a person knows to call if there is a problem on a project that may require a PII notification.

The insurance manager must be familiar with the requirements of the PII policy, both in terms of timing of any notification and also the level of detail required for a notification to be valid beyond dispute. They in turn must have the confidence to make sound decisions about whether a particular set of circumstances may or is likely to give rise to a claim. They must make sure they have sufficient information to make the correct call, taking advice from solicitors and the broker as necessary.

The insurance manager should be an individual with sufficient experience to recognise not only clear-cut instances when an issue should be notified, but also when notification is not necessary and when the broker should be consulted. If the notification can be trusted to the insurance manager, this frees up the project team to deal with the equally important client-facing practicalities:

- managing the client relationship to avoid the problem becoming a formal claim;
- taking remedial action as necessary;
- establishing a paper trail; and
- locating all important project documents in case they are needed to produce a legal defence to a formal claim.

The project team should bear in mind one golden rule, while all the time trying to maintain good relations with the client – *never admit liability*.

9.3 Risk management

Risk management is the process of seeking to reduce the number of opportunities for mistakes to occur, and as a consequence to reduce the number of claims that may be made against an architect. Effective risk management will also enable an architect to be better prepared to defend, and ideally defeat, claims when they do, inevitably, arise.

Insurers and brokers often offer, as part of their insurance package, risk management advice though newsletters, seminars and occasionally by

9

going into the business of the insured and carrying out a risk audit. There is a reason for this; the insurer has a vested interest in the ability of their insureds to manage risks and prevent, as far as possible, formal claims arising. It is of course also in the best interests of an insured architect to seek to manage risks proactively and take action to prevent claims. Architects who regularly notify claims tend to find that their premiums go up; and there are in any case always costs (management time, legal fees) which are incurred when dealing with a claim that may not be covered in full by insurance, even if the PII policy covers the claim itself. It is best to avoid the negative impact of claims by taking steps to manage them out. The RIBA Insurance Agency, with the RIBA Practice Department, has produced a 'Guide to Understanding Risk Management', which can be downloaded free of charge at:

• www.architectspi.com/Pages/RiskManagement.aspx

Underlying everything are the day-to-day decisions of individuals. How people act on a project and react to potential problems will govern how well an organisation manages risks. Some of the areas where experience, training and written guidelines can help individuals to make better decisions and consequently minimise risks are set out below.

9.3.1 Appointment of sub-consultants

This is not simply an insurance issue. Architects need to be alive to the risks associated with the appointment of sub-consultants. Does the sub-consultancy agreement always have to be a formal written agreement? The administrative hassle can be daunting; and when the agreement is finalised, how can the architect be sure that the sub-consultant's obligations fully cover the services and performance standards required, and fully protect the architect's position? If it is the architect's choice to appoint a sub-consultant, and if the sub-consultant is carrying out services for which the client is paying the architect, then the client is entitled to sue the architect in the event of any default.

In the absence of any restriction in the appointment, the architect is free to engage a sub-consultant to carry out any part of the services. A bespoke appointment is more likely to contain a clause requiring the architect to notify the client and obtain their consent to the engagement of the sub-consultant; sometimes in addition the client will have a right to approve the terms of appointment of the sub-consultant. The architect should seek wording in the appointment to the effect that consent cannot be unreasonably delayed or withheld, and retrospective consent should not be required for any sub-consultants already engaged by the architect prior to execution of the architect's own appointment.

Back to back: specific provisions

There are two critical issues an architect must deal with in a sub-consultant's appointment:

- the terms and conditions that apply to the appointment of the sub-consultant must be 'back to back' with the terms on which the architect was appointed, and
- the sub-consultant *must have adequate PII cover* in place.

Because of the need to be able to enforce these obligations against the sub-consultant if necessary, a written sub-consultancy agreement should always be executed, and if the architect's appointment is executed as a deed, so must be the sub-consultancy agreement – if not, the architect may have to face the final 6 years of exposure under their appointment with no scope for passing liability on to the sub-consultant. In addition, a written sub-consultancy agreement may be a pre-condition of the client's consent to the sub-consultant's engagement.

'Back to back' in this context is not an exact term of art; it is a common sense requirement best illustrated by giving examples. If the architect's appointment requires the architect to carry out their services:

'exercising all the reasonable skill, care and diligence to be expected of a competent and fully qualified architect, experienced in carrying out such services for projects of a similar nature, value, complexity and timescale to the Project'

it is not sensible for the architect to sign up the sub-consultant to carry out their services:

'exercising reasonable skill and care in accordance with the normal standards of its profession.'

In this example, the architect's standard is more onerous; the sub-consultant could complete their services fully in accordance with the terms of the sub-consultancy agreement but still put the architect in breach of their appointment with the client.

In addition to marrying up the basic standard of care in the appointment and the sub-consultancy agreement, there are often a number of obligations in the architect's appointment that should be specifically stepped down into the sub-consultancy agreement, for example:

- the obligation to provide collateral warranties;
- the provision of a copyright licence or assignment of copyright;
- the obligation to maintain PII cover at a specified level;

- the obligation to comply with statutory requirements or agreements with third parties.

Back to back: catch-all wording

As well as specific provisions 'stepping down' obligations from the architect's appointment into the sub-consultancy agreement, the architect should also consider including catch-all wording to avoid any risk of obligations slipping through the net:

'The Sub-Consultant warrants that it shall carry out and complete the Services and its other obligations under this Sub-Consultancy Agreement in accordance with the terms and conditions of the Appointment. In the event of any discrepancy between the terms of the Appointment and the terms of this Sub-Consultancy Agreement, the terms of the Appointment shall prevail.

The Sub-Consultant warrants that it has not and will not cause or contribute to the breach of any article, term or condition of the Architect's Appointment and shall indemnify the Architect in relation to any claims, proceedings, costs and expenses whatsoever incurred and howsoever arising under the Appointment due to the failure of the Sub-Consultant to perform and carry out the Services and/or obligations under this Sub-Consultancy Agreement .'

The indemnity wording above may be subject to the same objection as any indemnity wording in an architect's appointment – is it insurable? It may not be, in which case a more limited form of words covering the main point (that the sub-consultant must not cause or contribute to any breach of the architect's appointment) should be acceptable.

As part of the set of current RIBA Standard Form Agreements, the RIBA publishes Sub-Consultant Conditions to help facilitate sub-consultant appointments that are back to back with the RIBA Standard, Concise and Domestic Project conditions for the appointment of an architect.

9.3.2   **Recognising a potential claim and acting appropriately**

As discussed above, the main influence on the number of claims a practice is subject to, and the impact those claims have on the practice, will be the calibre of the individuals within the practice and the way in which they are trained and managed.

Everyone in the practice needs to know about the role of the insurance manager and the procedure for identifying and notifying potential claims to them. If there is no individual identified as insurance manager, there must be another clear and well-publicised procedure for passing information about potential claims up the management chain. All employees need to understand the PII policy requirements for prompt notification.

The practice must also have an adequate procedure for identifying circumstances likely to give rise to a claim and which must be brought to the attention of insurers as part of the PII renewal process. Part of the insured's duty of utmost good faith when completing its renewal paperwork is to bring potential claims, not previously notified, to the insurer's attention. The insurer cannot properly assess the risk of providing cover if the insured party has withheld information, whether deliberately or because the insured has made inadequate internal inquiries. If a PII policy is written or renewed on the basis of inadequate or incomplete information, the insurer may not be obliged to provide cover when a claim is made.

The flow of information internally is key to both processes: claims notification and full disclosure on renewal. If at all possible, the best and simplest practice is to have an insurance manager to act as a focus for the flow of information upwards, either directly from individual project team members or through their managers. Internal education is important; employees should be reminded regularly of the firm's notice and disclosure obligations under its PII policy and how to go about passing information on. Prior to renewal, it is good practice for the insurance manager to run seminars to remind staff of the importance of full disclosure of any potential claims as part of the renewal process. The insurance manager should then send out to all staff members (not just managers or senior staff) an e-mail or memorandum requesting information in respect of any circumstances that may give rise to a claim. Returns, positive or negative, must be compulsory.

Outside the renewal process, there has to be a clearly defined and understood route for information about a potential claim to get from the member of the project team dealing with the matter up to the manager, partner or director who will make the decision about whether or not to notify. Monthly meetings of managers are not necessarily enough. The risk of failing to notify a claim when a problem arises must be something at the forefront of the minds of project team members lower down the chain. Communication between managers is important, but the training given to all employees is arguably more important; if a project team member cannot identify a potential claim or does not know what to do when a problem arises, the process cannot begin.

9.3.3   Recruitment, management and training

Recruitment

Effective risk management starts with the quality of the people in your business, therefore it is important to ensure that only personnel of a suitable calibre are recruited.

- Check the qualifications claimed on a candidate's CV – ask for proof of the qualifications obtained by a candidate in the form of certificates from the relevant institution.
- Ask for references and take them up.
- Do not be afraid to check a candidate's practical ability – set a sample piece of work to be carried out.
- Interview promising candidates more than once.
- Conduct a less formal meeting with candidates – in addition to the formal interview process, it is often useful to invite promising candidates back for an informal meeting over drinks or lunch; the candidate may have the qualifications and experience, but an informal meeting may tell you more about what sort of person they are.

None of these checks guarantees the quality of a candidate – it is only really possible to get a full picture of a candidate's abilities and deficiencies when they begin work in earnest within the practice – but taking recruitment seriously can go some way to minimising the risk of taking on an unsuitable candidate.

- Ensure that all employees have a written contract of employment.
- Implement an initial probation period of up to 11 months for new joiners.
- Plan for a formal appraisal of a new joiner mid way through their probation period.

Management

There must in any practice be an established and understood management and reporting structure.

- Regular team meetings should be held to discuss both current projects and past projects where problems have been reported.
- Team members must have the confidence to raise issues without fear of being blamed.
- Individual managers should maintain spreadsheets listing the projects for which they are responsible; problems once identified should be noted in the entry for the relevant project, and should stay on the spreadsheet for discussion at each subsequent meeting until resolved.

- Managers should also meet regularly so that information about problems identified at project team level can be passed up the management chain, to the insurance manager if necessary.
- Meetings should always have an agenda, to ensure the discussion is as focused and productive as possible.

Effective management is also about assigning the right people to the right projects – the work must be appropriate for the particular qualifications, skills and experience of the team members.

- Once assigned, the work of the project team must be monitored and the proper level of supervision must be provided; different people will require different levels of supervision in different contexts, and *no-one* is too senior to be supervised.
- Effective supervision must also allow individuals to take responsibility in order to create a dynamic business.
- Supervision and review should be against objective standards set out in a policy applicable to the whole practice; some form of 'tick box' procedure may be useful as a starting point, but there has to be room for experienced managers to use their own initiative.

Training

Continuous professional development is important to maintain high standards of performance.

- The need for continuous professional development applies to staff at all levels.
- A practice should ensure that its know-how, precedents and intranet/library are up to date.
- There should be a standard procedure for knowledge sharing, ideally through an office intranet accessible by all members of project teams.
- Take advantage of training on legal, insurance and risk management topics that may be provided by your insurance brokers and solicitors.

9.3.4   **Office procedures**

It can be difficult to encourage staff within a practice to focus on such matters when they just want to get on with their core practice of architecture; but following correct office procedures and maintaining accurate records need to be seen as integral to the core practice. All staff should be trained to follow correct procedures.

- Maintain clear and comprehensive written records for every project – having proper records can make the difference between being able to defend a claim and having to accept liability.

- Keep notes of telephone conversations – a contemporaneous note is far more persuasive for a court or any tribunal than a note written up later from memory.
- Take contemporaneous meeting notes – make sure your notes are legible.
- Write the date on your notes.
- Date stamp incoming mail.
- Keep electronic and hard copy files and employ secretarial staff as necessary to maintain them in good, logical order.
- Establish a system for archiving and retrieval of files – files should be kept for a minimum of 16 years (the long-stop period for liability in negligence for latent defects is 15 years).
- Ensure that your computer system is properly maintained, secured and backed up.

9.3.5   Dealing with clients

It is essential that you develop a strategy for assessing the risk of taking on a potential new job. These pre-agreement matters are considered in detail in section 7.1.2 in the context of what the architect should look for in a client. An architect must also develop strategies for managing the relationship with the client during the course of the project.

- Record or confirm in writing the client's brief and all specific instructions.
- Ensure that all communication with the client is clearly understood and properly recorded.
- Record everything in writing – there is no way of telling which decisions or issues may become important later on in the project.
- Double check with the client that the more technical communications have been understood – those covering costs, timing and specification, for example.
- On a very practical level, avoid responding to an e-mail by answering points within the body of the initial e-mail – reply point by point in a new e-mail to avoid confusion.
- Make sure that all parties who should be copied in to an e-mail are in fact copied in.
- Ensure that professional appointment terms are properly handled – they must be recorded and agreed in writing.
- Make sure that, as well as the terms and conditions and schedule of services, the fee and schedule of fee payments is set out in writing.
- If at all possible, schedule fee payments to be monthly – in this way the architect can discover quickly, and take appropriate action, if the client misses a payment because they are in financial difficulty, rather than

continue to carry out work, possibly over several months, for which payment may never be received.

- Ensure that the client has the opportunity to make formal complaints through a specified point of contact under the professional appointment – few clients will be interested in litigation as a first step, and if the client has a way of making their displeasure known, through a process that gives the promise of a positive and cost-free outcome, then the client is likely to use that process. The architect can take steps to address the complaint and prevent the problem developing into a formal dispute.

9.3.6 Legal advice

One factor that should not be overlooked as a risk management tool is the importance of good legal advice, both when considering or drafting the terms of the professional appointment and during the course of the project in response to client queries or perceived potential problems. Legal advice is also vital as and when complaints are received or disputes arise – legal advice provides a framework within which the architect can manage the client relationship. If an accusation of professional negligence is made, you should never admit liability, but only your legal advisor will be able to tell you what the chances are of you actually being found to be liable. In such circumstances, your solicitor will be able to give advice on how best to manage your response to avoid giving away arguments that you could later use in your favour to reduce your liability, or your share of liability.

How do you find a good legal advisor?

As with all professional relationships, word of mouth is often the surest way, but there are a number of other routes to obtaining the services of a suitable legal advisor:

- your broker may have a recommendation;
- the RIBA runs a helpline which provides direct access to solicitors for an initial query; a professional relationship may flow from that if the enquiry becomes an ongoing matter Further details about the RIBA Chartered Membership benefits and services are available on the website www. architecture.com;
- the Law Society, the solicitors' professional body, has a website on which you may search for a solicitor by location and specialism: www. lawsociety.org.uk

You should in any case arrange a face to face meeting with a potential legal advisor, if at all possible, before agreeing terms with them. Good legal advice is not often cheap, and it is important to get a good feel for your advisor.

- Do they understand your business?
- Will they go the extra mile for you when you really need them?
- Will they provide free seminars on legal topics for you?

It is important that you are made to feel well looked after, and are made to feel that your work is important to your solicitor, because you will generally only be dealing with them in a neutral or negative context. They will draft and negotiate your appointment terms, which you will only need to rely on in the event of a dispute; they will be the call you make in a panic when an adjudication notice arrives from your client.

Chapter 10

Disciplinary proceedings and dispute resolution

This chapter:

- describes in detail the professional disciplinary procedures for architects;

- provides an overview of the main dispute resolution options;

- reviews in detail the theory and practice of statutory adjudication, arbitration, litigation and mediation.

10.1   Disciplinary proceedings

The codes of conduct of both the ARB and the RIBA impose subtly different obligations on architects in terms of their professional behaviour. Breach of either code will leave the architect liable to disciplinary action. Only the ARB, as a statutory body backed by the power of government, has the capacity to impose fines or take away the architect's right to practise architecture altogether, by suspending or striking off individuals from the Register of Architects. The RIBA for its part may caution members, reprimand members, or suspend or withdraw membership from those who fall foul of its disciplinary process. The RIBA controls who may use the title 'chartered architect' and who may use the letters 'RIBA' after their name. Removal of these and other benefits of RIBA membership can have a serious detrimental effect on an architect's ability to practise.

In fact, if an architect is found guilty by the ARB following its disciplinary process and is suspended or erased from the Register, it is very unlikely that the RIBA would not also impose a sanction upon that individual, assuming (and it is not always the case) that the registered architect is also an RIBA member. If the ARB's Professional Conduct Committee (PCC) has imposed any sanction on an RIBA member, that member will be given the opportunity to put a 'plea of mitigation' to an RIBA appraisal team as to why they should not be similarly sanctioned by the RIBA. If the ARB dismisses a case against a member which has also been submitted to the RIBA, an RIBA appraisal team will review the complaint and the member's response, and will then make a decision as to whether the RIBA will also dismiss the case or pursue an investigation.

In practice, though, the ARB and the RIBA disciplinary processes have slightly different functions. Generally, the ARB is a client-facing body, concerned with issues of competence; the RIBA is more broadly concerned with professional integrity. The likelihood is that a complaint from a member of the public will be made through the ARB process, whereas issues arising between architects will be directed to the RIBA. If a complaint is submitted to the ARB and the RIBA at the same time, the ARB's investigation will take precedence; the RIBA will require the member concerned to respond to a letter of enquiry in order to procure evidence from both sides for possible future reference, but it will then suspend any further investigation until the ARB reaches a decision.

10.1.1   Why is the ARB disciplinary process necessary?

From a consumer protection perspective, members of the public must be allowed, without risk of incurring legal costs, to raise in a public forum issues of unacceptable professional conduct or serious professional incompetence. To retain the confidence of the clients who instruct it, the profession must allow itself to be subject to this scrutiny. It is important also that the ARB is visible in performing its role; the list of guilty verdicts concerning cases of unacceptable professional conduct and serious professional incompetence is made publicly available, on the ARB website.

10.1.2   The ARB procedure in practice

The ARB Code sets out 12 standards dealing with:

- conduct and competence;
- client service; and
- complaints.

The Architects Act 1997 ('the 1997 Act') provides that failure by an architect to comply with the provisions of the ARB Code does not in itself necessarily constitute unacceptable professional conduct or serious professional incompetence. However, such failure may be taken into consideration in any disciplinary proceedings.

The initial complaint

It is extremely easy – and has to be, from a consumer protection perspective – for a member of the public to make a complaint to the ARB. A tick box complaints form is available on the ARB website, or alternatively the complainant may send a complaint to the ARB by post, fax or e-mail. There is no cost to the complainant at any stage of the process.

The ARB is given power under the 1997 Act to investigate just two possible 'offences':

- unacceptable professional conduct; and
- serious professional incompetence.

If the actions or omissions complained of may amount to either unacceptable professional conduct or serious professional incompetence, the ARB is empowered to investigate the complaint. As part of this initial process, the ARB will send a copy of the client's complaint to the architect and ask for comments. Any reply will be sent to the complainant and further comments requested. The architect is best served by engaging with the process from the outset: don't be tempted to ignore correspondence in the hope that the matter will go away – it won't. Failure to respond to the ARB regularly appears in its own right as 'unacceptable professional conduct' on the public list of adverse PCC decisions.

10

Formulation of the Investigations Committee and the PCC

An ARB Investigations Committee – a panel of three, always comprising one architect and two lay persons – then reviews the matter. The Investigations Committee may appoint an expert to produce further information; more usually further comments and documents are requested from the client and the architect in turn, and documentary evidence is gathered in this way. The Investigations Committee, independently or following receipt of a detailed report from its independent expert, will ultimately decide whether to:

• dismiss the complaint;
• give the architect a formal written warning; or
• refer the matter to the PCC for a full public hearing.

The architect will be informed of this decision. The Investigations Committee has a non-binding commitment to reach a decision within 12 weeks of receiving the complaint.

If the Investigations Committee recommends a formal public hearing, this will take place before the PCC. The PCC is another panel of three, always comprising an architect, a solicitor (usually also the chairman) and a lay member of the public. The public hearing cannot take place until the ARB has settled its case and formally set out the grounds for complaint and how these constitute either unacceptable professional conduct or serious professional incompetence, or both. The ARB's nominated solicitor, generally a senior lawyer at a City practice, who acts for the ARB as they would for any other client, puts together a 'Report from the Board's Solicitor to the Professional Conduct Committee'. This is in effect the same as the particulars of claim in litigation, or an adjudication referral. The unfortunate impression given is that this is a report from one part of the ARB to another part containing recommendations about the architect in question, and that the architect then faces an uphill struggle to convince the PCC not to follow the recommendations in the report.

The architect's defence

Once the solicitor's report is received by the PCC a provisional date for a public hearing will be set and the architect will be notified. It is up to the architect to serve a formal defence to the PCC prior to the hearing, along with any supporting documentary evidence and witness statements, to put their side of the story. There is a degree of flexibility about the hearing date (extensions of time are not uncommon) and the timing for service of the defence – officially, a defence should be served no later than 2 weeks prior to the hearing date, but there are no prejudicial consequences if for legitimate reasons this cannot be complied with. Unofficially, it is best practice not to serve any significant new documents any later than a week prior to the hearing date.

The hearing and the decision

The hearing itself is an approximation of a court procedure; it is adversarial and temperatures can rise. The ARB's solicitor acts as prosecutor and will directly question witnesses, including the architect. The architect or their legal representative may in turn 'examine' the complainant or any of the other witnesses, for or against them. The PCC panel may, and very often does, ask its own questions directly of witnesses. At the end of the hearing, which can last for several days in cases that involve complex issues or have otherwise generated a lot of paper, both the ARB and the architect get the chance to sum up their case. Sometimes the panel is able to give a decision on the day; in other cases, where a written decision seems appropriate, it can take months. The PCC is obliged to provide a decision as soon as practicable after the hearing, but this obligation is not as strict as it may appear; the PCC itself says when the 'hearing' ends. Logically, this may be expected to be the time when everyone stops talking and leaves the hearing venue to go home and await the decision, but the PCC has indicated in previous matters that the 'hearing' only ends when the panel finishes considering the evidence.

Mitigation, penalties and appeals

Once a decision of guilty or not guilty is given by the PCC, the architect has 30 days to request a third party review to consider any complaints of a procedural nature. The independent third party cannot consider the decision itself, and this is in no way an 'appeal' process. It is questionable what any architect would hope to achieve by requesting a third party review; perhaps if there was an obvious case of bias or unfairness, clearly evidenced, this would be something worth pursuing. At the end of the third party review process, the same PCC panel that gave the original decision is asked to decide whether there is anything in the independent reviewer's report that would mean its decision should be reconsidered. This, in truth, is an unlikely scenario.

Following the decision on culpability, if the verdict is guilty, the architect will be asked to provide a plea in mitigation for the panel to consider before making a decision on the appropriate penalty. This is not an opportunity to disagree with the decision itself; rather, it is a chance for the architect to persuade the panel that the penalty should be as light as possible,

10

for example because of the architect's previous good behaviour or their willingness to learn from the mistakes highlighted in the complaint, or because the available penalties would be excessive bearing in mind the facts of the matter or the particular circumstances of the architect.

Following mitigation – and again this decision may take weeks or even several months to come through – the PCC may:

- issue the architect with a formal reprimand;
- impose a fine of up to £5,000;
- suspend the architect from the Register for up to 2 years;
- permanently remove the architect from the Register.

The PCC may impose a combination of penalties; or, in rare cases, no penalty at all.

An aggrieved architect may take a case to the High Court within 3 months of the date of the decision, if they consider that the decision made against them by the ARB PCC is unjustified. Considering the likely costs of such a process, and the slim chances of successfully showing clear bias or some other blatant procedural unfairness, this should not generally be considered.

Once an architect becomes subject to the ARB's disciplinary process the effects can be profound, whether or not the architect is ultimately found guilty of serious professional incompetence or unacceptable professional conduct. If found guilty, the damage to your reputation can be hard to live down; you will not be entitled to recover the costs of defending yourself, whatever the outcome.

The best way to manage this process is to avoid having to engage with it.

Adopt strategies to ensure that you comply with the strict requirements of the ARB Code. Invest time in risk management more generally. If a client has a complaint, do not ignore it; if you engage with a complaint and manage the client appropriately at an early stage, there is every chance of avoiding a formal complaint being put before the PCC.

10.2   Dispute resolution: an overview

The nature of dispute resolution has changed dramatically in the past 15 years, in all areas but in construction in particular. On 26 April 1999 the Civil Procedure Rules (CPR) came into force, a single set of rules governing both the High Court and county courts. The overriding objective of the CPR (Rule 1.1(1)) is to enable 'the court to deal with cases justly.' This includes (Rule 1.1(2)):

(a) ensuring that the parties are on an equal footing;

(b) saving expense;

(c) dealing with the case in ways which are proportionate –

    (i) to the amount of money involved

    (ii) to the importance of the case

    (iii) to the complexity of the issues, and

    (iv) to the financial position of each party; and

(d) ensuring that cases are dealt with expeditiously and fairly

Everything in modern dispute resolution flows from this overriding objective, whether or not the method chosen is litigation; courts actively encourage parties to negotiate and mediate, where litigation would not be the most appropriate forum.

The upshot of the significant reforms to the civil justice regime through the Civil Procedure Act 1997, and to construction dispute resolution through the 1996 Construction Act, along with a shift in attitudes within the construction industry itself – being partly pragmatic and partly a reaction to these statutory changes – is far greater choice when it comes to dispute resolution.

Alternative dispute resolution

Alternative dispute resolution (ADR) – a generic term encompassing numerous different processes that allow for disputes to be settled outside of litigation and the court system – is actively encouraged under the CPR.

The most significant ADR processes are:

- negotiation – which may be structured to avoid a formal dispute, with an independent third party proposing an agreement that the parties may accept, or not;
- mediation – which has long been encouraged by the Technology and Construction Court;
- adjudication – referral to adjudication is now a statutory right under the Construction Acts; and
- arbitration – which is an adversarial process, with quite complicated rules set out in the Arbitration Act 1996. To some extent arbitration is perceived as a variation on litigation, rather than truly 'alternative', but it shares many positive features with other forms of ADR, such as the potential for time and cost savings.

The advantages, or otherwise, of ADR largely depend upon whether the nature and quality of the decision or recommendation resulting from the

10

process is such that neither party decides to resort to litigation afterwards. ADR, even arbitration, will generally be cheaper than going through the litigation process to trial, but if the parties subsequently litigate the same dispute anyway, the costs will obviously be more than if they had simply gone to court in the first place.

ADR is usually quicker than litigation, a benefit of not being weighed down with the best part of 1,000 years'-worth of procedural law. The time and cost benefits, along with a number of other factors, also combine to make 'collaborative' ADR, such as mediation (as opposed to 'adversarial' arbitration or adjudication), less stressful for the parties involved; the process is typically less reliant on the participation of lawyers and will usually be confidential, and the parties may find it less difficult to maintain a working relationship during and at the end of the dispute.

Perhaps the one inevitability of a professional career is that it will involve differences of opinion with clients and fellow professionals from time to time and, if the circumstances allow, that some of these differences may develop into disputes. Although the range of potential resolution processes available nowadays can seem bewildering, it must be better to have realistic alternatives for solving a problem more quickly and more cheaply than would have been possible in the past. As ever, the key is not to let a problem fester, but to seek professional legal advice at an early stage and to explore the options that now exist.

Do I need a solicitor?

Here, more than in any other aspect of an architect's professional life, it is vital to take independent legal advice. However experienced an architect is, they will benefit from legal assistance to guide them through any formal dispute resolution or disciplinary process. This is a counsel of perfection and some architects will simply have no way of affording legal fees; but, unfortunately, experience shows that the results speak for themselves when professional parties try to defend themselves without legal representation.

It is almost always a false economy to risk losing a case because of an unwillingness to incur legal fees. A good lawyer can make the difference between winning and losing: they can find the persuasive argument that may otherwise have been missed; or where there is no winning argument, they can present the case in such a way as to make the fight more even. Perhaps the good lawyer's greatest skill is to be able to tell an architect client when a case is not worth fighting.

10.3 Adjudication

Adjudication is a fast, relatively affordable, but adversarial dispute resolution procedure. Within a 28-day timescale, an adjudication produces a decision that is temporarily binding on the parties and enforceable by summary judgment in court. A losing party must generally pay up first before seeking to challenge the decision of the adjudicator in court proceedings or arbitration.

10.3.1 Adjudication under the 1996 and 2009 Construction Acts

Adjudication is the process that has dominated construction dispute resolution in the UK since it was introduced 15 years ago. Part II of the Housing Grants, Construction and Regeneration Act 1996 became law on 1 May 1998, bringing with it a regime for statutory adjudication, a new interpretation of a dispute resolution procedure that had been included as a contractual right in some construction contracts for many years previously. It is not possible for the parties to a construction contract, as defined by the 1996 Act, to prevent the Act from applying to their contract.

Initial worries about adjudication – its ability to deal with all types of disputes, the possibility that its availability would increase the number of disputes, concerns about how to enforce adjudicators' decisions – have largely fallen away. The success of statutory adjudication has been phenomenal.

Do the Construction Acts apply to my contract?

The Construction Acts apply, subject to some exceptions, to 'construction contracts', defined within the 1996 Act as contracts for the carrying out of 'construction operations'. This is given a broad meaning and expressly includes consultancy appointments for architectural design and advice on building, engineering, interior or exterior decoration and landscape design.

A collateral warranty is not a contract for the carrying out of construction operations so it is not possible, in the absence of an appropriate contractual term, to refer a dispute to adjudication under a collateral warranty.

Importantly for architects, an appointment with a residential occupier concerning work or services for a dwelling house or flat is not within the scope of the Acts. Neither the payment provisions, nor the right to refer disputes to adjudication, will apply to the contractual relationship between

10

an architect and such a residential occupier unless their appointment terms expressly incorporate the Construction Acts. If, for example, an architect contracts with a residential occupier on the basis of a standard form appointment such as the RIBA Standard Conditions or the RIBA Conditions for a Domestic Project, which provide for adjudication, then this will be available to resolve disputes, and the applicable adjudication scheme will be the RIBA Adjudication Scheme for Consumer Contracts. But it is important that this possibility is explained by the architect to their client at the outset if the architect has proposed such an appointment. A court is likely to find that it is not otherwise fair to impose a binding, fast-track dispute resolution procedure (carrying a significant administrative burden) on a residential occupier who would otherwise be outside the scope of the Act.

There is an extensive list of other works which are outside the definition of construction operations, and to which the Construction Acts therefore do not apply. An architect appointed to carry out services in relation to such works will not, in the absence of an appropriate contractual term, be able to refer disputes to statutory adjudication.

The Construction Acts apply not only to construction contracts that are in writing or evidenced in writing, but also to wholly or partly oral contracts (this was a change brought in by the 2009 Act). The old requirement for contracts to be 'in writing' was interpreted in some cases quite restrictively by the courts, and criticism of the effect of these decisions led to the removal of the requirement in the 2009 Act.

10.3.2 The adjudication regime in theory …

If a construction contract does not contain Act-compliant dispute resolution provisions, the Scheme for Construction Contracts (secondary legislation created to provide a practical framework for payment and adjudication where a contract does not) will be implied into the contract by law. If a construction contract contains a single provision that is not compliant with the Construction Acts' adjudication regime then the Scheme provisions will apply in full, overriding even those parts of the contract disputes clauses that do comply with the Acts. This can be contrasted to the equivalent position when a construction contract does not contain Act-compliant payment provisions; in such a case, the relevant payment provisions of the Scheme are implied into the contract, but not in full – only to the extent necessary to fill in the gaps.

The Construction Acts give each party to a construction contract the right to refer disputes arising under the contract to adjudication at any time.

Construction contracts must:

- allow the parties to give notice *at any time* of an intention to refer a dispute to adjudication;
- provide a timetable for securing the appointment of an adjudicator and referral of the dispute to them within 7 days of the initial notice;
- require the adjudicator to reach a decision within 28 days of the referral (not the notice) or such longer period as the parties may, after the referral, agree;
- allow the adjudicator to extend the 28-day period by 14 days with the consent of the referring party (the claimant) – the responding party (the defendant) does not have a say in such an extension;
- require the adjudicator to act impartially;
- enable the adjudicator to take the initiative in ascertaining the facts and the law;
- provide that unless they act in bad faith, or in bad faith omit to act, neither the adjudicator nor their employees or agents can be liable for any of their acts or omissions during the course of the adjudication.

The Acts also require a construction contract to provide that the adjudicator's decision is binding on the parties until the dispute is finally determined by legal proceedings or arbitration; this is why adjudication is, in theory, only 'temporarily' binding. The parties may agree to accept the decision of the adjudicator as finally determining their dispute, and evidence suggests that all but a tiny percentage of adjudication decisions are, in fact, the final word on the dispute in question, save for enforcement proceedings before a court.

10.3.3   ... and in practice

Instigating an adjudication

Whether you are considering making a referral to adjudication, or having to respond to a referral, there are a number of issues that have to be considered every time.

- Can it be said that there is a genuine dispute between the parties?
- Is your appointment a construction contract for the purposes of the Acts?
- Is your agreement one of those excluded from the operation of the Acts, for example because it has been made with a residential occupier?
- Are the rules for any adjudication set out in your appointment, or does the Scheme for Construction Contracts apply?

These are fundamentals. Adjudication will not be available in all cases, such as where there is no actual dispute or if the Acts do not apply to

10

your appointment; and if adjudication is available, the details of the rules under which the adjudication must be carried out can differ depending upon the wording of your appointment. To make sure these fundaments have been properly assessed in your case, it is very important to take specialist legal advice at the earliest possible stage.

If you are on the front foot, a solicitor will work with you to assess whether adjudication is available at all, and whether it is the right option in your circumstances. For example, what if you have had an instalment of fees withheld from you? The client may have followed the correct procedure for withholding, issuing the appropriate pay less notice and setting out the basis for not paying the notified sum in full, but what if you do not agree with the substance of the client's reasons for paying less?

Adjudication should be seen as part of a process of escalation of pressure to achieve a satisfactory solution

Most architects are understandably cautious about instigating adjudication proceedings against a client, even if a solicitor has advised that adjudication may be possible. A solicitor will help you to decide whether any other options are available and whether any other steps should be taken before getting to the point where a notice of intention to refer to adjudication is issued.

If you disagree with a pay less notice, make the client aware of your dissatisfaction. You may do this informally initially, at a meeting, but you should follow up your concerns in writing. Ask for clarification. Ask the client to reconsider and provide additional information in support of your position if necessary. If you have other contacts at a higher level within the client organisation, raise the matter with them. If you have gone as far as you can commercially with your argument, to the highest level of contact you have within the client organisation, and still not achieved a satisfactory solution, a decision needs to be made. If the money withheld is important enough to you, it will be sensible to raise legal arguments, suggesting that if the client still does not agree to pay the money they have withheld, there will exist between you a dispute. Additional pressure can be applied by giving the client a deadline by which to respond one way or another. Most clients will recognise this as a threat that adjudication may be looming, but the threat could be made even more explicit if the client still refuses to compromise.

When can there be said to be a 'dispute'?

There have been a surprising number of cases concerned with when a dispute can be said to have 'crystallised', but each case turns on its own facts and it is hard to draw general principles. A common sense approach is best. Simply saying 'a dispute now exists between us' will not be conclusive. But a client cannot be certain that a dispute has not crystallised if, for example, they repeatedly request vague 'additional information' as a tactic to give the impression that negotiations are ongoing and that they have not reached a final conclusion about the claim. Courts will typically take a purposive approach, giving the word 'dispute' its ordinarily understood meaning; sometimes it will be enough that the client has refused to admit the claim, or not paid it, even though the client has requested additional information.

It may be appropriate to increase pressure by having a solicitor send a letter to the client, formally making the same points and noting that a dispute now exists between the parties. Once a dispute exists, either party may give notice of their intention to refer the dispute to adjudication at any time.

Is it worth adjudicating?

If adjudication has been explicitly threatened and the client remains unwilling to compromise, you will be faced with the choice of following through with the threat, or backing down. Will the costs involved in preparing a case for adjudication, and the costs of the adjudication itself, outweigh the sum that may potentially be recovered by adjudicating? The costs of preparing a case can be greatly reduced if your paperwork is already comprehensive and up to date. If it is not, you may need to spend significant sums just to get to the stage where you have sufficient material to put a convincing case before an adjudicator. It is often sensible, when all the work has been done to make a convincing case, to issue this to the client in a final notice before the notice to refer to adjudication, rather than ambushing the client, to give them a final chance to compromise before both parties incur the costs of an adjudication.

Another important factor to consider is the likely damage that will be done to the client relationship by adjudication. A non-confrontational procedure, such as mediation, may be a viable alternative; will a confrontational procedure achieve the best result? There is no guarantee of success in adjudication. The most sensible approach, before deciding to adjudicate, is to gradually escalate the dispute, through commercial and legal channels, and to consider at each stage the viability of making a referral.

The course of an adjudication

If a dispute exists under a construction contract, notice of intention to refer the dispute to adjudication may be made at any time. A referral notice

10

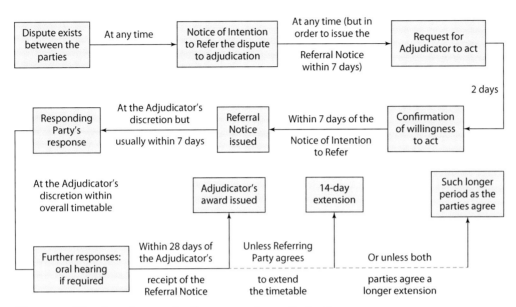

Figure 11 Timeline diagram for the course of an adjudication

must follow within 7 days, and the decision will follow within 28 days of the referral notice (Figure 11). This can mean that the referring party has taken many months to prepare its case, but the time for the adjudicator to deliver their decision will generally still only be 28 days after the date of the referral notice.

Since the 1996 Act first came into force, there have been concerns about the potential for referring parties to 'ambush' responding parties, swamping them with technical and legal argument that must be dealt with comprehensively in a formal response within a matter of days. The responding party cannot unilaterally extend the timetable for the adjudication, so the potential for ambush remains a real risk.

There can be no restriction on the right to give notice of intention to refer. It is even possible for a party to adjudicate a matter after it has issued proceedings in court concerning the same claim, although there has been one case (*Phoenix Contracts v Central Building Contractors*) in which a court decided that there could be exceptions to the statutory right and held that the referring party had waived its right to adjudicate because legal proceedings covering the same matter had reached an advanced stage. This is an exceptional decision, and seems unlikely to be followed in the light of previous judgments which have established that courts have jurisdiction to stay (prevent) court proceedings when a party exercises its right to adjudicate. Parties should work on the basis that if there is a statutory right, and there is a dispute, a notice of intention to refer to adjudication is possible at any time.

Appointment and referral

The Construction Acts contemplate the appointment of an adjudicator and referral of the dispute to them within 7 days of the adjudication notice. The parties may agree the identity of the adjudicator at this stage, or the adjudicator may have been named in the appointment. Often, the appointment will provide for an adjudication notice to be sent to an adjudicator nominating body – the Royal Institute of British Architects is one such nominating body. Raising spurious objections to the identity of the adjudicator is rarely a successful delaying tactic for the responding party; most adjudicators take a robust approach and will rarely reject an appointment in the absence of a compelling argument why they personally should not take the matter on.

There are various standard form terms of agreement for the appointment of an adjudicator, but many adjudicators also have their own standard terms. Either way, the adjudicator will want both parties to agree the terms of their appointment at the outset of an adjudication. That said, an adjudicator will generally never allow the timetable to slip because one party (usually the responding party expressing displeasure with the process) has not signed their appointment. The adjudicator will generally want at least one party to actually agree in writing to payment of their fees and expenses before proceeding, and it is obviously in the interests of the referring party to do this. The underlying contract or appointment will usually make both referring party and responding party 'jointly and severally' liable for the adjudicator's fees. This means that the adjudicator may recover the whole of their fees and expenses from either party; if one party refuses to pay their share, the paying party is left to take further legal action to recover a contribution from the non-paying party.

The referral notice must be limited in scope to the dispute identified in the original adjudication notice, but should contain all the relevant details, evidence, witness statements and copies of contractual documentation that the referring party needs to rely upon to make its case. Here is where the concern over 'ambush' of the responding party originates; only one dispute may be referred in any one adjudication, but the referral may be a lengthy document in itself, setting out many heads of claim within the single dispute, and the accompanying documentation can often amount to several lever arch files.

Once the adjudicator receives the referral, they will give directions for the future conduct of the adjudication, including timing for delivery of the response to the referral and any other rounds of communication that may be allowed. The adjudicator will typically allow communication by e-mail, for speed, but it is good practice to follow up e-mailed documents with copies by fax or post. The adjudicator will very often require the response to be served within a very short period; this puts the responding party at a disadvantage if the referral notice documentation is particularly bulky or contains a good deal of material that the responding party has not seen before.

The response and further replies

The various sets of available adjudication rules (as well as the Scheme for Construction Contracts, a number of construction industry bodies have produced Act-compliant standard rules, and there also exist amended and bespoke versions) provide for the adjudicator to dictate the timetable within the 28-day adjudication period; that includes setting a date for the defendant to serve their response to the referral notice. Often the timing will be tight, with a response required by the adjudicator within 7 days of the referral notice. In extreme cases, this can raise issues of natural justice, if it can be argued that the defendant is being denied a fair chance to construct their defence.

In the case of *CJP Builders v Verry* the adjudicator misdirected himself when approached by the defendant who sought an extension of time for serving their response to the referral notice. The applicable rules in that case would have allowed the adjudicator to grant the extension requested without reference to the referring party, but the adjudicator decided he had no discretion to grant the responding party's extension without the referring party's agreement.

The referring party agreed only to a shorter extension of time, and the responding party just failed to serve their response in time. The adjudicator refused to consider the response, and subsequently made an award in favour of the referring party. The court decided that the adjudicator had breached the rules of natural justice by effectively denying the defendant's right to be heard, and as a result his decision was unenforceable. This result may give encouragement to parties seeking extensions of time within the adjudication timetable, although an extension cannot be allowed to interfere with the delivery by the adjudicator of their decision.

Contents of the response and the responding party's tactics

The defendant's response should address fully all of the arguments raised by the referring party, and should contain all the material the defendant needs to rely upon to show that the referring party's claim should not succeed. It is not wise for the defendant to refuse to take part in the adjudication, even if they consider the claim to be obviously invalid.

Any challenges to the fundamentals of the process, most usually to the adjudicator's jurisdiction, should be made early and repeated as necessary throughout the course of the adjudication.

The best course of action for the defendant is to produce a substantive response to the claim as well as raising any possible jurisdictional issues. The defendant should participate in the process, but reserve their position in relation to the jurisdictional issues; this will allow them to raise the same arguments about the adjudicator's lack of jurisdiction in response to any proceedings brought by the referring party to enforce a decision in their favour. There is always a possibility, too, if the responding party raises a valid jurisdictional argument early on in the process, that the adjudicator will in fact decide that they are not able to continue to deal with the matter, and all parties could be saved a good deal of time and money.

Further replies and the likelihood of a hearing

The adjudicator is likely to allow the referring party a reply, and may grudgingly allow further replies if the parties can demonstrate that there is something new that needs to be replied to in the interests of justice. The adjudicator may direct that an oral hearing should be held, particularly if there is a factual dispute (rather than one involving the interpretation of documents) at the heart of the adjudication, and especially if a number of witness statements have been served with the referral and the response – the adjudicator may well be interested to see how well the various witnesses come across in person. At some stage the adjudicator may also seek specific responses from both parties to particular questions – these may be issued in a list and may give a hint as to the adjudicator's thinking about the matter as a whole.

The adjudicator's decision

There is no prescribed form for an adjudicator's decision. The Scheme requires that it should be given in writing, and it is sensible to request that the adjudicator gives reasons in their decision. Decisions delivered outside the 28-day period (or such longer period as may have been validly agreed) are very likely to be unenforceable if the losing party takes the point during enforcement proceedings.

10.3.4 **Enforcement, and resisting enforcement, of an adjudicator's decision**

If the losing party does not voluntarily comply with the decision, an adjudicator's award may be enforced through the courts by summary judgment. This is a fast-track litigation procedure, based on the claimant's application notice (accompanied by a supporting statement) appropriate

10

for cases where the court considers that the defendant has no real prospect of successfully defending the claim. A short hearing is involved; the court will give summary judgment if there is no other compelling reason why a full trial should be held.

In theory, the losing party is in a position where, even if they disagree with the award, they must pay up first and argue about the detail later, by bringing their own case to court to re-argue the points unfavourably dealt with by the adjudicator. In practice, losing parties often seek to avoid paying up by challenging the validity of the decision during the winning party's enforcement proceedings; even so, as will be seen below, the courts remain extremely reluctant to refuse to enforce an adjudicator's award in all but the most extreme cases.

The approach of the courts to enforcement

In order to give effect to the intention of Parliament and create a regime under the Construction Acts where an aggrieved party could take action quickly and cheaply to recover money owed to it, the courts have tended to take an extremely robust approach towards the enforcement of adjudication decisions. All other things being equal, as long as the adjudicator has provided a decision within the statutory timescale that provides an answer to the issues raised in the notice of adjudication, a court will enforce the adjudicator's decision. This remains the case even where the decision is patently incorrect, in law, procedure or fact. This principle was set out in the very first statutory adjudication case that came to court, *Macob Civil Engineering v Morrison Construction Ltd.*

If the adjudicator gives the wrong answer to the right question, there is generally nothing that the losing party can do to prevent enforcement. This can work in favour of architects who, along with contractors and sub-contractors, appear far more regularly as the referring party in adjudications than as the responding party.

Can a losing party ever successfully challenge enforcement?

If the winning party is in financial difficulties and it is arguably unlikely that the losing party will be able to recover their money later through court proceedings, this will not automatically make any difference – the loser must still pay. Courts have indicated that they will enforce an adjudicator's decision even in favour of a party who has entered into a company voluntary agreement – a binding agreement made between a company with severe financial problems and its creditors, setting out the amounts to be repaid by the debtor company. This might at first glance seem unfair to the paying party, but the courts are looking to protect the position of a winning party whose financial problems may have resulted from the paying party's original failure to pay fees due, in breach of contract.

Successful challenges are possible, generally on two grounds only:

- a lack of jurisdiction to make the decision, on the part of the adjudicator; or
- a breach of natural justice;

but the courts have set the thresholds extremely high, particularly in relation to breaches of natural justice; even the most blatant errors in procedure have not prevented enforcement of a decision that gives an answer to the issues contained in the adjudication notice. A rare example of a successful challenge on the basis of a breach of natural justice is the *CJP Builders v Verry* case, mentioned above, where the losing party was denied the opportunity to have their defence heard because of a procedural error by the adjudicator. Recent cases have also seen defences to enforcement proceedings on the basis that the adjudicators' decisions had been obtained by fraud; these arguments have not been entirely successful, and the threshold for proving fraud in these circumstances is again extremely high.

Adjudicators cannot (in contrast to arbitrators, for example) give a binding decision on their own jurisdiction, and jurisdictional challenges have been a constant feature of defences to enforcement proceedings since the 1996 Act first came into force. An aggrieved party may claim, for example, that the adjudicator's appointment is in some way defective; that the adjudicator has answered a question not referred to them; that there was no actual 'dispute'; or that there was no written contract, or at least not a construction contract for the purposes of the Acts.

The High Court and Court of Appeal have repeatedly taken a dim view of losing parties, as they see it:

> simply scrabbling around to find some argument, however tenuous, to resist payment

(this quote is taken from the judgment in *Carillion v Devonport Royal Dockyard*). For the most part the courts will, even in cases where they recognise that a technicality could invalidate an adjudicator's decision, find that the technical or theoretical breach did not, on the specific facts of the case, take place.

In summary, the 'pay now, argue later' principle, which Parliament intended to enshrine in the adjudication provisions of the 1996 Act, is

10

working well with the support of the courts. This suits architects, and is to the disadvantage of the paying party on any appointment to which the Construction Acts apply. Even if in a particular case there has been a breach of natural justice or a lack of jurisdiction, a court will continue to do its utmost to enforce any 'unaffected' part of the adjudicator's decision by severing out the unenforceable elements, as for example in the case of *Cantillon v Urvasco Limited*.

10.3.5 Ongoing issues for architects with statutory adjudication

Adjudication, if available under the appointment, is a useful tool for an architect. The possibility of an adjudication will help to concentrate the mind of a client who would otherwise not think twice before withholding fees. But although adjudication is relatively inexpensive (certainly compared with litigation, at least in former times) costs are still an issue. It is very hard for the referring party to frame their adjudication notice so narrowly that the responding party is severely restricted in terms of the material they may include in their response – the courts take a liberal approach to the material a responding party can introduce anyway – and the more complicated the adjudication becomes, the more expensive it will inevitably become. As well as increasing the cost, a failure to prepare for an adjudication with a wide scope can damage the referring party's chances of success.

The main problem is that, in contrast to litigation for example, statutory adjudication does not provide a mechanism for the recovery by the winning party of their costs. As a result, it is rarely commercially viable for a party to pursue adjudication, even if there is a very good chance of the claim being successful, for sums less than £10,000 to £15,000. Towards the end of a project an unscrupulous client may be encouraged to withhold relatively small sums, a few thousand here and there, without justification whilst remembering to serve the appropriate notices, safe in the knowledge that the architect will have limited options for recovery of these sums. Commencing an action in the small claims track of the county court may be an option to recover sums less than £5,000, but in reality if the client raises a plausible defence involving more than minor legal argument, the case is unlikely to remain on the small claims track and legal costs may escalate to a point where continuing the claim becomes economically unviable. The problem of recovery of costs was not, unfortunately, addressed by the 2009 Act.

One final point for the architect to bear in mind – it is never appropriate to take conduct of an adjudication on behalf of a client, or to agree as an additional service to draft or review an adjudication response or any other adjudication 'pleadings'. Client requests to do so should be politely refused; these are specialist legal tasks. Assistance with claims can be provided, as an additional service and for an additional fee, but should be limited to commenting on matters of fact or technical issues directly relating to the architect's own services.

10.3.6 Adjudication after the 2009 Construction Act

Contracts in writing

Following the coming into force of the 2009 Act on 1 October 2011, perhaps the most important change was the removal of the requirement for a construction contract to be in writing, or evidenced in writing, as a pre-condition for the availability of statutory adjudication. The 2009 Act repealed the equivalent section in the 1996 Act in full, allowing for parties to refer disputes under any construction contract, as defined by the Acts, regardless of whether the contract is wholly oral, partly oral, subject to variation orally, or even formed entirely on the basis of the conduct of the parties.

This should be a positive change. A disproportionate number of jurisdictional challenges in relation to adjudications under the 1996 Act were made on the basis that the adjudicator should not have accepted the referral because there was no written contract. Also, the requirement within the 1996 Act for a construction contract to be in writing was often interpreted restrictively by the courts, raising the question of whether parties were being denied justice under the 1996 Act regime in a way that arguably was not intended by Parliament when it framed the Act.

The 2009 Act regime potentially raises its own concerns, unfortunately. If there is no need for any contractual terms to be in writing, there is every chance that adjudications will become more focused on what exactly the contract terms are – a task that is not best suited to a summary procedure such as adjudication. The inevitable need for an adjudicator to hear oral evidence, about who agreed which contractual terms, may be expected to increase the costs of the average adjudication. The need for oral evidence may also possibly delay the process, even though the fundamental requirement for a decision within 28 days of the referral was unchanged in the 2009 Act. Another reasonable criticism is that the incentive for agreeing written contract terms – surely best practice – has been undermined.

Supporters of the 2009 Act would make the point that extending the scope of statutory adjudication to cover fully oral contracts is simply a

10

recognition of reality; by no means all parties have the time or inclination to agree written terms, and they should not be denied justice.

Even after the 2009 Act came into force, Act-compliant terms setting out the adjudication procedure need to be included in the contract and these need to be in writing; if they are not (as would inevitably be the case with any purely oral contract) the Scheme will apply. This requirement was retained in the 2009 Act to avoid any purely procedural disputes arising.

Other changes

The 2009 Act brought two other important changes to the statutory adjudication regime. The first was the formalisation of the ability of the adjudicator to correct their decision so as to remove any clerical or typographical errors arising by accident or omission. This so called 'slip rule' was assumed to be available to adjudicators anyway, following the case of *Bloor Construction (UK) Ltd v Bowmer & Kirkland (London) Ltd*, but the 2009 Act removes any doubt about the legitimacy of this procedure. The time allowed for correcting slips may be assumed (this is not set out expressly in the 2009 Act) to be a 'reasonable' period following delivery of the adjudicator's decision, but this does beg the question, what period is reasonable? There may also be challenges to decisions based on the scope of the corrections that an adjudicator may have made, or refused to make. It seems likely that some parties will try to exploit the slip rule to seek 'corrections' of fundamental decisions of fact or law, or it may be argued by a losing party that the adjudicator has exceeded their jurisdiction in correcting a slip.

The last important change brought in by the 2009 Act was the long overdue prohibition of contract provisions making one party (usually the referring party) solely responsible for the costs of any adjudication; these clauses became known as 'Tolent clauses', after the case which first highlighted the problem. Such provisions were always an unfair disincentive, effectively a fetter on a party's right to refer disputes to adjudication at any time, and at odds with the spirit of the original Act. This has been recognised by the courts already – in *Yuanda (UK) Ltd v WW Gear Construction Ltd* the court decided that such a provision was in conflict with the 1996 Act – so Parliament was right to formalise the law on this point. Because architects are far more often the referring party than the responding party in adjudications, they benefit from this change, along with other professional consultants and specialist sub-contractors.

A number of commentators have pointed out that, unfortunately, the wording of the 2009 Act in this respect is arguably not sufficiently clear to achieve the objective of outlawing Tolent clauses and it is likely that true clarification will only come once a case on this aspect of the 2009 Act comes before a court. Interestingly, the court in *Profile Projects Ltd v Elmwood*, a 2011 Scottish case based on the 1996 Act regime, decided not to follow the *Yuanda* decision and found that Tolent clauses were not prohibited by the 1996 Act. The *Profile Projects* decision seems partly to be based on the logic that 'The 2009 Act seeks to outlaw Tolent clauses, so the 1996 Act must have allowed them'. If that is indicative of how courts will view the 2009 Act then it will have achieved its aim of prohibiting Tolent clauses, however ambiguous its wording may be.

10.4 Arbitration

The parties to a commercial contract may choose to have disputes resolved by arbitration, as an alternative to litigation. Arbitration is an adversarial process which produces a binding award that may be enforced by the winning party upon application to a court. There are very limited grounds on which an award may be appealed against or set aside. The arbitration process mirrors to an extent the other available adversarial procedures (litigation and adjudication).

1. There is an initial notice.
2. The parties state their cases and disclose the evidence on which they intend to rely.
3. There is a hearing of the case.
4. The arbitrator makes an award.

Arbitration in England and Wales, including procedural aspects, is governed by the Arbitration Act 1996 ('the AA 1996').

An arbitration can only take place between two parties if they have agreed to it; the right to arbitrate, the identity of the arbitrator, and the procedure to be followed during the arbitration are all in the hands of the parties. Under a construction contract, the dispute resolution procedures available by default are adjudication and litigation. The parties have to make a positive decision to choose arbitration as a possibility.

Architects should always seek legal advice before instigating or responding to arbitral proceedings, or in relation to any other involvement in the process, for example as a witness.

10.4.1 Why choose arbitration?

Arbitration is a sensible choice in a project with an international dimension. Sometimes there may be doubts about the standard of the

10

local legal system, in which case the ability to refer disputes to trusted, independent and experienced international arbitrators is reassuring. If one of the parties to the contract is based overseas there is also an advantage – surprisingly, in a foreign country it can be far easier to enforce an arbitrator's award than the judgment of an English court. To date, 144 of the 192 states recognised by the United Nations are signatories to the 1958 New York Convention on the enforcement of foreign arbitral awards.

10.4.2 Positive features of arbitration

The AA 1996 gives arbitrators a good degree of freedom to be flexible about the procedure to be adopted in any given arbitration, and used creatively an arbitrator has the ability, through the AA 1996, to deliver high-quality justice quickly and cheaply, without an over-emphasis on procedural issues. It is questionable whether the current crop of arbitrators are making the most of the opportunities provided by the AA 1996 to provide such a service, and for domestic projects, adjudication and litigation remain the default choices.

The approach of the parties, and the choice of arbitrator, are crucial. The arbitrator has greater flexibility over the procedure to be followed than either the adjudicator in adjudication or the judge in litigation. Whether the parties to a contract receive the potential advantages of the arbitration process is to a large degree dependent upon their behaviour, and on the performance of the arbitrator.

Of prime importance to most participants in the process are quality, time and cost. The parties to an arbitration are free to choose their own arbitrator, so the arbitrator may be selected because of a specific technical expertise which is relevant to the case, going some way to ensuring a better quality of decision. The time taken over the decision-making process can enhance quality too, certainly in comparison with adjudication, which is acknowledged to be a 'rough and ready' procedure.

Generally, the arbitration process will be longer than an adjudication, in theory allowing for an enhanced quality of justice; but arbitration is usually a quicker process than litigation because the procedural rules are less prescriptive and the parties and the arbitrator are largely free to decide what the procedure will be and what the timescale will be. There is nothing in the AA 1996 that would prevent an arbitration from being conducted within the 28-day time period of an adjudication, or indeed any shorter period. The quicker the process is, the less it is likely to cost, and arbitration typically strikes a middle ground between adjudication and litigation in terms of the overall cost.

One other aspect of arbitration that helps to reduce costs is that in most cases the parties will only produce as evidence the documents on which they intend to rely; contrast this with the 'disclosure' process in litigation, where the parties are obliged to provide huge numbers of documents, both favourable and unfavourable to their cases, at an early stage in the process. The legal fees incurred by lawyers in obtaining and reviewing disclosed documents during litigation can be huge.

The arbitrator has the power to award costs as part of their final decision. The general rule is that the loser pays, unless there is evidence as to why the costs should be allocated differently; for example, if the loser made a realistic offer to settle earlier in the process that was rejected by the winning party.

Arbitration is a private process, and the proceedings are confidential. If parties are keen to avoid damaging public revelations, arbitration offers this benefit, but this is an advantage shared by all procedures other than litigation. Finally, the parties may be keen to have a 'once and for all' decision made about their dispute, and arbitration allows the parties to agree that any right of appeal is waived. This is really only an advantage if you get the right decision.

10.4.3 Disadvantages of arbitration

A perception of arbitration is that it is probably best suited to complex, high-profile, high-value disputes with an international dimension – where ensuring a high-quality final decision, privacy and ease of enforcement are the most serious issues. Yet one of the major disadvantages of arbitration is that the arbitrator has no power to order that other parties should be 'joined' into the original dispute if they have connected disputes with one of the original parties. It is by no means uncommon for multiple parties to be involved in high-value construction disputes, and arbitration is not set up to deal with that possibility, potentially leading to several overlapping arbitrations taking place at the same time, with the potential for increased costs and inconsistent decisions.

Other disadvantages of arbitration are the flipsides of the potential advantages. The procedural rules can be applied flexibly, but the arbitrator does not have the same powers as a court to insist on compliance with the rules and deadlines they set out. The arbitrator may be a specialist in the particular technical areas with which the case is concerned; but if the case turns on a legal issue, the parties would have been better served by a judge. Timing, and consequently costs, are not necessarily going to be an improvement on litigation if the parties do not co-operate and the arbitrator is not sufficiently strong.

10

The parties to an arbitration must also bear in mind one significant cost that is never an issue in litigation – the arbitrator's own fees, which may be considerable. The parties will still be paying legal costs in the same way as they would in an adjudication or litigation.

Finally, what of the quality of the decision? The disclosure process in litigation is often very expensive, but the advantage is that a party cannot easily hide documents that are damaging to its case. The absence of full disclosure could easily mean the difference between winning and losing a case.

It is arguable that the AA 1996, while providing a great deal of procedural flexibility, is simply not prescriptive enough. The stakes involved in the sort of technically complex, high-value cases that would otherwise be suitable for arbitration are too high for many parties to feel comfortable with accepting the relative uncertainty of the arbitration process.

10.5 Litigation

10.5.1 Why choose to litigate?

Litigation is an adversarial dispute resolution process involving a trial that is open to the public and leading to the judgment of a court. Parties may choose to negotiate or mediate, or there may be a referral to adjudication, but in the background will usually be the potential for litigation to finally decide a dispute; parties would need a particular reason to choose arbitration as the fallback position rather than litigation. Even so, it is far more rare for a dispute to be the subject of litigation than, say, adjudication.

The procedure adopted in litigation is decided by the judge on the basis of their application of the Civil Procedure Rules (CPR). The judgment is final and binding, subject to a right of appeal to a higher court. Parties who choose litigation can expect a high quality of justice delivered by judges of the Technology and Construction Court (TCC), who are among the very best in the world; but it is also well known that litigation can involve costs out of all proportion to the sums in dispute and may take years to reach a conclusion.

Whether as claimant, defendant or witness, you should never engage in the litigation process before seeking legal advice. Some disputes, if particularly high value or legally complex, may seem obvious candidates for litigation rather than, for example, adjudication. But generally litigation is best viewed as the last option for a dispute that cannot be settled in another way. There is no construction dispute whose subject matter would be too complex for the TCC; but choosing to litigate a low-value dispute is not wise. The court may decide that a party who proceeds with litigation when other, cheaper alternatives may have been more appropriate should be unable to recover its legal costs in full, even if successful.

10.5.2 How does litigation work in practice?

In construction disputes, before an action can be commenced in court, the parties are obliged by the CPR to comply with the Pre-Action Protocol for Construction and Engineering Disputes ('the Protocol') (Figure 12). Parties who fail to comply with the Protocol and launch straight into litigation are likely to be punished in costs by the court if the matter proceeds to trial. The Protocol applies to all construction disputes, specifically including 'professional negligence claims against architects' (Protocol paragraph 1.1). Some actions are exempt from the application of the Protocol, for example actions to enforce an adjudicator's decision.

The Protocol sets out a mechanism for the parties to provide information about their respective cases that is as full as possible, as soon as possible. The idea is to save the parties' costs; with early access to all the relevant information, parties are in a better position to assess the strength of their own cases and decide whether it is worth carrying on with the fight, and in this way it is hoped that many cases will settle early. Unfortunately, the side effect of compliance with the Protocol is that parties are obliged to spend significant sums of money right at the start of the litigation process to develop their cases.

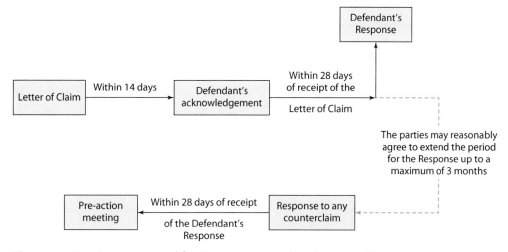

Figure 12 Pre-Action Protocol for Construction and Engineering Disputes

Building your case

During this initial phase and throughout, you should work closely with your solicitors. Do not be tempted to hold information back; there is nothing to be gained by giving the false impression, to your own legal advisors, that your case is stronger than it really is. Adopting such an approach is likely to lead to significant sums of money being wasted in the long term.

There will generally be a good deal of correspondence before a claim begins to become formalised, but the first Protocol requirement is that the claimant sends a letter of claim, setting out a brief summary of its claim and in broad terms what it is seeking – usually damages. The defendant is given a set time to respond with a letter detailing its own position, and following this exchange the Protocol timetable provides for a pre-action meeting to narrow the issues. At this stage, paragraph 5.4 of the Protocol explicitly requires the parties to:

> consider whether some form of alternative dispute resolution procedure would be more suitable than litigation.

Commencement of the action, through to trial

An action is said to be 'commenced' (for the purpose of statutory or contractual limitation periods on bringing actions) when the claimant issues a claim form in the court. The claim form is then served on the defendant, along with a document setting out the particulars of the claim, within a period set by the CPR. After this, the defendant will file an acknowledgement of service, and then a formal defence to the claim, along with any counterclaim it may wish to make. Parties will typically be advised at this stage, if not before, that it is necessary to engage a barrister ('counsel') to advise on the content of the documents lodged with the court; it will be counsel's role to present their party's case before the court at trial and in the various pre-trial hearings, such as the case management conference discussed below.

A judge will have been assigned to the case at the outset and at this point the judge will require a case management conference – a short hearing in court – to settle the timing and procedure of the case up to trial. The judge issues directions to the parties covering such issues as the disclosure of relevant documents, exchange of witness statements, the preparation of the bundle of papers to be used and referred to in court during the trial, and the date of the trial itself. Prior to trial the judge will require a pre-trial review hearing and, if no settlement can be reached, the case proceeds to trial on the appointed day or days, followed by the judgment of the court.

The vast majority of cases settle before this point. Legal fees for solicitors and counsel over the course of a trial can be very significant.

10.5.3   How litigation is changing to reduce costs

The overriding objective of litigation under the CPR is to deal with cases justly, and that requires 'proportionality' – the costs involved in litigation must be proportionate to the value of the case to the parties. But it is surprising how often litigation seems to take on a life of its own and parties seem unable to break out of the process. A solicitor should always be able to advise you if you are in danger of throwing good money after bad. If a solicitor advises compromise or settlement, this advice should be taken at face value – it is a matter of professional competence for a solicitor not to encourage a client to waste money by pursuing a cause with only a slim chance of success.

Even with the support of good legal advice, litigation can be a painful and unpredictable process and, bearing in mind the financial costs and management time involved, is best avoided if at all possible. The Jackson Report (*Review of Civil Litigation Costs: Final Report*, 14 January 2010) proposed changes to the system to better limit the costs of litigation. It is clear the courts are concerned that some parties are prevented from seeking justice (or from properly defending themselves) because of the continuing and well-rehearsed criticisms of civil litigation – the procedures are too complex, the process takes too long, litigation is consequently too expensive, and as a result is financially too risky for the participants. The Jackson Report is aimed at promoting access to justice, because parties, particularly in the construction industry, are increasingly looking to alternative means to resolve disputes. In practice this means adjudication, which, although intended to be only temporarily binding, is in the vast majority of cases the last word on the dispute. Parties do not relish the prospect of fighting their case again in court if they have lost an adjudication.

The Government agreed to implement the vast majority of the reforms proposed in the Jackson Report, and most of the relevant provisions came into force on 1 April 2013. Still for most cases for most architects, litigation is not the most appropriate option, even if it is commercially viable at all.

10.6   Mediation

The most popular and effective dispute resolution mechanism is negotiation. The term 'mediation' covers a broad range of approaches, but at its most fundamental level mediation is simply negotiation conducted through, and given structure by, an independent third party. Mediation is a consensual process, not a confrontational or adversarial process like litigation, adjudication or arbitration. The outcome is largely down to the parties; no binding award can be imposed on them without their consent. However, if the parties agree that the mediation settlement is to be framed as a contract, it may be enforced through legal proceedings in just the same way as any other binding contract. Only at this point does the process become binding upon the parties.

Mediation had been available as an option in this country since 1990 and the arrival in London of the Centre for Effective Dispute Resolution (CEDR), but its popularity has steadily increased since it became officially part of the litigation process when the CPR came into force in 1999. If the parties to a contract take their dispute to court, the court will almost always encourage them to make a genuine attempt to settle their differences through mediation; a party is likely to suffer costs consequences at the hands of the court if they fail for no good reason to engage with some form of alternative dispute resolution process and simply ploughs ahead with litigation. In this sense mediation is less 'voluntary' than it used to be.

Many other parties elect to mediate even without this encouragement, in an effort to preserve working relations in spite of the dispute, and avoid resorting to a confrontational dispute resolution procedure. Most standard form contracts provide for mediation as an option, rather than as something that must be pursued. The RIBA Standard Conditions provide in clause 9.1 that the parties may attempt to settle any dispute or difference 'by negotiation or mediation, if suitable'. Any construction dispute, however complex, may potentially be suitable for resolution through mediation if the parties are willing to make the process work. More detailed information about the mediation process and tactics for a successful mediation can be found in the RIBA's *Good Practice Guide: Mediation* (2009).

10.6.1 How does mediation work?

The mediator's role will vary according to the requirements of the parties. In some cases they are required only to give structure to the discussions; in other cases they are required to give their opinion on the merits, either of the case as a whole or some particular aspect or aspects of it.

Mediation is private and confidential, and will always be conducted on a 'without prejudice' basis – meaning that if the mediation fails, details (such as any offers to settle, or other concessions or admissions) cannot be released to any subsequent tribunal, be it a court, arbitrator or adjudicator. The parties will need to have agreed to mediate before it can happen; the details of how the mediation will be conducted and who will act as mediator can be hard-fought negotiations in themselves.

Once the details are agreed, a formal mediation agreement (made between the parties and the mediator) is usual, providing among other things for confidentiality and preventing the parties from calling the mediator as a witness in any future proceedings. The process is then relatively quick and cheap. To be effective, the parties should prepare thoroughly, and parties should generally be accompanied at the mediation by their legal representatives, but there are important cost savings to be made if the mediation produces a settlement and the parties avoid having to engage in a confrontational dispute resolution procedure. The parties' working relationship may also be preserved.

When is the right time to mediate?

There is a balance to be struck. The sooner the parties submit to mediation, the greater are the potential cost savings; but if the parties have not developed their cases thoroughly enough before mediating, the effectiveness of the mediation will be limited. The parties will not have a sufficiently strong grasp of the strengths and weaknesses of their cases to know when a good settlement is being proposed.

Prior to the mediation, it is common for the mediator to ask for written statements of the parties' respective positions, along with key documents, to enable the mediator to understand the background to the dispute. On the day, or days, of the mediation, there may be an initial meeting of the parties and mediator together, during which the parties state their cases and the mediator looks for areas of compromise. The open-session format may continue, or the parties may break out into separate rooms and conduct the mediation through the mediator carrying out 'shuttle diplomacy'; in such circumstances, the mediator will only be allowed to pass on to one party information given to them in confidence by the other if they are specifically given permission to do so. The skill of the mediator is to focus the thinking of the parties and suggest areas for compromise.

10.6.2 **Advantages of mediation**

Speed and cost efficiency are the two main advantages of a successful mediation; mediations normally last no longer than 2 to 3 days. There is also evidence (in *The Fourth Mediation Audit* by CEDR, 11 May 2010) to suggest that the settlement rate is very high, with up to 75% of cases

10

settling 'on the day' and a further 14% settling shortly afterwards. There is, though, word-of-mouth evidence to suggest that as the number of mediations overall has increased, the settlement rate has been decreasing.

Is there still an advantage in mediating, even if a settlement is not achieved? It is hard to argue against the logic of taking a chance on mediation, notwithstanding the additional cost, because the benefits if successful are potentially so great. Particularly if a court has suggested that the parties attempt mediation, there is no advantage in refusing to try. And even if a settlement is not reached, it is likely that the mediation process will have focused the thinking of the parties on the most important areas of difference between them and will in all likelihood save costs and lead to a settlement sooner than may otherwise have been the case.

10.6.3 Disadvantages of mediation

As mediation becomes part of the normal litigation process in every case, it is likely that there will be an increasing number of unwilling parties to mediations, which seems likely to affect the success rate and also lead to more (and more creative) legal challenges to mediation agreements. Such challenges may serve to undermine some of the basic principles of mediation, for example confidentiality. In the case of *Farm Assist v DEFRA* the court made clear that what parties do or say in a mediation will not necessarily remain confidential if it is 'in the interests of justice' for a court to be told the details.

One further issue is the additional cost of an unsuccessful mediation. This may not be a huge amount in the grand scheme of complex litigation that goes to a full trial; but if it is obvious that one or other party is unwilling to compromise and is simply going through the motions, the money spent on mediating is being thrown away. Compromise is always a necessary element of a mediation settlement. This presents another potential disadvantage – a party with a very strong case may be presented with a settlement that is below their level of expectations, and feel compelled to agree it rather than risk incurring further legal costs by taking their case through an adversarial dispute resolution process. There is no guarantee that reasonableness will be rewarded; the success or otherwise of a mediation is largely dependent on the attitude of the parties.

Table of cases

Table of legislation

Glossary

ADR: alternative dispute resolution – a term used for any type of dispute resolution procedure other than litigation through the court system. Examples include arbitration, adjudication and mediation.

Assignee: a party to whom the benefit of a contract is assigned.

Assignment: the transfer of the benefit of a contract to a new beneficiary. In the absence of any restriction in the contract, the benefit may be assigned by agreement between the current beneficiary and the incoming beneficiary without reference to the party performing the obligations. In order for a legal assignment to be fully effective, notice in writing must be given to the party performing the obligations under the contract. Only the benefit of a contract can be assigned in this way, not the burden; the transfer of the burden of a contract is only possible through novation.

Assignor: a party who assigns the benefit of their contract.

Beneficiary: the party having the benefit of a particular contract. The term is often used to mean the party having the benefit of a collateral warranty.

Benefit: in the context of a contract, the benefit is the right to require performance by the other party. So for an architect, the benefit is essentially the right to enforce the client's payment obligations; for the client, the benefit is the right to require the architect to provide the agreed services.

Building contract: the legal agreement between the employer and the contractor setting out their respective rights and obligations. To avoid confusion, it is good practice to refer to this document as the 'building contract' or 'main contract', rather than simply 'the contract'.

Burden: in the context of a contract, the burden includes all of the obligations that must be performed for the other party; for example, the client's obligation to pay the architect's fees, or the architect's obligation to carry out the services.

Claimant: in a civil legal action, such as an action to recover damages for breach of contract or negligence, the claimant is the party making the claim and asking the court to make an award in their favour.

Condition precedent: in a contract, a condition precedent is something which must be done by a party in order for another entitlement to be activated. So, for example, a bespoke professional appointment may say that it is a condition precedent to payment that collateral warranties are provided when requested.

Contemporaneous: happening at the same time as something else. For example, it is good practice for an architect to make a contemporaneous note of any client meetings.

Contract: an agreement recognised by law as creating rights and imposing obligations which are legally binding on the parties who made it.

Contractor: the builder carrying out the construction works on a project for the employer. It is good practice to refer in contracts and correspondence to the "main contractor" to avoid confusion with sub-contractors, for example.

Contractor's proposals: a document prepared by the contractor and forming part of the building contract, showing how the contractor will carry out and complete the works in accordance with the employer's requirements.

Defendant: in a civil legal action, the defendant is the party against whom the action (or 'claim') is brought by the claimant.

Employer's requirements: a document produced on behalf of the employer by its design consultants and forming part of the building contract, describing the project that the employer wants the contractor to carry out and complete.

JCT: the Joint Contracts Tribunal Limited, whose members include bodies representing various interest groups within the construction industry – developers, local authorities, contractors, consultants and specialist contractors. Since 1931 the JCT has been producing standard forms of building contract, guidance notes and other documents for use in the construction industry.

LADs: liquidated and ascertained damages – these are damages for breach of contract, the level of which has been agreed in advance by the parties. The most common use of LADs is in relation to delay damages within building contracts.

Novation: the legal mechanism enabling one of the parties to a contract to transfer both the benefit and the burden of the contract to an incoming party. Novation often occurs in the context of a design and construct project, where a client wishes to transfer the rights and obligations under their appointments with the design team to an incoming design and construct contractor.

Privity of contract: the legal doctrine which states that only the parties to a contract are bound by its terms. This doctrine is subject to certain exceptions, for example the rights which third parties may be entitled to by virtue of the Contracts (Rights of Third Parties) Act 1999.

Professional appointment: the contract between a client and a professional consultant. This may be referred to as simply an 'appointment'.

SBC: shorthand for the JCT's Standard Building Contract. The SBC may be used when a 'traditional' procurement route has been chosen, as opposed to design and construct, for example.

Set-off: a defendant in a civil action may have a cross-claim against the claimant which can be set off against the amount claimed. The defendant may use the cross-claim in this way to defend themselves against the claimant's action and reduce, or even cancel out altogether, the claim.

Third party: in the context of a particular contract, a third party is any legal entity, person or business, that is not a party to that contract.

Timeous: a contract may require a party to perform a particular obligation 'timeously', meaning 'in good time' or 'sufficiently early'. Contractual notices are often required to be given timeously.

Tort: a non-contractual civil wrong recognised by law as causing a harm for which the victim of the tort is entitled to seek a legal remedy. The most widely recognised tort is negligence.

Further reading and resources

Chapter 1

www.bailii.org

www.justice.gov.uk/about/hmcts

www.legislation.gov.uk

www.parliament.uk

Baker, J. H. *An Introduction to English Legal History*, 4th edn (2002) Oxford University Press.

Cross, R. and Harris, J.W. *Precedent in English Law*, 4th edn (1991) Oxford University Press.

Endicott, T. 'Law and Language', *The Stanford Encyclopedia of Philosophy*, Fall 2010 edn, Edward N. Zalta (ed.) (2010) Stanford University.

Hart, H.L.A. *The Concept of Law* (1961) Oxford University Press.

Hart, H.L.A. 'Definition and Theory in Jurisprudence', *The Law Quarterly Review* 70 (1954).

Irvine of Lairg (Derry). 'The Law: An engine for trade', *The Modern Law Review* 64: 333–349 (2001).

Kelly, J.M. *A Short History of Western Legal Theory* (1992) Oxford University Press.

McLuhan, M. and Fiore, Q. *The Medium is the Massage* (1967) Penguin Books.

Marmor, A. *The Pragmatics of Legal Language*, Draft Legal Studies Research Paper No 08-11 (2008) University of Southern California Law School.

Slapper, G. and Kelly, D. *The English Legal System*, 2013–2014 edn (2013) Taylor and Francis.

Williams, G. 'Language and the Law', *The Law Quarterly Review* 61/62 (1945/1946).

Chapter 2

Baatz, N. *Construing Construction Contracts: Principles, policies and practice*, Society of Construction Law paper 165 (2010).

Bowling, J. *'It started out so well…' Construction Contracts and Letters of Intent*, Society of Construction Law paper D116 (2010).

Furmston, M. and Tolhurst, G.J. *Contract Formation* (2010) Oxford University Press.

O'Farrell, F. *Professional Negligence in the Construction Field*, Society of Construction Law paper 157 (2009).

Peel, E. *Treitel on The Law of Contract*, 13th edn (2011) Sweet & Maxwell.

Phillips, R. *A Guide to Letter Contracts*, 3rd edn (2012) RIBA Publishing.

Rogers, W.V.H. *Winfield & Jolowicz on Tort*, 18th edn (2010) Sweet and Maxwell.

Wevill, J.T. *The Protection of Expectations When Work is Performed Under a Letter of Intent* (2003) MSc thesis, King's College London.

Chapter 3

Anderson, M. and Warner, V. *Execution of Documents*, 2nd edn (2008) The Law Society.

Blackler, T. and Wevill, J.T. 'Principles: Appointments', *RIBA Journal* 108(6) (2001).

ICAEW. *Partnership Agreements, Standard 1: Helpsheet 10* (2010) The Institute of Chartered Accountants in England and Wales.

Lawson, R. *Exclusion Clauses and Unfair Contract Terms*, 10th edn (2011) Sweet & Maxwell.

McKendrick, E. *Goode on Commercial Law*, 4th edn (2010) Penguin Books.

RIBA. *A Client's Guide to Engaging an Architect: Guidance on hiring an architect for your project* (2009) RIBA Publishing.

Chapter 4

Ostime, N. and Stanford, D. *Architect's Handbook of Practice Management*, 8th edn (2010) RIBA Publishing.

Phillips, R. *Good Practice Guide: Fee Management*, 2nd edn (2012) RIBA Publishing.

Phillips, R. *Guide to RIBA Agreements 2010* (2010) RIBA Publishing.

Phillips, R. *A Short Guide to Consumer Rights in Construction Contracts* (2010) RIBA Publishing.

Sinclair, D. *Leading the Team: An architect's guide to design management* (2011) RIBA Publishing.

Chapter 5

The British Council for Offices. *Good Practice in the Selection of Construction Materials 2011* (2011) BCO

Bailey, J. *Construction Law* (2011) Informa.

Bainbridge, D. *Intellectual Property*, 9th edn (2012) Pearson.

Blackler, T. and Wevill, J.T. 'Principles: Copyright', *RIBA Journal*, 108(5) (2001).

Choat, R. 'You Asked Me for a Contribution: Are net contribution clauses fair?', *Building Magazine* (1 May 2009).

Construction Industry Council. *Indemnities in Consultants' Appointments*, CIC Liability Briefing (2009) CIC.

Devlin of West Wick (Patrick). *The Judge* (1979) Oxford University Press.

Gelder, J. *Ban the Ban: Materials blacklists* (November 2005) The National Building Specification.

Mavers, L.A. *Timeless Melody* (1990) Go! Discs Music Ltd.

Redmond, J. '"Valid" Doesn't Mean "True": Withholding payment', *Building Magazine* (4 September 2009).

Sheehan, T. *Good Practice in the Selection of Construction Materials* (1997) Ove Arup & Partners.

Chapter 6

Construction Industry Council. *Novation of Consultants' Appointments on Design and Build*, CIC Liability Briefing (2008) CIC.

Furst, S. and Ramsey, V. *Keating on Construction Contracts*, 9th edn (2012) Sweet & Maxwell.

Metham, M. *It's Not Our Liability: We Novated the Contract!* (2009) Berwin Leighton Paisner LLP.

RIBA Insurance Agency. *Guide to Reviewing Contract Documentation* (undated) RIBA Publishing.

Uff, J. *Construction Law*, 11th edn (2013) Sweet & Maxwell.

Chapter 7

Bickford-Smith, S. and Sydenham, C. *Party Walls: Law and Practice*, 3rd edn (2009) Jordans.

Clamp, H., Cox, S., Lupton, S. and Udom, K. *Which Contract?*, 5th edn (2012) RIBA Publishing.

Collins, J. and Moren, P. *Good Practice Guide: Negotiating the Planning Maze*, 2nd edn (2009) RIBA Publishing.

Evans, H. *Guide to the Building Regulations 2011 Edition* (2010) RIBA Publishing.

Jamieson, N. *Good Practice Guide: Inspecting Works* (2009) RIBA Publishing.

Klimt, M. 'Legalese: Project managers can help projects finish on time, but clients shouldn't pay for the same service twice', *Architects' Journal* (10 November 2011).

Morrow, N.S. *Party Walls: A practical guide* (2010) RIBA Publishing.

Ostime, N. *RIBA Job Book*, 9th edn (2013) RIBA Publishing.

Sinclair, D. *Assembling a Collaborative Project Team* (2013) RIBA Publishing.

Sinclair, D. *Leading the Team: An Architect's Guide to Design Management* (2011) RIBA Publishing.

Chapter 8

Birkby, G., Ponte, A. and Alderson, F. *Good Practice Guide: Extensions of Time* (2008) RIBA Publishing.

Chappell, D. *Construction Contracts: Questions & answers*, 2nd edn (2010) Taylor & Francis.

Lavers, A. *Early Termination by the Client in the Event of the Contractor's Non-Performance*, Society of Construction Law paper 166 (2011).

Lupton, S. *Guide to SBC11* (2011) RIBA Publishing.

PLC Construction. *Ask the Team: How do I terminate a JCT contract?* (2010) Practical Law Company.

Chapter 9

Construction Industry Council. *Asbestos-related Claims and Professional Indemnity Insurance*, CIC Liability Briefing (2008) CIC.

Construction Industry Council. *Professional Indemnity Insurance for Construction Consultants*, CIC Liability Briefing (2008) CIC.

Construction Industry Council. *Professional Indemnity Insurance – The dangers of changing insurers*, CIC Liability Briefing (2008) CIC.

Construction Industry Council. *The Implications of Consultants Appointing Subconsultants*, CIC Liability Briefing (2009) CIC.

Godfrey, P. *Good Practice Guide: Insurance* (forthcoming) RIBA Publishing.

Luder, O. *Good Practice Guide: Keeping Out of Trouble* (2012) RIBA Publishing.

MacPherson, C. *Notifying your Insurer: Getting it right* (5 October 2009) Allen & Overy LLP.

Marsh, A. *Seminar on Risk Management* (undated) Fishburns LLP.

Merkin, R. (ed.) *Insurance Law – An introduction* (2007) Informa.

O'Sullivan, S. 'Claims Perfection', *New Law Journal* (24 September 2010).

O'Sullivan, S. 'Playing the market', *New Law Journal* (17 September 2010).

RIBA Insurance Agency, *Guide to Understanding Risk Management* (undated) RIBA Publishing.

Chapter 10

Binmore, K. *Game Theory: A very short introduction* (2007) Oxford University Press.

Centre for Effective Dispute Resolution. *The Fourth Mediation Audit* (2010) CEDR.

Coombes Davies, M. *Good Practice Guide: Adjudication* (2011) RIBA Publishing.

Coombes Davies, M. *Good Practice Guide: Arbitration* (2011) RIBA Publishing.

Grossman, A. *Good Practice Guide: Mediation* (2009) RIBA Publishing.

Gwilliam, R. *Open Season for Ambush? How 'Disputes' Have Changed,* Society of Construction Law paper D110 (2010).

Neuberger of Abbotsbury MR (David). *Equity, ADR, Arbitration and the Law: Different dimensions of justice,* The Fourth Keating Lecture, Lincoln's Inn (2010).

RIBA. *It's useful to know… Guidance to help understand the architect's role in a building project and what happens if things get difficult* (2008) RIBA Publishing.

McCartney, P. and Dain, A. 'Is construction mediation changing?', *Construction Law Journal* 26(7) (2010).

Packman, C. *The Adjudication Provisions of the Construction Act 2009,* Society of Construction Law paper D111 (2009).

Pickavance, J. 'Keeping a lid on costs', *Construction Law* (August/September 2009).

Reynolds, M. 'Crossing the Rubicon', *Construction Law Journal* 26(2) (2010).

Richbell, D. *Mediation is the Only Way to Justice,* Society of Construction Law paper D114 (2010).

Roeg, N. and Cammell, D. *Performance* (1968) Warner Bros.

Tackaberry, J. *Flexing the Knotted Oak: English arbitration's task and opportunity in the first decade of the new century* (2002) Society of Construction Law.

Uff, J. *How Final Should Dispute Resolution Be?,* Society of Construction Law paper 164 (2010).

Vinden, P. *Using Adjudication to Resolve Disputes When One of the Parties is Insolvent,* Society of Construction Law paper D112 (2010).

Index